59.95

The definition of 'Englishness' has become the subject of considerable debate, and in this important contribution to 'Ideas in Context' Julia Stapleton looks at the work of one of the most wide-ranging and influential theorists of the English nation, Ernest Barker. The first holder of the Chair of Political Science at Cambridge, Barker wrote prolifically on the history of political thought and contemporary political theory, and his writings are notable for fusing three of the dominant strands of late-nineteenth and early-twentieth-century political thought, Whiggism, Idealism, and Pluralism. Infused with a strong cultural sense of nationhood, Barker's writings influenced a broad non-academic audience, and their subsequent neglect graphically demonstrates the fate of a certain vision of Liberal England in the generation after the First World War. With, however, the erosion of a particular sense of Englishness, Barker's ideas have begun to assume renewed resonance.

IDEAS IN CONTEXT

ENGLISHNESS AND THE STUDY OF POLITICS

IDEAS IN CONTEXT

The books in this series will discuss the emergence of intellectual traditions and of related new disciplines. The procedures, aims, and vocabularies that were generated will be set in the context of the alternatives available within the contemparary frameworks of ideas and institutions. Through detailed studies of the evolution of such traditions, and their modification by different audiences, it is hoped that a new picture will form of the development of ideas in their concrete contexts. By this means, artificial distinctions between the history of philosophy, of the various sciences, of society and politics, and of literature may be seen to dissolve.

The series is published with the support of the Exxon Foundation.

A list of books in the series will be found at the end of the volume.

ENGLISHNESS AND THE STUDY OF POLITICS

The social and political thought of Ernest Barker

JULIA STAPLETON

Department of Politics, University of Durham

CAMBRIDGE
UNIVERSITY PRESS

Published by the Press Syndicate of the University of Cambridge
The Pitt Building, Trumpington Street, Cambridge CB2 1RP
40 West 20th Street, New York, NY 10011-4211, USA
10 Stamford Road, Oakleigh, Melbourne 3166, Australia

First published 1994

Printed in Great Britain at the University Press, Cambridge

A catalogue record for this book is available from the British Library

Library of Congress cataloguing in publication data

Stapleton, Julia,
Englishness and the study of politics: the social and political
thought of Ernest Barker/Julia Stapleton.
p. cm. (Ideas in context: 32)
Includes bibliographical references.
ISBN 0 521 46125 1 (hc)
1. Barker, Ernest, Sir, 1874–1960 – contributions in political
science. 2. Political science – Great Britain – History. I. Title.
II. Series.
JC257.B34S73 1994
320'.092–dc20 93–35733 CIP

ISBN 0521 46125 1 hardback

VN

For my parents

Nothing is more certain, than that our manners, our civilization, and all the good things which are connected with manners, and with civilization, have, in this European world of ours, depended for ages upon two principles; and were indeed the result of both combined; I mean the spirit of a gentleman, and the spirit of religion. The nobility and the clergy, the one by profession, the other by patronage, kept learning in existence, even in the midst of arms and confusions, and whilst governments were rather in their causes than formed.

Edmund Burke, *Reflections on the Revolution in France* (1790)

Contents

Acknowledgements

I began the research for this book while I was at the University of Sussex and wrote it when I moved to Durham. I have received considerable support in these and other places, and it is a pleasure to acknowledge my most pressing debts.

I would first like to thank Nicolas Barker for his illuminating responses to my questions about his father's life and work, and for kindly granting me permission to publish extracts from Ernest Barker's unpublished letters. I am also grateful to the Master and Fellows of Peterhouse, Cambridge, for allowing me to consult the Barker Collection in the Ward Library and to reproduce a photograph of Barker which is held there. Pamela Cromona was especially helpful in making the collection available. Two anonymous readers for Cambridge University Press gave close attention to the manuscript and made valuable suggestions for improvement. Staff at the Inter-Library-Loans sections of Sussex and Durham University Libraries were of great assistance in tracing obscure material. The School of Social Sciences at the University of Sussex financed several trips to libraries in London and Oxford. I was especially fortunate at Sussex in working with John Burrow and Donald Winch. Their interest and example have provided a vital stimulus to my research subsequently.

At the University of Durham, I would like to thank the Research and Initiatives Committee for awarding me a research grant in 1991–2. This enabled me to devote a large part of the year to writing, as well as funding research in Cambridge. I owe thanks to my colleagues in the Department of Politics for giving me priority in the assignment of computers, and for providing a congenial atmosphere in which to work. I am particularly indebted to Bob Dyson for covering the bulk of my teaching while I was on sabbatical, and for patiently enduring much idle chatter about Barker. Anthony Fletcher generously gave his time to read and make challenging comments on five of the chapters. Finally, I am grateful to Helen Corr for her friendship and good humour which sustained me considerably while writing this book.

My largest debt, however, is to Stefan Collini, who has continued to encourage me since supervising my Ph.D. thesis. I have been much inspired by his work on British intellectual history in the nineteenth and twentieth centuries. In addition, I have benefited greatly from his acute comments on drafts of all the chapters. While he is not responsible for the imperfections which remain, his advice has been invaluable. I offer heartfelt appreciation to him, in particular.

I gratefully acknowledge access to and permission to quote from unpublished correspondence and manuscripts from the following:

Balliol College, Oxford, concerning the A.L. Smith Papers and a memorandum from Barker 'On the need for the redistribution of the work prescribed for the School of Modern History' (1908)

University Library, Birmingham, concerning correspondence in the C.T. Onions Papers and Francis Brett Young Papers

The Bodleian Library, Oxford, concerning the papers of Lord Bryce, Lionel Curtis, Gilbert Murray, J.L. and B. Hammond, A.E. Zimmern, F.S. Marvin, H.A.L. Fisher and The Round Table

The British Library, Oriental and India Office Collections, concerning the William Archer Papers

The British Library of Political and Economic Science concerning the papers of Graham Wallas and Violet Markham

The Brynmor Jones Library, University of Hull, concerning the H.J. Laski Papers

University of Cambridge, Secretary General of the Faculties, concerning material of the General Board of Faculties

University of Cambridge, Faculty Board of History, concerning the Minutes of the Board

University of Cambridge, The Registry, concerning the names of the electors to the Chair of Political Science

H. Guy-Loë concerning the correspondence of Elie-Halévy

International Institute of Social History, Amsterdam, concerning the H.J. Laski Papers

John Rylands University Library of Manchester concerning the T.F. Tout Papers

University Library, Keele, concerning the A.D. Lindsay Papers
King's College London, concerning King's College London Archives
Peterhouse, Cambridge, concerning the Ernest Barker Papers
Public Record Office, concerning Treasury and Board of Education files (Crown copyright)
Keeper of the Archives, University of Oxford, concerning Oxford University Archives
University College, Oxford, concerning the Clement Attlee Papers
University Library, Sussex, concerning the papers of Maurice Reckitt and Leonard Woolf
Yale University Library, concerning the Walter Lippmann Papers

INTRODUCTION

The 'national character' of Barker's thought

ENGLISHNESS AND POLITICAL SCIENCE

On 24 May 1948, Ernest Barker (1874–1960) dined at the Athenaeum with Sir Edward Bridges, Permanent Secretary of the Treasury and Official Head of the Civil Service. He was there to discuss how Bridges might resolve a feud which had arisen between Bridges and the Foreign Office over that part of Bridges' title which referred to his 'headship' of the Civil Service. Bridges had inherited this role from one of his predecessors, Sir Warren Fisher, who had revived its association with the Treasury in 1919. But the dust of the constitutional wrangling at that time had never settled, a certain Sir Walford Selby in the Foreign Office persistently alleging that the Treasury's possession of the headship had effectively 'paralysed' his department, and wreaked much other havoc in British government besides. The latest figure whom Selby had sought to recruit to his cause was Barker, evidently unaware of Barker's friendship with Bridges.

Barker offered a possible solution to Bridges' difficulties in a correspondence which followed the dinner. With his usual unfailing courtesy and scholarly command, he informed Bridges of a similar problem which had confronted Elizabeth I. Upon her accession, she had been forced to find an alternative term for the *Caput* – or headship – of the Church of England in the monarch's title, this having lapsed during Mary's reign. Elizabeth's solution was simple. It entailed – in the words of Barker's mentor, F.W. Maitland, which he quoted – the substitution of *Caput* with 'a new and happy *et cetera*' after 'Governor of the Realm', while she played for time in devising the Supremacy Act of 1559. Barker urged Bridges to find a similar way of 'etceterating' himself without losing overall control of the Civil Service. Steeled by Barker's support, Bridges successfully defended his role as head of the Civil Service before the Prime Minister's Office, and also fended off the challenge of a Private Members' Bill which would divest him of this responsibility.[1]

The above anecdote provides a revealing introduction to the work of one of the most prominent political scientists in Britain during the first half of the twentieth century. Barker was the first holder of the Chair in Political Science at Cambridge between 1928 and 1939; author of the still widely used *The Political Thought of Plato and Aristotle* (1906), an authoritative translation and interpretation of Aristotle's *Politics* (1946), and such key texts in post-war political theory as *Reflections Upon Government* (1942) and *Principles of Social and Political Theory* (1951); and he was also one of the founder members of the Political Studies Association in 1950. These are just a few of the ways in which he made his mark upon the discipline of politics. But his encounter with Bridges underlines his extensive connections and influence outside the academic world as well. Indeed, Barker became something of a national figure in his lifetime. Heir to a prominent late-Victorian ideal of the university as a training ground for public service, he distributed his substantial intellectual energy widely. He performed government work through his chairmanship of the Hadow Committee on 'the Education of the Adolescent' in 1926; his directorship of 'politico-military' courses for army officers in Cambridge during the Second World War; and his chairmanship of the Books Commission of the Allied Ministers of Education in 1942.[2] Moreover, he served on numerous voluntary and educational bodies ranging from the National Council of Social Service to the Conference of Educational Associations, and the Extra-Mural Board in the University of Cambridge.[3] Finally, he wrote voluminously for lay audiences, not least for the 'middlebrow' section of English society whose cultural tastes and outlook become the subject of considerable paternal interest among certain sections of the cultivated elite in interwar

[1] The correspondence relating to this incident is in files T199/352 and 353 at the Public Record Office. I am indebted to Richard Chapman for this reference. The dispute over the headship of the Civil Service is lucidly analysed in R.A. Chapman, *Ethics in the British Civil Service* (London, 1988), 23–32.

[2] Barker's role in the Hadow Commission is discussed in chapter 5 below. He referred to this involvement in the 'politico-military' courses at Cambridge at the outbreak of the Second World War in his autobiography, *Age and Youth: Memories of Three Universities and Father of the Man* (London, 1953), 210–12. His chairmanship of the Books Commission is discussed in chapter 8 below.

[3] On his work for the National Council for Social Service see chapter 6 below. His addresses as President of the Conference of Educational Associations are printed in *Education*, 6 January 1950, 3–4; and 13 January 1950, 43 and 49. As Chairman of the Rural Areas Committee of the Extra-Mural Board at Cambridge University, he wrote a foreword to H.E. Poole, *Perspectives for Country Men* (London, 1942).

Britain.[4] Thus, whether addressing students of history and politics at Oxford between 1899 and 1920, and at Cambridge between 1928 and 1939; or community service volunteers and the readership of intellectually lightweight journals such as *The British Weekly*, *England*, *John O'London's Weekly* or *Far and Wide* in the 1940s and 1950s;[5] or indeed, Sir Edward Bridges at the Athenaeum in 1948, his ambition remained the same: that of spreading academic learning beyond the confines of the university, bringing scholarly and humane values to bear in all walks of national life, and elevating and unifying the latter as a consequence.

Yet despite the renown which Barker achieved in his lifetime, his work as a whole has nonetheless eluded the attention of historians since his death in 1960. This book seeks to remedy this neglect by illuminating his place in both political inquiry and cultural self-reflection in Britain during the first half of the twentieth century. Its central thesis is that Barker's large scholarly output and high public profile derived from a broad and humanistic conception of the discipline of politics, one with considerable scope for articulating an influential definition of English national culture in a period of shifting and emasculated public identities. As J.H. Grainger has argued, when the commercial and industrial pre-eminence enjoyed by Britain began to falter at the end of the nineteenth century and its remaking as a world power became imperative, rival versions of the English *patria* emerged. The inclusive *patria* of mid-Victorian Britain could no longer be assumed, largely because of the very success of the empire in diffusing England abroad coupled with increasing social diversity and disunity at home.[6] Early-twentieth-century assertions and contestations of the nature of Britishness in the guise of 'Englishness' have become the subject of much recent historical interest.[7] But while the contributions to this genre by literary critics,

4 On this elite attempt to 'uplift' tastes and standards among the general public in the light of the development of the mass-communications industries, see D.L. LeMahieu, *A Culture for Democracy: Mass Communication and the Cultivated Mind in Britain Between the Wars* (Oxford, 1988), especially chapter 4.

5 E. Barker, 'Mr. Gladstone', *The British Weekly*, 20 May 1948, 7; 'The English character and attitude towards life', *England*, September 1950, 6–9; 'Should we read Plato?', *John O'London's Weekly*, 45, 1283, 19 April 1946, 1; 'The significance of the crusades', *Far and Wide*, Winter 1950–1, 33–6.

6 J.H. Grainger, *Patriotisms: Britain, 1900–1939* (London, 1986), 20–1, 26.

7 For example, R. Colls and P. Dodd (eds.), *Englishness: Politics and Culture, 1880–1920* (London, 1986); C. Shaw and M. Chase (eds.), *The Imagined Past: History and Nostalgia* (Manchester, 1989); B. Doyle, *English and Englishness* (London, 1989); R. Samuel (ed.), *Patriotism: The Making and Unmaking of English National Identity*, 3 Vols. (London, 1989); and S. Collini, 'The Whig interpretation of English literature: literary history and national identity', in *Public Moralists: Political Thought and Intellectual Life in Britain*, 1850–1930 (Oxford, 1991).

novelists, poets, composers, artists, journalists, and politicians have now been substantially documented, little work has appeared on constructions of English nationhood in the political thought of the period. This domain played an equally important role in the process of national introspection at the turn of the century, the cultural particularity of 'England' still being widely associated with its enduring polity and the liberal political values which sustained it.[8] Barker was especially significant among British political thinkers in satisfying a deep yearning for national self-understanding and reassurance in rapidly changing and threatening times. He did so by tying the interpretation of the political world to broad issues in English national development, and these in turn to European civilisation more widely.

Of course, despite their claims to universality, all attempts at national projection arise from particular social experiences, beliefs, and values. To this general rule Barker's meditations upon the 'character' of England were no exception. It will become apparent in the following chapters that the 'England' which he framed through a catholic understanding of political science was securely anchored in Establishment institutions and practices, balanced only by the religious and cultural influences of Nonconformity. This partial snapshot of English life was nonetheless made to rest on foundations which were sunk deep into the archaic soil of English society. It was essentially a rearguard defence of the political order which prevailed before the First World War, albeit adapted to embrace the limited social as well as constitutional rights which characterised what one historian has termed a 'redeployed liberalism' in British government subsequently.[9] Furthermore, it was aimed as much at the challenge of the 'technocratic' middle class as at socialist and Labourite England. What Barker was mainly concerned to defend was a 'gentlemanly' ideal of government – that which was based upon liberal learning rather than trained expertise.[10] Through bracketing the former with 'Englishness', he sought to extend the wider set of values upon which it was based to all 'Englishmen', representing it as a vital embodiment of both their personal and national character.

In this light, it is easy to dismiss Barker's project of cultural

[8] As D. Smith notes of the period between 1885 and 1921, 'Liberalism had become Englishness'. 'Englishness and the liberal inheritance after 1886', in Colls and Dodd, *Englishness*, 255.

[9] S. Hall and B. Schwarz, 'State and society, 1880–1930', in M. Langan and B. Schwarz (eds.), *Crises in the British State, 1880–1930* (London, 1985), 27.

[10] This tension between the old (gentlemanly) and the new (technocratic, managerial) ideal of professionalism in the state is absent from Harold Perkin's otherwise excellent study, *The Rise of Professional Society: England since 1880* (London, 1989).

inclusion as a specious attempt to spread certain class imperatives and ideals beyond their natural constituency and lifespan. Barker's staunch commitment to 'gentlemanly' England, his conception of its ripeness for imperial export, and of its significance in the history of Western civilisation certainly struck some contemporaries as unbearably smug and naive. One such critic was Harold Laski, who had been one of Barker's pupils at Oxford early in the century. Reviewing *Reflections Upon Government* in 1942, he denounced the primacy of 'concepts' over 'experience' in the political theory of his former teacher. He was also scathing about Barker's definition of democracy as simply 'government by discussion', regardless of where discussion might lead. Laski caustically continued,

> It is easier to think [this way] amid the dreaming spires of Oxford or in the loveliness of the Cambridge backs in June than if one is a blacklisted miner in a Welsh coalfield or a share-cropper trying to fix a decent price on his puny holding in Alabama. A democratic state validates its character by the level of rights that it maintains; and the weakness of Professor Barker's definition is his complete indifference to the fact that the level is urgent.[11]

It is true that Barker was apt to underestimate the degree of social inequality and conflict, particularly in Britain; and no doubt the peace and calm of Oxbridge life was instrumental in softening the impact upon him of class divisions and social unrest in the world outside, as Laski suggested. In this sense, Barker was far out of step with the left sympathies cultivated by many intellectuals in the interwar period. Their scorn for the rigid class hierarchies and parochialism of 'England' – a stance that was epitomised in R.H. Tawney's *Equality* (1932), the *New Statesman*, and the Left Book Club – spelt almost complete rejection of the inherited nation to which Barker was so firmly attached.[12] But, as will become clear in the following chapters, he was not wholly blind to inequalities of economic and political power in modern society; nor, correspondingly, was he impervious to issues of economic and social justice in political argument.[13] Moreover, his tendency to gloss over the full extent of

[11] H.J. Laski, *New Statesman and Nation*, 4 July 1942, 14–15.

[12] Grainger, *Patriotisms*, 345–7.

[13] As Barker wrote to Laski on 15 January 1944 following a periodic crisis in their relations, '[w]hen I speak of disliking your views, I do not mean that I dislike communism, or socialism, or any other variation on the theme of common property. Some measure of common property is a necessary ingredient of any modern society; and you and I would only disagree on the question, "How Much?" It is your views on social method, and the general process of society, which [drive?] me away from you. I have never thought, and can never think, that a good end sanctifies bad means.' Laski Papers, The Brynmor Jones Library, University of Hull.

privilege and disadvantage in society deserves comment which goes beyond obvious references to his class bias and cloistered academic environment. For example, it needs to be set alongside his wider Hegelian concern that the state should be safeguarded against 'capture' by all 'partial' interests, be they those of labour, capital, single nationalities, or whatever. Of further interest are the way in which he marshalled a number of diverse but ultimately reinforcing strands of early-twentieth-century political theory in support of his consensual and elysian picture of England; the authority he commanded in doing so; and his strikingly eirenic intellectual temperament and literary style. The latter led him to seek reconciliation between a multitide of conflicting ideas, movements, and even cultures, and to praise others whom he perceived as performing similar good works.[14] Finally, if his vision of England was hopelessly blurred, nevertheless his ideals continue to accord with general political sentiment in the West.[15] It will therefore add to our understanding of the place which that sentiment occupies in contemporary discourse if one of its systematic expressions earlier in the twentieth century is elucidated.

CONSENSUS, CONCILIATION, OPTIMISM

These various points of interest relating to Barker's work will be considered in the course of the book. In the first three chapters, for example, I emphasise the substantial common ground between the three main sources of Barker's political thought in the late-nineteenth and early-twentieth centuries: Idealism, Whiggism, and Pluralism. This is well illustrated in his writings before the First World War. In particular, I underline the extent to which the concerns of Idealism and Pluralism – as well as Whiggism, more obviously – were informed

[14] For example, he hailed Gandhi in precisely these terms. Contributing to a volume of essays in honour of Gandhi's seventieth birthday, he wrote: 'I should therefore celebrate in Mr. Gandhi the man who could mix the spiritual with the temporal, and could be at the same time true to both. I should also celebrate the man who could be a bridge between the East and the West.' E. Barker, 'Gandhi as bridge and reconciler', in S. Radhakrishnan (ed.), *Mahatma Gandhi: Essays and Reflections on his Life and Work* (London, 1939), 61.

[15] For example, the former President of Czechoslovakia, Václav Havel, writes in a similar spirit to Barker in asserting his conviction that: 'we will never build a democratic state based on rule of law [*sic*] if we do not at the same time build a state that is – regardless of how unscientific this may sound to the ears of a political scientist – humane, moral, intellectual and spiritual, and cultural'. *Summer Meditations on Politics, Morality, and Civility in a Time of Transition* (London, 1992), 18. The comparison between Barker and Havel is not as wide as it might appear at first glance given Barker's admiration for the Czechoslovak Republic and its leaders. See below ch. 8, p. 186.

by shared images of English national character and development, inspiring reverence for, rather than detachment from, the latter.

It was this combined legacy which Barker carried forward into the second quarter of the twentieth century, his writings serving to highlight an important channel in which the three intellectual currents ran after they lost their pre-First-World-War momentum. Over time, he changed the weight of each strand in his thought, although he never dispensed with any of them completely. Most importantly, he began to distance himself from Idealism in the 1930s, at the same time moving closer to the Whig tradition than he had perhaps been inclined to do in earlier years. The dimensions and extent of this shift should not be exaggerated. It would certainly be mistaken to interpret it in terms of the contrast between a 'radical' and 'iconoclastic' temper of his early career and 'conservative' disposition later in life.[16] Even when the reforming impulse of T.H. Green's Idealism most seized him – at the same time he wrote *The Political Thought of Plato and Aristotle* – a deep-seated wariness about social and political change is also revealed in his arguments. The constitutional image of the state in which this concern was grounded and which was strongly projected in Whiggism had always competed for his allegiance with the Idealist model of the state as a moral community; it merely gained a stronger hold upon him than previously in the interwar years and beyond. The political values associated with constitutionalism were by no means absent from Idealism, as will be seen in chapter 1. But they were perceptibly overshadowed by an emphasis upon the state's responsibility for strengthening moral goodness and social solidarity. Barker's intellectual development was largely grounded in his attempt to balance these two political visions between which he was torn: of an impersonal, legal state concerned purely with external acts, on the one hand, and a state which was responsible for social justice and reform, on the other.

Underlying his ambivalence at this level of political theory was the deeper tension he felt between the claims of personal liberty and the priorities of collective life. It was an old liberal dilemma, complicated in Barker's case by his embrace of Pluralism. This brought groups into the delicate legal relationship which in his view had to be established among the various actors in political society. He regarded the conflict

[16] Dermot Morrah, review of Barker's *Essays on Government*, *Times Literary Supplement*, 12 January 1946, 16. Morrah was a journalist for *The Times*, and had been one of Barker's students at Oxford. E. Barker, *Age and Youth*, 83.

between individuals and groups, individuals and the state, and groups and the state as ineradicable, although it might be tempered through the rule of law and parliamentary democracy. Always, however, Barker's primary sympathy ran with the individual, free scope for whose development he regarded as 'the general moral ideal' of the modern world. (It was one which in his view was applicable to both men and women alike. Notwithstanding his sense of the threat which the individual rights of women posed to the cohesion of the family and society at large as currently constituted, he advocated the granting of degrees to women at Oxford in the early part of the century, emphasised the importance of careers to women and also greater ease of divorce. In this case, as in other major social issues of the day, his approach was one of enjoining progress through cautious and gradual experiment rather than by the admittedly unanswerable but often destructive appeal to 'logic'.)[17] His reservation of a large margin for privacy and even solitude in social and political thought formed a constant refrain in his work from its earliest period at the turn of the century. At a time when 'collectivist' enthusiasms are assumed to have set the tone for political debate,[18] his perpetual stress upon the value – indeed the 'ultimate' value – of 'the personal' and 'the private' calls for exploration and explanation. Indeed, it would add to the already convincing case for revising the standard view of the period.

Barker's concern to shield individuals against the gregarious pressures of modern life was rooted in a strongly spiritual understanding of human nature, society, and history. It was one which was especially reinforced by the Italian Idealist, Benedetto Croce. He made few references to Croce's work and failed to develop the interest he began to take in it in the 1920s.[19] But he was nonetheless considerably inspired by it, and knew Croce personally.[20] In a review of Croce's

[17] E. Barker, 'History and the position of women', in Z. Fairfield (ed.), *Some Aspects of the Women's Movement* (London, 1915). On his support for the higher education of women, see *Age and Youth*, esp. 98–100. He urged girls to pursue careers in his speeches at school prize-days. See for example *Brighton and Hove Herald*, 17 December 1938.

[18] Such a view has been advanced most recently by W.H. Greenleaf, *The British Political Tradition*, 4 vols. (London, 1983–8). See the persuasive criticism of Greenleaf's catch-all categories of 'Collectivism' and 'Libertarianism' by P. Morriss, 'Professor Greenleaf's collectivism', in *Politics*, 12, 1 (1992), 34–7.

[19] See his address 'History and Philosophy' delivered before the Historical Association in 1922, reprinted in *Church, State, and Study* (London, 1930).

[20] Barker described himself as a 'friend and admirer' of Croche in a review entitled 'Catholicism and Fascism', *Manchester Guardian*, 21 October 1941.

History as the Story of Liberty which appeared in English translation in 1941, he praised its author as 'the greatest man of our times, in pure activity of thought and pure courage of the will'.[21]

In the light of the privileged place which individuals held in Barker's thought, we may say that the tensions in the latter reflect the ineliminable tensions he discerned in society. Moreover, it is clear that he found no single political theory of his formative intellectual years which was adequate to the task of comprehending these multi-layered rifts, let alone resolving them. Still, a *modus vivendi* between competing political forces had to be reached, and this called for as broadly based a political philosophy as it was possible to construct. His pursuit of this aim produced a number of recurrent preferences and aversions in his writings, to which it will be well to draw attention at the outset of this book.

The first was a love of compromise or balance between contending arguments and perspectives in political theory, leading him to identify both their merits and defects, and the possibilities of their alignment accordingly. It was a stylistic trait which appeared in his earliest book, *The Political Thought of Plato and Aristotle*, prompting one reviewer – Sidney Ball – to apply the approach to Barker himself. In other words, Barker's painstaking concern to emphasise both the advantages and disadvantages of particular political philosophies had good points and bad points itself. Ball wrote: 'Mr. Barker, indeed, seems to show a laudable anxiety to preserve a balanced judgement rather than to fix impressions . . . [However] the argument is not only of the nature of a see-saw, . . . it is apt at times to remain there.'[22]

This inveterate liking for even-handedness and receptiveness reflected his keen, conservative embrace of moderation in political life, the need to refrain from pushing either political principles or demands to extremes; thus shorn of their excesses, they might be accommodated with their rivals. Such a proclivity is not only evident in his approach to the three key influences upon his thought outlined above; it also shaped his treatment of the many other political outlooks to which he turned his attention. Even extremist ideologies such as Communism and Fascism, he ventured to suggest in 1937, might contain some grain of 'Truth' which would repay the effort of listening.[23]

[21] His review of Croce's *History as the Story of Liberty*, transl. by S. Sprigge, was for *The Observer*, 23 March 1941. [22] *International Journal of Ethics*, 17, 4 (1907) 517–22.

[23] E. Barker, 'The conflict of ideologies', in *The Citizen's Choice* (Cambridge, 1937), 20.

Second, and related to Barker's determination to produce a 'balanced' political theory and to allow all political creeds a hearing, was his unremitting desire to have the best of all worlds existing side by side. An emphatic aversion to theoretical purity left considerable scope in his mind for the realisation of opposing ideals and approaches at different levels of social life and thought respectively. This explains his simultaneous embrace of an impersonal state but a communitarian model of society; his conception of the importance of both nationalism and internationalism to human life, and of both law and moral philosophy to political science; his emphasis upon the need for both solitude and society in equal measures; and his combining of a conservative appreciation of the value of hierarchy with a liberal belief in the value and possibility of 'equality of opportunity' in English society. These are just a few examples of Barker's penchant for having it both ways rather than siding with one at the expense of the other.

A third characteristic of Barker's work which again bears upon the first and second is his antipathy to intellectual fashion. Permanently on his guard against that which was novel, sensational, and exciting, he can frequently be found warning against the intransigent opposition to traditional beliefs inherent in many new currents of thought, and their liability to shake the social and political world to its deepest foundations. It was a typically Burkean approach to intellectual innovation, accentuating the strident and abstract forms which such change invariably took. He certainly treated the more jarring versions of Pluralism in this way, although at the same time seeking to tame them for addition to an inherited stockpile of widely accepted national beliefs. However, from other dislocating intellectual developments he kept well clear. For example, he dismissed Freud's theory of the unconscious;[24] he was seemingly unaware of the existence of the Bloomsbury circle while he was the Principal of King's College London between 1920 and 1927;[25] he thought ill of T.S. Eliot's modernism;[26] and he eyed the term 'ideology' – a newcomer to the

[24] He wrote: '[h]ow astonished the Greeks, who walked in the light of clear cool reason, would be, if they knew that good Greek names would one day be attached to misty fumes arising from "the unconscious".' *Reflections on Family Life* (London, 1947), 22.

[25] E. Barker, *Age and Youth*, 151.

[26] Barker to Francis Brett Young, 10 March 1948, University Library, Birmingham, MS. FBY 2546. In this letter to a poet he much admired, Barker expressed astonishment that Eliot had been awarded the Order of Merit. The letter is worth quoting at length. 'I have met him, and I have read a good deal of his verse and prose; but I count him what we call in universities B+ – i.e. a second-class man somehow pushing his way up into the first class. And he makes such a parade of learning, which I sometimes doubt. I once put my foot into it heavily with him. I

vocabulary of English political thought in the 1930s – with intense suspicion, regarding it as the new 'confessionalism' of modern times.[27] In this latter respect, he took up a stance which was more fully worked out by Michael Oakeshott, who taught with Barker at Cambridge in the 1930s and to whom Barker attempted – albeit unsuccessfully – to pass on his Chair when he retired.[28]

The truth was that Barker detested controversy. He not only disliked being embroiled in it himself; he also shrank from that which was generated by the heat and smoke of the monolithic warring groups and their rancorous 'doctrines' which in his perception had come to dominate the political life of modern societies. He preferred the comforting balm of a liberalism which presupposed broad agreement upon political fundamentals, one which had sustained the English nation – especially – through many troubled times and which was sufficiently flexible to be adapted in the light of new concerns and pressures. This characteristically Whiggish optimism about the capacity of liberalism to absorb all that was worthy in opposing ideologies extended to much else besides, constituting a fourth distinguishing feature of his intellectual approach. In the face of some of the darkest moments in twentieth-century history he was quietly confident that European polity could weather the worst political storms, even – varying the metaphor slightly – finding a silver lining in some of them. For example, much troubled though he was by Communism and Fascism in the interwar years, nonetheless he managed to extract at least some solace from their emergence. He concluded his address of 1937 on 'The Conflict of Ideologies' on a characteristically upbeat note thus: 'It is not altogether evil that great gusts of doctrine should sweep over [our continent] and vex it. It may

had just been to a performance of "Murder in the Cathedral," and I was dining at King's College afterwards. I saw Maynard Keynes, and I went up to him and said, "What a pastiche T.S. Eliot's play is – bits of Aeschylus patched into bits of Shakespeare." "Hush," said Keynes, "he is standing next to me." He was; and I think he heard me. I did not repent.' Barker consoled Brett Young (on perhaps not receiving an award), with the words 'Fashion in literature is wilder than fashion in women's dress.' Barker had warmed to Eliot by 1953, but he confided to Brett Young that 'I don't want him to be the next Poet Laureate, as I suppose he will be.' Barker to Brett Young, 6 April 1953, MS. FBY 2547.

27 E. Barker, Preface to the Fourth Edition of *National Character and the Factors in its Formation* (1927, London, 1946), xvi. See also his 'The conflict of ideologies'. Both pieces convey the alien nature of the term 'ideology' for an English political theorist in the 1930s and 1940s.

28 Oakeshott undertook his *The Social and Political Doctrines of Contemporary Europe* (Cambridge, 1939) at Barker's suggestion. On this and Barker's wish that Oakeshott might succeed him in the Cambridge Chair, see the anonymous obituary for Oakeshott in *The Times*, 22 December 1990.

even be counted for good that Europe should be so much one that it can be vexed, like a single sea, by all these embattled winds of conflicting ideologies.'[29] His undiminished propensity to look on the bright side, to stress the positive above the negative, is not the least noteworthy – indeed perplexing – aspect of his thought, underpinning his deep attachment to the politics of civility and restraint. This attitude contrasts sharply with the despondency which overcame many of his contemporaries – for example, L.T. Hobhouse and G.M. Trevelyan – after the First World War shattered all their hopes for a world that was rooted in progress, reason, and humanity.[30] The grounds for Barker's optimism will become clear in due course, these ranging from the good fortune he experienced in early life to the Aristotelian primacy he always attached to 'ideals' in political analysis.

ACADEMIC PROFESSIONALISM AND PUBLIC EDUCATION

In chapters 7 and 8, I suggest that Barker's unwavering confidence in English national traditions was central to his intellectual and cultural authority. At a time of acute national crisis, his emphasis upon the gainly and solid character of England and its institutions was in heavy demand. Whether as a seasoned writer for the Central Office of Information (COI),[31] for popular journals such as those mentioned at the beginning of this introduction, or as the editor of that glowing account of the national identity – *The Character of England* (1947)[32] – Barker painted gently mocking but ultimately endearing portraits of the national self.

Throughout his life, and not simply in periods of crisis, Barker appointed himself guardian and interpreter of the national culture. This led him to engage in informed commentary upon all aspects of national life and thought, and also international affairs. He did so in cultivated weekly and fortnightly reviews such as *The Listener*, *The Spectator*, *The Contemporary Review*, and *The Fortnighly Review*,[33] as well

29 E. Barker, 'The conflict of ideologies', 21.

30 On Hobhouse, see S. Collini, *Liberalism and Sociology: L.T. Hobhouse and Political Argument in England, 1880–1914* (Cambridge, 1979), Epilogue; on Trevelyan, see D. Cannadine, *G.M. Trevelyan: A Life in History* (London, 1992), 86–9.

31 His contributions to COI literature included *British Constitutional Monarchy* (1944, 1952), *Winston Churchill* (1945), and *Cultural Influences in Britain* (1948).

32 See ch. 7 below.

33 For example, 'Group idols and their loyalties', *The Listener*, 18 July 1934, 98; 'John Hampden', *The Spectator*, 25 June 1943, 587–8; 'The contact of colours and civilisations', *The Contemporary Review*, November 1930, 578–87; 'The movement of national life, 1910–1935', *The Fortnightly Review*, May 1935, 513–26; and 'The new reign', *The Fortnightly Review*, March 1936, 257–66.

as in 'low-to-middlebrow' forums. Furthermore, he was a leader and feature writer – and prolific reviewer – for influential newspapers such as *The Times* and the *Manchester Guardian.* He confessed in his autobiography that he had perhaps too freely mixed scholarship and journalism at times, although overall he felt that he had not crossed them unduly.[34] Yet in the best tradition of the Victorian 'man of letters', Barker acted upon the assumption that scholars were responsible for informing and leading a wider public – indeed in his case, the public at large – shaping its primary attitudes, values, and outlook.[35] The importance he attached to such an enlarged conception of his role was reinforced when he became a visiting professor at the University of Cologne in 1947, drawn temporarily out of retirement by the British Council to help re-establish political studies there. Confronted with the erudite but aloof tradition of *Wissenschaft*, Barker underlined – as a result of his experience – 'the general social duty' of the university, 'which should lead it to co-operate with the people, and with popular movements and organizations'. If the German academic community needed to recover its standards first, nevertheless Barker hoped that in future it would ally itself with 'the general movement of democracy in the community at large'.[36]

So extended a conception of his pedagogical function raises general issues in the history of intellectual life in Britain, going beyond the development of the discipline of politics with which Barker was primarily associated during his career as an academic teacher and writer. Indeed, the inclusiveness of his social, political, and cultural thought is unintelligible without appreciating his overriding concern, which was touched upon earlier in this introduction: to diffuse the culture of the educated class far down the social scale. At the same time, such action would preserve the cohesiveness of the intelligentsia itself against the forces of intellectual fragmentation in the modern age. What light does this ambition shed upon the professionalisation of academic disciplines in the same period? As Barker was the first holder of one of the earliest British Chairs in political science this wider question is by no means irrelevant, and will repay some consideration at the beginning of this book.

It is certainly inappropriate to lament Barker's failure to live up to

[34] E. Barker, *Age and Youth*, 223–4.

[35] For my understanding of the role and social position of Victorian intellectuals, I am much indebted to Stefan Collini's *Public Moralists*, and also his 'Intellectuals in Britain and France in the twentieth century: confusions, contrasts – and convergence?', in J. Jennings, *Intellectuals in Twentieth-Century France: Mandarins and Samurais* (Oxford, 1993).

[36] E. Barker, *Age and Youth*, 207–8.

an arbitrary ideal of 'professional' political science, as the author of one of his obituaries implicitly did in 1960. Another of his pupils at Oxford earlier in the century, George Catlin, readily conceded that Barker had been a 'great political philospher' and teacher. But at the same time, he condescendingly maintained that: 'There are those . . . concerned in an older tradition with taking Political Science seriously and who might have hoped great things from the foundation of a new Chair in a major university, for whom Ernest Barker's appointment, in terms not of the great tutor but of the greater subject, could only be regarded as a disaster.'[37] It is true that Barker equated 'political science' with social and political theory, embracing history, law, and moral philosophy as well. Accordingly, he distanced himself from those who sought to transform the discipline into an 'exact science'. However, his rejection of such models stemmed from the general educational role – both within and beyond the university – which he assigned to all modern subjects more than from intellectual prejudice itself. Political inquiry in an historical and theoretical rather than a natural scientific mould would simultaneously inform and integrate, raising the level of cultural awareness and sense of common identity in England (which he always used unproblematically as a synonym of 'Britain'). It was this motivation which sustained him throughout his professional life, making even his most learned work broadly accessible.

How is this objective best placed in the literary world and cultural politics of the first half of the twentieth century? Most obviously, Barker's numerous public commitments suggest that the Victorian model of the 'literary statesman' had by no means become obsolete in the twentieth century, despite the sharp slump in its fortunes after the First World War.[38] The broad didactic role of the nineteenth-century intellectual continued to appeal to members of the expanding academic profession, as well as to a dwindling number of freelance literary figures such as Belloc and Chesterton.[39] Anxious to secure the widest moral and cultural authority rather than the limited acclaim

[37] G.E.G. Catlin, 'Sir Ernest Barker, 1874–1960', *Proceedings of the British Academy*, 46 (1960), 349.

[38] D.G. Wright, 'The Great War, government propaganda and English "men of letters" 1914–16', *Literature and History*, 7 (1978), 93–100.

[39] T.W. Heyck claims that literary figures such as Belloc and Chesterton, in addition to 'socialists involved with the intellectual and political enlightenment of the working class', were the only survivors of the tradition of the Victorian 'Men of Letters' in the early-twentieth century. This is surely an exaggeration. He certainly seems to pre-date considerably the advent of 'the detached thinking of university people' at the end of the nineteenth century. *The Transformation of Intellectual Life in Victorian England* (London, 1982), 228–9, 236.

of academic circles only, many of the professional scholars in twentieth-century Britain stayed loyal to the heritage of their 'amateur' predecessors – those who contributed to the extensive 'higher journalism' of Victorian England and wrote books for a learned but essentially non-specialised audience. A keen desire to put their intellectual talents at the service of the public was characteristic of Gilbert Murray, G.M. Trevelyan, G.P. Gooch, Harold Laski, A.D. Lindsay, R.G. Collingwood, William Beveridge, H.A.L. Fisher, and Barker himself, to name a few examples.[40] Most of these figures maintained the close connections with the political elite from which much of the status and self-confidence of their predecessors had derived;[41] most, also, perpetuated the late-Victorian and Edwardian conflation of the worlds of thought and action, serving government itself as well as other organisations in the public sphere; and all remained committed to the polymathy of the Victorian intelligentsia, the humanities and social sciences constituting a seamless web through which public as well as scholarly opinion might be advanced. Their concern to forge links with general audiences contrasts sharply with the stance of literary modernists with which one recent commentator has associated twentieth-century intellectuals generally, both in Britain and elsewhere in the West.[42] Instead of turning their backs upon lay audiences in revulsion against the 'barbarism' of mass culture, the academic writers in question earnestly sought to educate it. This was especially true of Barker. After underlining the extent to which 'our learning and our culture' had been made by 'private scholars' in the nineteenth century, he urged their successors – the university teachers of his own era – to 'keep a rich humanity at the same time that [they] acquire a large erudition'.[43]

[40] The 'public service' motivation of these figures is well brought out in the following studies: F. West, *Gilbert Murray: A Life* (New York, 1984); M. Moorman, *George Macaulay Trevelyan: A Memoir* (London, 1980), and Cannadine, *G.M. Trevelyan*; F. Eyck, *G.P. Gooch: A Study in History and Politics* (London, 1982); H.A. Deane, *The Political Ideas of Harold Laski* (New Haven, 1955); D. Boucher, *The Social and Political Thought of R.G. Collingwood* (Cambridge, 1989); D. Scott, *A.D. Lindsay: A Biography* (Oxford, 1971); J. Harris, *William Beveridge: A Biography* (London, 1977); and D. Ogg, *Herbert Fisher, 1865–1940: A Short Biography* (London, 1947).

[41] Collini, *Public Moralists*, 58. In some cases, these connections now extended to an international as well as a national political elite. For example, Barker was well acquainted with General Smuts, Mahatma Gandhi, and Czech leaders such as Thomas Masaryk, Jan Masaryk, and Eduard Beneš.

[42] J. Carey, *The Intellectuals and the Masses: Pride and Prejudice among the Literary Intelligentsia, 1880–1939* (London, 1992).

[43] E. Barker, *Universities in Great Britain: Their Position and Their Problems* (London, 1931), 9.

Indeed, in seeking to diffuse the riches of scholarship beyond the educated public itself, some twentieth-century writers proved more ambitious than their counterparts in mid- to late-Victorian England. The growth of interest in adult education at Oxford and Cambridge Universities earlier this century well illustrates this concern. It was a campaign which Barker enthusiastically espoused, particularly through his scheme for 'People's Colleges' in the 1940s. Here, he urged the expansion of the model of adult education which had been established by the Workers' Educational Association a few decades previously, to embrace periods of residential study as well as evening classes. This would enable working men and women to become 'better citizens', better 'because more aware of the history, politics, and the economics of their community, and more alive to the treasures of its literature and all its culture'. His democratic impulses with respect to learning even led him to suggest that owners of country houses and mansions unable to afford their upkeep might generously donate them to the cause of 'People's Colleges'.[44] Earlier in his life he pursued a similar goal, becoming advisory editor of a six-volume *International University Reading Course* which brought together 'crowned masterpieces of eloquence' from a broad array of national literary traditions.[45]

This continued aspiration among twentieth-century scholars for wide cultural influence provides a primary context in which Barker's work as a political scientist must be situated. His task was particularly aided in the 1930s and 1940s by the 'common culture' which developed in Britain. This has been attributed by D.L. LeMahieu to the new mass-communication industries of that time, such as radio, cinema, and gramophone, combined with the existence of economic depression amidst relative affluence. The latter produced a 'heightened sense of social responsibility' among the better off in society, reinforcing the cohesive effect of the new media in which 'audiences, standards, and tastes' converged.[46] Unlike, for example, J.B. Priestley, who attempted to create an 'authentic' culture for a rapidly growing middle class in the 1930s, Barker and some of his academic contemporaries attempted to incorporate that stratum within the

[44] E. Barker, 'For adults: The idea of People's Colleges', in R.A. Scott-James (ed.), *Education in Britain: Yesterday, To-day, To-morrow* (London, 1944).

[45] This curious publishing venture, aimed no doubt at the working-class autodidact, was published in London somewhere beween 1917 and 1920. Barker's involvement possibly came about through his friendship with Lord Bryce, who contributed five pages of 'Hints on Reading' in vol. 1 before the reader plunged into the next 3,000 pages.

[46] LeMahieu, *A Culture for Democracy*, 227–36.

culture of higher learning.[47] The Second World War gave further momentum to the movement towards cultural integration in Britain, fixing a high premium on the celebrations of Englishness which Barker largely composed from the relevant insights of early-twentieth-century political science. Indeed, the public significance which the discipline of politics attained through its deployment in Barker's exposition of the national culture was similar to that which had been marked out – with some degree of success – for English studies in the Newbolt Report of 1921. Entitled *The Teaching of English in England*, the report urged scholars of English to become what Brian Doyle has termed 'national intellectuals'. Their task was to enlighten popular audiences on 'the English spirit' as reflected in the national literature, thus providing a firm basis for social unity.[48]

OUTLINE AND SCOPE

As suggested by the contextual themes above, the approach of this book is chiefly historical. Accordingly, the order of the chapters follows a roughly chronological sequence. Chapter 1 focuses upon the significance of Barker's north-country upbringing for his political outlook later in life, together with the formative influences of Idealism and Whiggism during his education in the Literae Humaniores and Modern History Schools at Oxford towards the end of the nineteenth century. Chapter 2 turns to his early work on classical political thought as a lecturer in history at Oxford at the turn of the century, emphasising the contemporary resonance he found in it for clarifying the nature of society, the state, and the individual. In particular, this chapter highlights his interest in Greek conceptions of the relationship between politics and law, the context of this interest in late-Victorian associations between Englishness and law, and his attempts to steer political science in a legal and historical rather than a philosophical direction as the battle-lines emerged over a 'Modern Greats' School. Chapter 3 considers Barker's contribution to Pluralist thought in the second decade of the twentieth century, stressing the centrality he accorded to voluntary association in English national development. The uses of government propaganda to which Barker set political theory in the First World War provide the focus of chapter 4. But particular attention is paid there to the ideals of

[47] On Priestley, see LeMahieu, *A Culture for Democracy*, 317–33.

[48] On the Newbolt Report, see Doyle, *English and Englishness*, ch. 2.

multinationalism and internationalism which developed out of his castigation of 'exclusive' nationalism in Germany, ideals which he continued to uphold thereafter. The issue of nationalism continues in chapter 5. This turns to the interlocking themes of national character and education in Britain which preoccupied Barker while he was Principal of King's College London in the 1920s. Chapter 6 analyses Barker's work at Cambridge subsequently, outlining the renewal of his hopes for a political science that was closely tied to law, his growing interest in natural law, and his alarm at the intensification of group identities across Europe which in many countries had resulted in the supersession of democratic by totalitarian governments. Chapters 7 and 8 discuss Barker's interpretations of Englishness in the Second World War and beyond. The Conclusion looks briefly at his posthumous reputation as a political thinker, emphasises the liberal-conservative character of his outlook, and assesses the fate of his view of England together with the contemporary relevance of his work more widely.

In general, the chapters are based upon Barker's published work. There is little unpublished material among his papers at Peterhouse, Cambridge, with which his *oeuvre* may be supplemented. He appears to have destroyed most of the letters and documents he received once he had dealt with them, following – no doubt – a notable Victorian concern to protect his privacy from posthumous invasion.[49] However, this disposal exercise has not adversely affected the following account, the central focus of which is his social and political thought. I have seldom mentioned events in his personal life and background, and then only in so far as they shed light on the primary subject-matter of the book. The advantage of writing about a thinker such as Barker who was blessed with longevity and who also succeeded in publishing the main things he had to say about the world is that little intellectual business remained unfinished at the time of his death.[50] There are no fragments, therefore, which need to be pieced together from manuscript sources. Where appropriate, though, I have made use of letters to his

[49] See P.N. Furbank, 'Posers for posterity: self-protection and self-projection in the great Victorian authors', review of M. Millgate, *Testamentary Acts: Browning, Tennyson, James, Hardy* (Oxford, 1992), *Times Literary Supplement*, 17 July 1992, 3–4.

[50] Only two of his projects seem to have fallen by the wayside: first, a history of English and American political ideas during the American Revolution and second, a study of 'the political career and philosophy of Burke'. But even these appeared, in the form of a number of extended essays, in his *Essays on Government* (Oxford, 1945) and *Traditions of Civility: Eight Essays* (Cambridge, 1948). See his Preface to *Essays on Government*.

friends and colleagues which survive in various private and public collections. I have also incorporated archival material with regard to his proposals for political (and social) science at Oxford and Cambridge Universities during his years of service there, and also his involvement in the Books Commission during the Second World War.

Barker was not an exceptionally original thinker, being far too fond of eclecticism to have attained that status. Nevertheless, his contribution to English political and cultural thought was a highly nuanced one. As such, it found a broad appeal in academic, official, and popular circles alike. My fundamental aim in writing this book has been to capture the singularity of his work and the public concerns which it addressed. Consequently, I have sought to clarify the reasons why Barker held certain beliefs and not others; the various factors in his life and milieux which shaped the intellectual and temperamental dispositions I outlined earlier; the place of his thought within the political debate of its time; and the way in which his ideas shifted slightly but nonetheless significantly during successive phases of his career. In general, I have attempted to keep my own expressions of sympathy and antipathy to a minimum, although the reactions of contemporaries to his writings do feature in the analysis. Finally, while I have endeavoured to give as rounded a picture as possible, I do not pretend to have given an exhaustive account of his work; that feat is precluded by its scale and range.

CHAPTER 1

Lancashire, Idealism, and Whiggism: the making of an English political scientist

HOME AND SCHOOL

The frustrated ambition of working-class scholars at the end of the nineteenth century is well captured in the hero of Hardy's novel, *Jude the Obscure* (1895). Having immersed himself in centuries of learning during every spare moment for well over ten years, Jude Fawley's dreams of formal study were brutally shattered by the Masters' indifference at the hallowed Colleges of 'Christminster' – Oxford in thin disguise. The lowest rungs of the 'ladder of opportunity' for which Jude yearned were not installed until 1902 when the Balfour Education Act laid the foundations of public secondary education in Britain. However, it was not entirely unknown for boys of poor birth to satisfy keen intellectual aspirations before the passage of that Act. A number of factors helped to smooth the path to academic distinction from the most unlikely backgrounds. These included various scholarship schemes, luck, generous benefactors, good voluntary educational institutions in the locality, and the invaluable Cassell's *National Library of Classical Literature.*

For example, Barker's friend and fellow-Mancunian, George Unwin, enjoyed many of these 'advantages' in an environment where public educational provision was meagre. The son of a publican turned shopkeeper, he left school at the age of thirteen to become a clerk in a Stockport hat-making firm. But he soon developed a wide knowledge of philosophy and literature, chiefly through the stimulus of the Stockport literary society, the local Mechanics Institute, and the Unitarian Church. This won him places at Cardiff and Oxford Universities, from where he went on to become an eminent economic historian.[1]

[1] G. Unwin, *Studies in Economic History: The Collected Papers of George Unwin*, ed. R.H. Tawney (London, 1927), xi–xii.

Unwin was exceptional in winning university scholarships without previously attaining a bursary for secondary education. Barker's experience of gaining scholarships from a much earlier age – in his case, the age of twelve – was more common among the university entrants of his generation who came from humble origins. Yet the element of chance was as important in his intellectual good fortune as it was for Unwin. The headmaster of his village school at Bredbury on the Cheshire border with Lancashire was requested to prepare the son of a local businessman for the scholarship examination to Manchester Grammar School. In this unprecedented exercise in the village, Barker was recruited as a 'pace-maker'. He had already developed a large appetite for books which he borrowed from neighbours who looked kindly upon him or from the school itself. As a result, he far outdistanced what he liked to regard – with characteristic modesty – as 'the real candidate', and he joined the Grammar School in 1886.[2] From a small, overcrowded cottage on his grandparents' farm on the lower slopes of Werneth Low, where he was born in 1874, he began a course of upward social mobility that led him to the heart of the British Establishment.[3]

As will become apparent at several points in this study, Barker himself saw nothing exceptional in his success. He would certainly have disliked any comparison between his own circumstances and those of Jude Fawley, finding the latter 'too pathetic to be true to life'. In any case, he believed that there was no reason at the turn of the century for 'a man who was hungry for knowledge to go unregarded about the Oxford streets': a Non-Collegiate Body and the Delegacy 'for the extension of teaching beyond the limits of the University' existed to prevent such pitiful spectres.[4] Still, fate had been as kind to him as it had been cruel to Jude, and his fundamental attitudes and outlook were shaped accordingly. In particular, conscious that he owed his whole career to scholarships of one kind or another, he became a firm advocate of that route to higher education from less prosperous homes, rather than a system of loans or concurrent employment.[5]

[2] E. Barker, *Age and Youth: Memories of Three Universities and Father of the Man* (London, 1953), 253–5.

[3] In his usual upbeat way, he liked to think that the 'stars had been auspicious in the year of my birth', sharing it – as he did – with G.K. Chesterton, Geoffrey Dawson (editor of *The Times*), Chaim Weizmann, Winston Churchill, James Mallon (Warden of Toynbee Hall) and Lord Sandwich. Barker to M.B. Reckitt, 17 December 1953, Reckitt Papers, University of Sussex Library, 13/1.

[4] E. Barker, *Age and Youth*, 71.

[5] E. Barker, *British Universities* (London, 1946), 21.

The place at Manchester Grammar School released Barker from the career as a schoolmaster at an elementary school which had previously been appointed for him; but it by no means cleared away all the financial and psychological obstacles he faced in his drive to become a scholar. He relied heavily upon winning prizes to overcome the resistance of the male members of his extended family who disdained his non-remunerative existence in the world of books. Through these achievements, he also contributed to the incidental expenses he incurred in school attendance which the stretched resources of his home could not meet.[6] Further encouragement came in the form of supplementary coaching and the loan of books from some of the masters. Such supports enabled his education to reach a point at which it acquired discipline and direction. He eventually specialised in classics, particularly Greek, laying the foundation of his lifelong admiration for the ancient world. As he emphasised in his autobiography, it was from a love of the classics that all his other intellectual interests stemmed, including the subject in which he was later to hold a chair.[7] Henceforth, Greek political thought and institutions, in particular, became the cardinal reference-point for his understanding of political science.

The best of classical educations was not the only factor in Barker's early life in Lancashire which concentrated his mind on politics and political science; the *Manchester Guardian* came a close second. As he reflected in 1931, this newspaper was one of two things about Manchester – the other being the Grammar School – which he would never forget: 'I remember buying it and reading it when I was a boy. I read it with more understanding as I grew up; and from it, perhaps, I learned such lessons of political wisdom as I have mastered, and acquired the tastes that have since conducted me to a Chair of Politics.'[8] An equally important stimulus to his political interests – and along the same lines as the *Manchester Guardian* – was his father. While his relationship with George Barker – a miner-cum-'general handyman' – seems to have been a distant one, he readily imbibed his Liberal politics. Gladstone, in particular, won his father's praise, and Ernest Barker followed suit. Gladstone's personality, he recalled on the fiftieth anniversary of the death of the elder statesman in 1948, 'coloured and even controlled' his memories of boyhood and youth.[9] Many of the political ideals and causes which Barker later embraced

6 E. Barker, *Age and Youth*, 258, 270. 7 E. Barker, *Age and Youth*, 262–3, n.1.
8 'When I was in Manchester', *The Times*, 31 December 1931.
9 E. Barker, 'Mr. Gladstone', *The British Weekly*, 20 May 1948, 7.

were leaves from Gladstone's book, though they were not exclusive to the latter. These included democracy, Home Rule, sound public finance, national self-determination, and the primacy of morality in the conduct of political affairs. An aspect of Gladstone's persona which Barker was in a better position than his father to appreciate was the figure he cut as a 'scholar-statesman', and a classical scholar at that. This, combined with Gladstone's great powers of oratory, reminded Barker of Pericles. It was a satisfying contemplation for a fellow 'Greats' graduate from Lancashire. Most of all, however, Barker's Gladstonian roots shaped his keen sensitivity to the importance of individual liberty and the incursions which state and society could often make upon it.

Such an attitude was reinforced by his character as well as by filial loyalty. For example, he recalled in his autobiography his antipathy as a boy towards organised games. He sought an outlet for his cricketing instincts at home with his seven brothers and sisters (of whom he was the eldest) rather than teams at school. Long, solitary walks under the inspiration of Wordsworth were another of his preferred forms of exercise. Indeed, he openly confessed to a certain 'awkwardness' in company, the result of a 'home-keeping' temper and the rural setting in which he grew up. His studies seem to have provided all the stimulation he needed during his youth: 'Outside the cottage', he declared, 'I had nothing but school; but having my school, I had everything'.[10]

It was not that he was embarrassed by his early environment; or at least, if he was, he realised the foolishness of his attempts to conceal the modesty of his home from his more affluent contemporaries.[11] Later in life, at any rate, he frequently counted its blessings and extolled them against pessimistic accounts of working-class life in the era of modern capitalism. In 1934, for example, he wrote to thank J.L. Hammond for his latest book – written with Barbara Hammond – entitled *The Bleak Age*. This argued that the material advantages which the working class enjoyed in industrial civilisation were greatly outweighed by a new poverty of spirit. Barker strongly resisted this conclusion, suggesting that all was not gloom in the poorer quarters of nineteenth-century towns and villages.

[10] E. Barker, *Age and Youth*, 292. I was alerted to this passage by Michael Oakeshott's *The Voice of Liberal Learning: Michael Oakeshott on Education*, ed. Timothy Fuller (Yale, 1989), 40. Oakeshott uses it to exemplify a concept of education – now rapidly fading – in which school is the centre of a boundless imaginative universe.

[11] E. Barker, *Age and Youth*, 269.

I was born sixty years ago in a little cottage, with one of the two rooms on the ground having a stone floor, and the other nothing but plain . . . earth. I suppose it was bleak; and yet all the memories that survive in my mind about it are curiously warm and kind. My father played his old violin, and sometimes sang; we grew up among chequered joys and troubles. I used to hear from my great grandfather, who survived till I was 12 or more, tales of an earlier day. There were bleak things in those tales; but there were also things (like stories of fast trips at over 4 miles an hour in a 'packet' on the canal) that used to please me.[12]

Nevertheless, both the relative isolation and simplicity of his boyhood surroundings enhanced his diffident tendency, setting limits to his identification with the many organisations he subsequently joined. While fully appreciating the importance of society to human fulfilment, he was careful not to over-expose himself to it. As he wrote in his autobiography: 'Whenever I have belonged to a group, and have found the group cultivating and expecting the quality called *esprit de corps*, I have instinctively shied at the expectation. Institutionalism has seemed to me a sort of infectious disease, which I have been anxious not to catch.'[13]

This aversion informed Barker's social and political theory at every point. The great store which he set by privacy is nicely caught in a book which he wrote in 1939. There he urged recognition of the 'duty of solitude' as 'the ultimate duty which a man owes to himself, to others through himself, and to the self which is behind himself and all other selves'. The duty of solitude ranked higher even than responsibility to one's family, neighbour, and the state.[14] He paid homage to the Puritans for this insight, a sympathy which arose from the Nonconformist faith in which he had been brought up. As we shall see, it was not the only grounds on which he upheld their legacy.

LATE-NINETEENTH-CENTURY INDIVIDUALISM

The ambivalence which Barker felt towards society, the state, and voluntary groups was by no means unique among political thinkers during his intellectually formative years. In part the product of his character and background, it was also a response to the vulnerability of liberalism at the end of the nineteenth century. Influenced by the

[12] Barker to J.L. Hammond, 6 October 1934, MS. Hammond 18, fol. 225, Bodleian Library.
[13] E. Barker, *Age and Youth*, 304.
[14] E. Barker, *The Values of Life: Essays on the Circles and Centres of Duty* (London, 1939), 108–9.

growing demand for legislation in the economic and social realms, concerted attempts were made in many intellectual camps to close the gap between the individual and society which that ideology was alleged to have opened up. This task seemed the more urgent in the eyes of contemporaries as the extension of the state now went beyond the economic infrastructure of 'telegraphy, insurance, annuities, postal order, and parcel post'. Of far deeper import for G.J. Goschen – writing in 1883 – was 'the growing interference with the relations between classes, its increased control over vast categories of transactions between individuals and the substitution in many dealings of trade and manufacture, of the aggregate conscience and moral sense of the nation, for the conscience and moral sense of men as units'.[15]

A common justification of this new type of state action was that – in the words of the Idealist philosopher Bernard Bosanquet – 'society is the moral essence of the individual'.[16] But rarely was a philosophical and political synthesis achieved without reservation and equivocation. This was largely due to the long shadow cast over English political thought at the turn of the century by the tenacious belief of an earlier generation in the primacy and importance of individual moral agency. That conviction – it is becoming increasingly clear – rarely condoned unrestrained egoism on the basis of an atomistic conception of society.[17] This was often obscured in early-twentieth-century endeavours to discredit the 'abstract individualism' imputed to 'classical' Liberalism in order to give the collectivist state a clear run. In effect, however, the continuing resonance of the Victorian language of character – one which was by no means oblivious to a wider public good – limited the purchase of holistic concepts of society in the collectivist enthusiasm of the time. In this sense, it is more correct to speak of the re-orientation of individualism as a perspective on society, morality, and politics at the turn of the century, rather than its displacement. In general, society continued to be regarded as

[15] G.J. Goschen, *Laissez-Faire and Government Interference* (London, 1883), 3–4; quoted in W.H. Greenleaf, *The British Political Tradition*, vol. 1, *The Rise of Collectivism* (London, 1983), 30.

[16] B. Bonsanquet, 'The antithesis between individualism and socialism philosophically considered' (1890), in *The Civilization of Christendom and Other Studies* (London, 1893), 308.

[17] For this revisionist view of Victorian 'individualism' as associated with the concepts of character, moral strenuousness, and even altruism rather than economic selfishness, see Stefan Collini, *Public Moralists: Political Thought and Intellectual Life in Britain, 1850–1930* (Oxford, 1991); on the wide range of attitudes towards the relationship of individuals to society and the state in 'old liberalism' see A. Vincent, 'Classical liberalism and its crisis of identity', *History of Political Thought*, II (Spring 1990), 143–61.

a function of individuals, albeit individuals who impacted strongly on one another, who were imbued with a sense of mutual obligation, and achieved some kind of common identity. The changed tone of this individualism consisted mainly of the elevation of the state as a key variable in both individual character and social cohesion, a development which owed much to the prominent place which poverty occupied in the late-Victorian 'moral imagination'.[18]

The strength of 'moral individualism' across a wide spectrum of nineteenth-century political thought is best appreciated by examining the two chief influences in Barker's education after he left Manchester Grammar School in 1893: Idealist philosophy and Burkean political ideas. Despite their very different lineage and language, the two streams of thought shared the same double-faced nature. On the one hand, exponents of both underlined individual liberty and spontaneity as the cardinal political values; but on the other, they stressed that these priorities were dependent upon a wider, group freedom identified primarily with the nation. Barker encountered Idealism and Burkeanism in the Literae Humaniores and Modern History Schools at Oxford respectively, after winning a scholarship to Balliol College. He declared his allegiance to Idealism in his earliest work, and also singled out in his autobiography a number of Idealist thinkers who had particularly impressed him as an undergraduate. By contrast, it was not until later that he explicitly identified with the Whig historiography which formed the main vehicle of Burkean thought in the nineteenth century.[19] Consequently, in the following account, the influence of Idealism will be more apparent. Nevertheless, as will be seen in the next chapter, his first publications were steeped in Whig assumptions and values, albeit unacknowledged and largely unattributable to specific individuals within that tradition.

LITERAE HUMANIORES AND PHILOSOPHICAL IDEALISM

The idealist revival of the last quarter of the nineteenth century was inextricably linked with the distinction which Literae Humaniores –

[18] G. Himmelfarb, *Poverty and Compassion: The Moral Imagination of the Late Victorians* (New York, 1991).

[19] As J.W. Burrow has remarked, 'it is in historiography rather than in theoretical statement that we find the fullest expressions of Burkean political ideas in nineteenth-century England'. *A Liberal Descent: Victorian Historians and the English Past* (Cambridge, 1981), 131.

or 'Greats' – achieved in this period.[20] First expounded in the lectures of T.H. Green and the writings of F.H. Bradley, British Idealism gave purpose and intellectual coherence to Oxford's most prestigious and exacting School. In turn, its further development was directed by this association. There were a number of reasons for the closely intertwined fortunes of Idealism and Greats in the heyday of the latter. First, the dominance of Plato and Aristotle in the Greats curriculum gave Idealism a more secure and lasting hold at Oxford than it ever achieved at Cambridge in the equivalent Moral Sciences Tripos.[21] Second, the high premium which Idealist thinkers since Hegel attached to the state reinforced the ethic of public service which Oxford – particularly Literae Humaniores – now inculcated.[22] Third, Idealism located the roots of contemporary institutions and thought in antiquity, tracing a developing sense of human solidarity back to the Greeks, especially. It thus underlined the contemporary relevance of classical literature and history as the basis for understanding the ideas and institutions of the modern world.

The central Idealist belief in a sense of 'the common good' as the foundation of society was part of the late-Victorian reaction against perceptions of the atomistic individualism in nineteenth-century political thought mentioned above, and identified mainly with Utilitarianism.[23] It both reflected and reinforced the growing movement towards social reform and democracy as English society seemed to acquire a greater sense of collective national purpose. In attempting to clarify the opportunities and dangers attendant upon these changes, Idealist philosophers and also other classical scholars turned to ancient Greece. They regarded the Greek city-states as a model of society organised around the principles of obligation and citizenship rather than individual rights, from which many modern lessons could be learned. Aristotle's *Ethics*, in particular, became a seminal guide to the increasingly 'civic' nature of English political life, overshadowing – if not entirely displacing – its previous association with Christianity.

[20] On 'Greats' in its most flourishing period, see R. Symonds, *Oxford and Empire: The Last Lost Cause* (London, 1986). A recent and illuminating work on British Idealism is P.P. Nicholson, *The Political Philosophy of the British Idealists: Selected Studies* (Cambridge, 1990). This contains an extensive bibliography of writings both by and on the Idealists.

[21] P. Robbins, *The British Hegelians, 1875–1925* (New York, 1982), 46.

[22] On the transformation of Oxford from a theological seminary to a centre for training political and administrative elites after the reforms of the mid-nineteenth-century, see A.J. Engel, *From Clergyman to Don: The Rise of the Academic Profession in Nineteenth-Century Oxford* (Oxford, 1983). See also Lewis Campbell, *On the Nationalization of the Old Universities* (London, 1901).

[23] Collini, *Public Moralists*, 325.

As F.M. Turner has argued: 'Democracy, empire, military preparedness, international economic rivalry, an expanding bureaucracy, national insurance, school lunches, and national education, to mention only a few political developments, had made citizenship a category of thought and association to which an increasingly large number of values and experiences adhered.'[24]

As an undergraduate at Balliol College reading Greats, Barker was fully exposed to Idealist thought. He had joined the college in 1893. In that year Edward Caird – an influential Idealist philosopher and friend of Green, although more of an Hegelian – became Master following the death of Benjamin Jowett. Jowett had himself been instrumental in the revival of Idealism in Britain. Idealism had also flourished at the college through Green, who had been a Fellow there before his early death in 1882. At Balliol, Barker enjoyed Caird's counsel in philosophy. Indeed, he so impressed Caird that the latter encouraged him in a rather premature application for the Chair in Philosophy at the University of Glasgow at the outset of his academic career.[25] But while, ultimately, Caird failed to turn his charge into a philosopher, he did succeed in imparting a good many of his 'views and . . . idioms'.[26] It was probably Caird, along with like-minded tutors such as J.A. Smith, who directed Barker's reading in philosophy towards the Idealists. He certainly absorbed Kant, Hegel, Green, and Bradley in the course of his studies for Greats. Equipped with this Idealist orientation, he developed an interest in the interpretation of political thought, if not in political philosophy itself.

Barker's first book, *The Political Thought of Plato and Aristotle*, published in 1906, reflected a growing interest among scholars of his generation in the history of political ideas written from an Idealist perspective.[27] Its arguments will be examined in the next chapter.

[24] F.M. Turner, *The Greek Heritage in Victorian Britain* (New Haven, 1981), 358. On the Idealist reading of contemporary anxieties about democracy and collectivism into Greek political thought, see pp. 432–46. Here Turner focuses on the work of R.L. Nettleship, Bernard Bosanquet, and Barker. See also his account of Alfred Zimmern's *The Greek Commonwealth: Politics and Economics in Fifth-Century Athens* (Oxford, 1911), 259–62. This work contained themes which were similar to the Idealist interest in the Greeks.

[25] E. Barker, *Age and Youth*, 194.

[26] E. Barker, *Age and Youth*, 318.

[27] The influence of Idealism on the history of philosophy has scarcely been explored. Some moves in this direction in relation to Bosanquet have been made by C. Parker, 'Bernard Bosanquet, historical knowledge, and the history of ideas', *Philosophy of the Social Services*, 18 (1988), 213–30. Besides the contributions of Bosanquet and Barker to this area, there are also those of John MacCunn, D.G. Ritchie, and C.E. Vaughan. These were also rooted in Idealist thought. See J. MacCunn, *Six Radical Thinkers: Bentham, J.S. Mill, Cobden, Carlyle, Mazzini,*

Here, it is appropriate to note the influence of Green on the book, which its author acknowledged at the outset. Claiming to have gained his 'general conception of political science' from Green's *Principles of Political Obligation*, Barker declared: 'it is with his teaching that I have contrasted, or (more often) compared, that of Plato and Aristotle'.[28] A eulogy to Green which he made in 1915 reveals the precise attraction which Barker found in his leading Idealist mentor, revealing as much about Barker's conception of and preoccupation with English culture as it does about Green's political philosophy. Green, he wrote, had 'seized the philosophy of Greece and of Germany, and interpreted it for Englishmen with a full measure of English caution, and with a full reference to that deep sense of the "liberty of the subject" and that deep distrust of "reason of state", which marks all Englishmen'. In this way, Green had remained true to the liberal tradition of J.S. Mill. Mill in his turn – according to Barker – was fully alive to the sense which Green later developed of the 'spiritual foundations of society'.[29] However, Green had corrected Mill's individualism with a more socialised conception of human action. Green, Barker maintained, had put paid to Mill's flawed idea of 'self-regarding' actions; and he had substituted the truer distinction – for the purpose of defining the scope of the state – between 'outward actions necessary and valuable for the maintenance of rights – actions which the state can secure by external force because they are external and actions proceeding from an inward will'.[30]

This claim certainly sounded a keynote of Green's political philosophy. For Green, the state had a duty to secure the social conditions in which individuals could exercise the full range of their capacities as freely as possible. In particular, the function of the state was to create a propitious climate for 'the growth of self-reliance, with the formation of a manly conscience and sense of moral dignity, – in short, with the moral autonomy which is the condition of the highest

T.H. Green (London, 1910); D.G. Ritchie, *The Principles of State Interference: Four Essays on the Political Philosophy of Mr. Herbert Spencer, J.S. Mill, and T.H. Green* (London, 1891), *Natural Rights: A Criticism of Some Political and Ethical Conceptions* (London, 1894), and parts of *Darwin and Hegel, with Other Philosophical Studies* (London, 1893) and *Studies in Political and Social Ethics* (London, 1902); Vaughan's main works were *The Political Writings of Jean Jacques Rousseau* (Cambridge, 1915); and *Studies in the History of Political Philosophy Before and After Rousseau*, 2 vols. (Manchester, 1925).

28 E. Barker, *The Political Thought of Plato and Aristotle* (London, 1906), vii.

29 E. Barker, review of J. MacCunn, *Six Radical Thinkers, International Journal of Ethics*, 20, 2 (1910), 220.

30 E. Barker, *Political Thought in England from Herbert Spencer to the Present Day* (London, 1915), 58–9.

goodness'. (It was an ideal of arduous self-development which did indeed have strong echoes of Mill, and which Barker constantly played up in his renditions of Idealism.) But the state could not promote moral goodness directly, Green thought, having defined the latter in terms of voluntary contributions towards 'the common good'; the 'disinterested or unselfish morality' which he exhorted as the object of all human endeavour could not be forced.[31] He was optimistic that the state's indirect role in promoting this 'true morality' could be realised with only a minor extension of its duties to encompass land reform, elementary education, temperance, and restrictions upon freedom of contract in employment.[32]

Green's Idealism was thus quite compatible politically with the 'Manchester' liberalism of Cobden and Bright to which he was consciously indebted. This called for an end to 'abuses' in public life, such as those which were embodied in protectionism and an Established Church. Green worked firmly with this grain of political moralism in mid-Victorian liberalism, if he did not adopt all of its causes. It was one to which Gladstone, especially, had given much practical effect.[33] Indeed, recent historians have stressed that Green's primary contribution to political radicalism was to clothe its underlying moral ethos in philosophical language, his specific policy proposals being ancillary to this end.[34] He expanded the horizons of radicalism by – in Melvin Richter's words – 'lead[ing] a reaction against that aspect of [it] which made no demand for a personal contribution to the social good'.[35] Yet it is important to recognise that in doing so he introduced a distinct emollient element into English liberalism, as will become clear later in this chapter.

Barker could not fail to have been attracted to Green's theory of the state, given its deep roots in liberal radicalism. He shared the northern, provincial, Nonconformist ambience of that force in mid-nineteenth-century politics. Following Green's lead, though, he dropped the war against 'privilege' which had galvanised it then (not

[31] T.H. Green, *Lectures on the Principles of Political Obligation*, ed. B. Bosanquet (1895; London, 1931), 39–40.

[32] T.H. Green, *Liberal Legislation and Freedom of Contract* (London, 1881).

[33] This connection between the moralism in mid-Victorian liberalism and Gladstone is emphasised by R. Bellamy. 'T.H. Green and the morality of Victorian liberalism', in R. Bellamy (ed.), *Victorian Liberalism: Nineteenth-Century Political Thought and Practice* (London, 1990), 132.

[34] S. Collini, *Liberalism and Sociology: L.T. Hobhouse and Political Argument in England, 1880–1914* (Cambridge, 1979), 45; and Bellamy, 'T.H. Green and the morality of Victorian liberalism', 132.

[35] M. Richter, *The Politics of Conscience: T.H. Green and his Age* (London, 1964), 269–70, 291.

least, perhaps, because he found no doors to the political and educational Establishment closed against him).[36] Barker's Nonconformism was especially important in drawing him to Green and the political tradition in which he stood, as it was for other second-generation Idealists like A.D. Lindsay.[37] Brought up in the Congegationalist faith at the seventeenth-century chapel of Hatherlow in Cheshire, he would have been much moved by the ideal of spontaneous moral community at the heart of Green's political thought.[38] It is true that the same Puritan background set limits to his identification with Green's political vision; as we have seen already, Barker flinched from society in excess, both in his personal life and in his tastes in political theory. In this he departed from Green for whom 'ascetic altruism' was the essence of the good life, and for whom – as Alan Milne has remarked – conflict between personal interest and the common good was unimaginable.[39] Green's insistence upon the virtue of unremitting self-sacrifice reflected the social gospel of Evangelicalism, a force which had melded with the earlier Nonconformist traditions of his family but which was absent from Barker's religious roots. Still, Green's political prescriptions and his sense of the sanctity of individual personality which underlay them were less demanding than his ethical ones, and clearly harmonised with the religious and ideological temper of Barker's home. Like Green, he inducted Nonconformity to a central place in his political theory, a theme which will become more apparent still when we turn to his role in the Pluralist movement.

Barker was also attracted to the work of two other leading Idealist thinkers in Britain: F.H. Bradley and Bernard Bosanquet. These, like Green, offered insights which illuminated his early environment, particularly his sense of its relative 'classlessness'. He was to make much of the latter in his writings on Englishness after the Second World War, arguing vehemently against analyses of 'England' which emphasised its class divisions. Such interpretations were, he believed, products of the southern part of the country, quite alien to those who

[36] On Barker's attempt to induct Nonconformism into mainstream Englishness, see ch. 5 below.

[37] Lindsay brought out the Puritan basis of Green's political beliefs in his Introduction to the latter's *Lectures on the Principles of Political Obligation* (1895, London, 1941). Lindsay's Idealism is contrasted with Barker's in ch. 6 below.

[38] This suggestion has been persuasively advanced by F.M. Turner, *The Greek Heritage in Victorian Britain*, 441.

[39] Richter, *The Politics of Conscience*, 257; A.J.M. Milne, 'The common good and rights in T.H. Green's ethical and political theory', in A. Vincent (ed.), *The Philosophy of T.H. Green* (Aldershot, 1986), 69.

were accustomed to the 'industrial democracy' of the north.[40] Green's Idealism was less promising on this score than that of his contemporaries. Green had notoriously raised doubts about the extent to which the gin-drinking denizens of London yards were included within the pale of Victorian society, a concern which was echoed in his comment about the social divisions engendered by the culturally central concept of the 'gentleman'.[41] By contrast, Bosanquet was more sanguine about the homogeneity of English society, expressing ideas with which Barker could readily identify and which were later to inspire his theory of national character. Bosanquet's philosophy, maintained Barker in 1915, represented a 'fuller social experience [than that of Green], the fruit of new social experiments, which suggests that the essentials of character are the same throughout the social whole'.[42] Bradley's philosophy of 'my station and its duties' could also be invoked in support of an agreeable image of English society, one which was held together by the bonds of mutual occupational service rather than class conflict. This was especially so given that Bradley denied that stations were inexorably 'fixed' at birth,[43] his allowance of a degree of occupational mobility according well with Barker's conception of the fluidity of English social structure, to which his own success bore witness. We shall find echoes of these Idealist assumptions and commitments throughout Barker's *oeuvre*, so it is important to be aware at the outset of the strong regional identities which attracted him to them. They were reinforced, however, by the cultural beliefs articulated in Burkean Whiggism.

MODERN HISTORY AND BURKEAN WHIGGISM

After obtaining a First in Greats in 1897 Barker joined the Modern History School at Oxford. His aim in doing so was to prepare himself for the Home Civil Service examination, a demanding exercise which favoured the generalist. In the event, his extra year at Oxford settled his vocation as a scholar rather than an administrator. He had gained Firsts in both Greats and Modern History, and in 1899 he added to these accomplishments a prize fellowship in Classics at Merton College Oxford. The fellowship was to run for seven years. However, the income it generated was not munificent and was certainly

[40] E. Barker, 'The English people', *Britain Today* (July, 1943), 15–19.
[41] Collini, *Public Moralists*, 31. [42] E. Barker, *Political Thought in England*, 72.
[43] Nicholson, *The Political Philosophy of the British Idealists*, 40.

inadequate by itself to maintain a married don, which Barker became in the following year. He therefore sought an additional academic position. The first post which fell vacant was a Lectureship in Modern History at Wadham College which he secured in the same year as the Merton fellowship. This appointment marked the beginning of his 21-year association with the Oxford Modern History Faculty, holding associate tutorships at St John's College in 1909 and then New College in 1913. In the words of a contemporary, he proved to be 'one of the most (if not the most) successful history lecturers in the University'.[44]

The ease with which Barker moved between the two subjects is not only a comment on his intellectual versatility; it also reflects the extent to which classics was seen to provide the linchpin of all other areas of the Humanities at this time. This common background created, as Barker himself pointed out in his autobiography, a *lingua franca* which made light of disciplinary boundaries.[45] In the case of history, the route which Barker and many of his colleagues had taken from Greats created an instant sympathy with the work of the French historian Fustel de Coulanges. As H.A.L. Fisher recalled, 'Fustel had travelled the high road which leads from the ancient to the modern world. It was exactly the route which I proposed to follow.'[46] In similar words, Barker himself introduced one of his later works.[47]

Throughout the period in which Barker was associated with it, the Oxford Modern History School was intellectually centred in Whig

[44] W.H. Stevenson to T.F. Tout, 3 December 1908, Tout Papers, The John Rylands University Library of Manchester, 1/1143/4. This – and two other letters between Stevenson and Tout (4 and 7 December 1908) – concerned Barker's application for the tutorship at St John's College in 1908. The correspondence provides a revealing insight into Barker's character and the qualities which well equipped him for a college post. The college would overlook the fact of his being married – and in addition, not baptised – thought Stevenson. More important was his 'brilliant university career'; his 'charmingly frank and often, almost naive, nature that wins most hearts'; his 'wise tolerance of aberrations from the highest standards of religious and social morality . . . both in the eyes of the authorities and of the undergraduates'; and his 'moderate and . . . [un]obtruded' religious and political views. In these respects Stevenson compared Barker with Maurice Powicke, Barker's chief rival for the post, who shared Barker's Nonconformist upbringing and would soon share his married status as well. The implication of Stevenson's letter, however, was that Powicke's views were not as flexible as Barker's. I am much indebted to Peter Slee for drawing these letters to my attention.

[45] E. Barker, *Age and Youth*, 17.

[46] H.A.L. Fisher, *An Unfinished Autobiography* (Oxford, 1940), 71.

[47] E. Barker, *From Alexander to Constantine: Passages and Documents Illustrating the History of Social and Political Ideas, 336 B.C.–A.D. 337* (Oxford, 1956). The aim of the book, he declared, was to 'build a bridge – or rather lay stepping-stones . . . – across the six centuries of time between the emergence of the hellenistic world of great states and solemn kings and the appearance of that Christian world of Church and State in which we still live and have our being'. Preface.

historiography. The Whig interpretation of English history had increasingly lost its sectarian edge in the nineteenth century, becoming – instead – the 'national' interpretation of the English past.[48] Initially focusing upon the Whig settlement of 1688 but later extending back to the early Middle Ages and the Teutonic invasions, nineteenth-century Whiggism told a story of national unification which successfully transcended class, racial, and linguistic barriers; of the uniqueness of the English political system with its fine balance of local and central forces; of the successful brokerage of 'progress' and 'tradition'; and of the gradual securing of English constitutional liberty and representative institutions.[49] Whiggism maintained a particularly powerful presence at Oxford in the second half of the nineteenth century due to the influence of William Stubbs, Regius Professor from 1867 to 1884.[50] Stubbs' *Select Charters and other Illustrations of English Constitutional History* (1870) and his three-volume *Constitutional History of England* (1874–8) supplied to the Modern History School what the works of Plato and Aristotle gave to Greats: that is, authoritative texts which set the intellectual tone of the School as a whole. In the 1880s, Stubbs' works were accompanied by J.R. Green's *Short History of the English People* (1874) on the School's syllabus.[51] This addition strengthened the hold of Whiggism on the study of history at Oxford, carrying its characteristic themes of English liberty and continuity into the realm of social history.

Two other historians also came to share Stubbs' influence on the study of history at Oxford: Paul Vinogradoff and F.W. Maitland.[52] These figures represented a new wave of 'professional' historians who consciously distanced themselves from the 'literary', narrative style of historical study which Whiggism was important in sustaining in the nineteenth century. They revered Stubbs because he did much to break this 'amateur' mould through the high premium he set upon the use of original documents. It is true that they rejected Stubbs' 'presentist' view of the English past, a characteristic feature of the Whig approach which perceived in historical events a steady upward

[48] Burrow, *A Liberal Descent*, 295.

[49] I have only attempted to identify nineteenth-century Whiggism in its broadest outlines here. On the nuances of this genre, see Burrow, *A Liberal Descent*.

[50] According to J.P. Kenyon, Stubbs 'moulded the greater part of the Oxford history syllabus, almost single-handed, into the form it retained until the 1960s'. *The History Men: The Historical Profession in England since the Renaissance* (London, 1983), 169.

[51] Kenyon, *The History Men*, 164.

[52] The precise nature of their influence will be examined in ch. 2 below.

progression towards the existing political order.[53] It was on this account that their work on medieval history seemed more credible than that of Stubbs to a younger generation of historians anxious to cultivate 'impartiality' as a critical mark of scholarship. In 1936, for example, Barker praised Maitland for interpreting 'the manor, and feudalism, and the Middle Ages in general, instrinsically and by their own light . . . This, to my mind, is the difference between Maitland and Stubbs. Great as Stubbs was, he wrote his *Constitutional History of England* in spectacles – the spectacles of Victorian Liberalism.'[54] Yet, while eschewing anachronism in historiography, the new 'professional' historians clung to the notion that history was a discipline of profound moral and political significance. Moreover, many continued the reverence for English political institutions which had been a cardinal attribute of Whiggism, whether in its 'amateur' or 'professional' guise. Again, while determined to overcome the insularity of the Whig tradition, a new generation of historians – Acton, Bury, and Maitland, for example – nevertheless brought to the study of West European and American history the same preoccupation with the development of political and intellectual liberty which English history had inspired in their Whig predecessors.[55] Finally, the transition to 'professionalism' in English historiography left virtually intact the nineteenth-century belief – rooted in the combined forces of Liberal Anglicanism and romantic nationalism – that 'national character' constituted the moving force in history.[56] Barker's work as an historian and political scientist was to reflect all these changes and continuities in Whiggism at the turn of the century.

[53] On the reaction against Whiggism at the turn of the century see P.B.M. Blaas, *Continuity and Anachronism: Parliamentary and Constitutional Development in Whig Historiography and in the Anti-Whig Reaction between 1890 and 1930* (The Hague, 1978). For a stimulating and persuasive attempt to go beyond the amateur/professional dichotomy in characterising the transition in English historiography at the turn of the centry to a recognition of the many different forms which professionalism took, see J.W. Burrow, 'Victorian historians and the Royal Historical Society', *Transactions of the Royal Historical Society*, 5th series, 39 (1989), 125–40.

[54] E. Barker, 'Maitland as a sociologist', *The Sociological Review*, 29 (1937), 123.

[55] R. Jann, *The Art and Science of Victorian History* (Columbus, Ohio, 1985), 228.

[56] C. Parker, *The English Historical Tradition since 1850* (Edinburgh, 1990), 12 and 41; J.R. Green's organic understanding of the English nation is discussed in Jann, *The Art and Science of Victorian History*, 145–7. On Maitland's evident continuity with this tradition of attributing generic characteristics to the English nation, see ch. 3 below. The nation as a collective subject had not always featured so strongly in Whiggism as it did from the middle of the nineteenth century onwards. The focus of the Whiggism of the early nineteenth century, as typified by Macaulay, was more personal and heroic. See Burrow, *A Liberal Descent*, 104–6.

THE UNITY OF BARKER'S EDUCATION

For all their differences of subject-matter and intellectual orientation, there were several cross-currents between the historiography and the philosophy which Barker encountered at Oxford and which underpinned his subsequent adherence to both. Not least important, in Whiggism and Idealism alike much emphasis was placed on the cohesiveness of English society, a quality which was attributed to an homogenous English character as most powerfully expressed (J.R. Green aside) in the nation's political life. The importance of the concept of national character in Idealist thought – as well as in Whiggism – is evident in Bosanquet's praise of Vico and Montesquieu; they had laid the foundations of Idealism by recognising 'the fundamental unity of a national civilisation'. As a consequence, 'national mind and character [had taken] its unquestioned place in modern social theory'.[57]

It is true that, as Christopher Parker has pointed out, the Whig understanding of national character was permeated with 'nominalist' assumptions. He maintains that 'the strength of the English myth, the matter of England, was that, however paradoxically, it embraced the concept of individualism'. That is, for English historians towards the end of the nineteenth century, it was individual Englishmen rather than a transcendent 'national person' who achieved and sustained the institutions (and more importantly, the Constitution) embodying the nation's capacity for freedom.[58] The full-blown kind of organicist thinking which subordinated parts to the whole manifestly failed to penetrate English historiography, a barrier which it was to encounter in Barker's political thought as well.[59] Idealism, of course, existed to combat all individualist heresies, its protagonists emphasising the conceptual priority of society over the individual. Nevertheless, none of the English Idealists attributed an independent existence to society, nor to the state for that matter. Even Bosanquet, who is often regarded as lacking Green's reserve by attributing reality to the

[57] B. Bosanquet, *The Philosohpical Theory of the State* (London, 1899, repr. 1965), 39.

[58] Parker, *The English Historical Tradition*, 45.

[59] For example, using the term 'nominalism' in the opposite of Parker's sense that names are pure fictions, Barker denounced in 1937 'the nominalistic ideology' of the times. By this he meant the same false conception that only names exist, and that the individuals behind the 'labels' are insignificant, to which Parker regards the nineteenth-century historical tradition in England as similarly adverse. His attack was all of a piece with his unease at the power and divisiveness of groups in modern society. He wrote that '[one] creates a noun of assemblage: one worships that noun, and hates another noun of the same type.' *The Values of Life*, 45–6.

General Will of society, emphasised that the latter existed *only* through the minds of its members.[60] The distance, then, between Idealism and Whiggism was limited, and less important than their shared philosophical and cultural perspectives.

To explore this common ground further, there is an obvious Burkean backdrop to the Idealism of both Green and Bosanquet. Thus, Green rivalled the emotional heights which Burke scaled in praising patriotism and its derivation from 'a common dwelling place with its associations, from common memories, traditions, and customs, and from common ways of feeling and thinking which a common language and still more a common literature embodies'.[61] The connection beween Burke and Green was obvious to contemporaries, as can be seen from the sympathetic account of Green's thought which was given by John MacCunn in 1910. In his book *Six Radical Thinkers* MacCunn stressed Green's advice to his students to read Burke.[62] For MacCunn, Green could almost be taken for a conservative rather than a radical on account of his strong religious instincts, his respect for his predecessors, and his 'reverent appreciation of existing social and political institutions'. What marked him off from conservatism was his 'passion for the ideal' and 'rational faith in the future'.[63] Yet there was no inconsistency here for MacCunn; Green's writings prompted the reflection that 'it is entirely possible for a philosophy to be radical without ceasing to be conservative'.[64]

MacCunn evidently found the crucial link between Green's radicalism and his conservatism in his keen sensitivity to patriotic impulses. MacCunn was a fervent disciple of Mazzini, whose democratic and humanitarian nationalism Green himself had imbibed in his youth.[65] Certainly, he saw Green's writings on the English Civil War as the key to understanding the liberal-conservative tone of his

[60] Nicholson, *The Political Philosophy of the British Idealists*, 208. A. Simhony has helpfully suggested that the majority of British Idealists upheld a notion of 'relational organicism' rather than 'holistic organicism'. As she argues, these thinkers believed that 'the social good is . . . neither separate from, nor more valuable than, the well-being of individuals'. She is not entirely convinced that Bosanquet may be included in this analysis of British Idealism. 'Idealist organicism: Beyond Holism and Individualism', *History of Political Thought*, 12, 3 (1991), 533.

[61] Green, *Political Obligation*, 1931 edition, 130. On the 'national exclusiveness' of English liberalism since Green, see P. Rich, 'T.H. Green, Lord Scarman, and the issue of ethnic minority rights in English liberal thought,' *Ethnic and Racial Studies*, 10 (April 1987), 149–68. Rich's thesis fails to stand up to the strong element of cosmopolitanism in English liberalism, even state-centred varieties such as Idealism. Certainly, this study emphasises the ecumenical dimension in Barker's liberalism.

[62] MacCunn, *Six Radical Thinkers*, 229.

[63] Ibid., 237

[64] Ibid., 223.

[65] Richter, *The Politics of Conscience*, 81.

Idealism, an emphasis which was indeed well placed. In his 'Four lectures on the English Revolution' (1867) Green had lavishly praised the Protectorate established by Cromwell, revealing his identification with the Puritanism with which he had strong ancestral connections.[66] He regarded Cromwell as a man of great honour who had been confronted with an insuperable task: that of overcoming the factionalism and fanaticism of the burgeoning Nonconformist sects, while at the same time preserving them from encroaching 'ancient interests', specifically those of Laud's Anglican sacerdotalism. Reinforcing the rehabilitation of Cromwell during the second half of the nineteenth century,[67] Green highlighted his 'genuine and persistent effort' to govern constitutionally, as reflected in the 'instrument of government' which he issued following the dissolution of the Rump parliament. Green was particularly impressed by English Independency, of which he saw Cromwell as a close sympathiser; and he much revered the leader of the Indepedents, Sir Henry Vane. It was from Vane that he derived the ideal of 'religious citizenship' which he pressed upon late-Victorian England. Vane – and Cromwell – he felt, had achieved that rare combination of beliefs in liberty of individual conscience, on the one hand, and the needs of civil life, on the other. There was no parallel to this delicate balance between the 'inward' and 'outward' life elsewhere in Europe following the Reformation; religion either succumbed to Jesuit destruction of the political fabric of nations, as in Spain, southern Germany, or France, or princely control, as in northern Germany.[68] A revealing comment by MacCunn as to why this should have been so for Green is that the latter distinguished his heroes from the majority of Puritans by their respect for the 'traditions, the habits, the common feelings and interests, even the prejudices which stood rooted in the national character'.[69] It was something of a gloss, reflecting MacCunn's own passionate devotion to Burke, but the remark nonetheless captures the high premium which Green placed upon historical continuity and national unity as hallmarks of Englishness. One way of interpreting this stance is to follow the suggestion made earlier that Idealism injected a conciliatory tone into interpretations of Nonconformist political thought at the end of the nineteenth century. This has been singularly absent

66 Ibid., 40. 67 On this see Blaas, *Continuity and Anachronism*, 140–53.

68 T.H. Green, 'Four lectures on the English Revolution' (1867), in *The Works of T.H. Green*, ed. R.L. Nettleship (3 vols., London, 1889) vol. III, 282, 284.

69 MacCunn, *Six Radical Thinkers*, 222.

previously, as Matthew Arnold's searing attack on Nonconformity in his *Culture and Anarchy* (1869) makes clear.

So while for Green the Commonwealth may have failed in the short term, subsequently it left a more enduring legacy as the 'great spring of political life in England'. Central to this legacy were the dissenting bodies, whose 'vigorous growth' had been secured by Cromwell's sword.[70] For Green, they represented the cornerstone of spiritual and political freedom in England, a new variation on an old Whig theme that dovetailed with a growing interest in the role which voluntary societies had played in English national development.[71]

Bosanquet's ideas on the centrality of national character also possessed a familiar Burkean ring. This is apparent in his notion of the social mind which underlay all human institutions, rules, and culture. He was at pains to point out that responsibility for these achievements could not be attributed to particular individuals; the products of civilisation belonged 'to the unconscious reason and providence of nature rather than the definite foresight of man'.[72] As Parker has aptly commented, the examples which Bosanquet brought to bear to illustrate this point formed a 'delightfully Victorian, even Whiggish selection', including as they did 'the British Constitution, the unity of Italy, the science or philosophy of the nineteenth century, and the English language and its literature'.[73] The same conclusion about the immersion of Bosanquet's Idealism in English thought and experience is drawn by Nicholson. He argues that Bosanquet did more than explain Hegel to the English; rather he gave Hegelian ideas a concerted English application. Hegel had emphasised the inadequacies in Rousseau's theory of the General Will, specifically the way in which Rousseau had tied its expression to voting rather than *Sittlichkeit*, the values and beliefs of a society implicit in all its varied institutions, not simply those of government.[74] Bosanquet found the most mature example of this essentially pluralist picture of civil society of England, with its deep-rooted experience of self-government and voluntary organisation. Answering the charge from abroad that the English mind was fundamentally deficient in logic, he argued

70 Green, 'Four lectures on the English Revolution', 364.
71 This will be explored in ch. 3 below.
72 B. Bosanquet, 'Old problems under new names', in *The Civilisation of Christendom and Other Studies* (London, 1893), 112–13. Quoted in Parker, 'Bosanquet, historical knowledge, and the history of ideas', 215.
73 Parker, 'Bosanquet, historical knowledge, and the history of ideas', 215.
74 Nicholson, *The Political Philosophy of the British Idealists*, 204 and 218.

passionately that 'there is not, and never has been, a national mind more highly endowed than the English'. The English people unquestionably excelled in 'concrete logic, the creative spirit of things'; hence their two main strengths of poetry and politics. What better example of English practical logic than 'the great organised institutions which have sprung unaided from the brain of our wage-earning class'.[75]

Thus, the English Idealists were as much attuned to the force of national character and tradition in historical development, particularly that of their own country, as the Whig historians and their successors. Of course, they recognised other loyalties and identities as well as that of the nation, and they were by no means devotees of all nationalist causes.[76] In particular, the ideal of internationalism engaged their interest as much as that of nationalism, as will be seen in chapter 4 below. But the support which the idea of national character elicited among Idealist thinkers, and the way in which it veiled a more specific absorption in the traits of the English nation is a significant one. Moreover, the hold of this idea upon the Idealist imagination grew especially strong after the generation of Green and Bosanquet. This can be seen in two works which emerged in the 1920s. Both J.S. Mackenzie's *Arrows of Desire: Essays on our National Character and Outlook* and Barker's *National Character and the Factors in its Formation* represented a late crop of Idealist reflections upon the nature of Englishness.[77] Furthermore, while the Idealism of Green and Bosanquet purported to treat the *idea* of the state in general, it was often constructed around some resonant images of English society and history, together with associated cultural values. Here too, Idealism seemed to dovetail with Whiggism in the importance which its adherents attached to democracy, political order, constitutionalism, and a high capacity for political organisation as the core of English

[75] B. Bosanquet, 'The teaching of patriotism' (1911), in *Social and International Ideals: Being Studies in Patriotism* (London, 1917), 18–19. See also his 'The English people: Notes on national characteristics', *International Monthly*, 3 (1901), 71–116. The Pluralist strain of Bosanquet's thought will be further examined in ch. 3 below.

[76] This point is well argued by John R. Gibbins in his 'Liberalism, Nationalism and the English Idealists', *History of European Ideas*, 15 (1992), 491–7.

[77] J.S. Mackenzie, *Arrows of Desire: Essays on our National Character and Outlook* (London, 1920). Mackenzie admitted in the preface that some aspects of the subject he addressed were 'not specially within the writer's province'. (He was Professor of Logic and Philosophy at University College Cardiff.) His dedication to his task in the absence of 'a more intimate knowledge of history and literature, of anthropology and social conditions' indicates the importance he attached to the subject, particularly in the aftermath of war. On Barker's *National Character and the Factors in its Formation* (London, 1927), see below ch. 5.

national identity. Finally, the Idealists were by no means averse to according England a unique place in the unfolding of human Reason as a result of these accomplishments. This conception of England as an elect nation is best illustrated in a lay sermon by Edward Caird – his Scottishness notwithstanding – at Balliol College in 1898. There he asserted 'our claim' to be 'a *chosen people*, with a special part to play in the great work of civilisation and of Christianity'. A passage which followed is worth quoting at length for its fine Whiggish (and again, Pluralist) intonations:

> it was in this country . . . that the great movement towards political freedom was first initiated; indeed, it was carried to a considerable point of advance, when it had hardly begun in any other country . . . [T]here was from an early time at once greater liberty for individuals and a more ready reaction of the opinions of the people upon government. At the same time, with this freedom of the individual and as the complement of it, there has gone a great facility of association . . . It is perhaps not too much to say that this country first showed to the modern world the immense power that lies in the associated action of free citizens, and proved that its greater vitality, its combination of subordination with independent initiative, makes it more than a match for the mechanical drill of despotism.[78]

It can be seen, then, that at least at the historiographical and cultural levels explored above, Barker's dual intellectual heritage was mutually reinforcing, lending a certain consistency to his work from the start.[79] Indeed, much of his *oeuvre* served to strengthen the Whiggish tone which Idealism had already acquired in England, and to strengthen Whiggism at the same time. The net effect of Barker's writings was to retain the close contact between ideal and reality upon which his philosophical mentors – particularly Green – had insisted. For Barker the ideal was not laid up in another world, as the keener exponents of Idealism such as Plato and Carlyle had claimed, but pervaded existing institutions and activities, particularly English ones. This by no means sanctioned political quiescence. While Green and Bosanquet framed their maxims for state intervention in negative terms – those of 'hindering hindrances' and 'removing obstacles' to moral freedom – this nonetheless registered the need for at least some growth of legislative activity. It was a formula for state-sponsored

[78] E. Caird, 'The nation as an ethical ideal' (1898), *Lay Sermons and Addresses Delivered in the Hall of Balliol College, Oxford* (Glasgow, 1907), 112–13.

[79] This will become further apparent in ch. 3 below, in a discussion of the meeting-point of Whiggism and Idealism in Pluralist political theory.

social reform with which Barker had little difficulty, seeming – as it did – to indicate the path of cautious, piecemeal change that he found so congenial in Burke's political thought. In the next chapter we will see the two deposits of intellectual capital from which he worked coming together on this point, while beginning to fracture at another level: the nature of the state.

CHAPTER 2

The polis, law, and the development of political studies at Oxford, 1900–1920

QUESTIONS OF INTELLECTUAL IDENTITY

The Whig-tinged Idealism which Barker acquired as an undergraduate at Oxford decisively shaped the content of his first book, *The Political Thought of Plato and Aristotle* (1906). This book was by no means an exercise in disinterested scholarship; rather, it was part of a wider quest in Barker's generation – noted in the previous chapter – to illuminate recent changes in English political life against the backdrop of ancient Greece. As he insisted in the Introduction:

> The city-state was different from the nation-state of to-day; but it was only different in the sense that it was a more vital and intense form of the same thing . . . In studying it we are studying the ideal of our modern States: we are studying a thing, which is as much of to-day as of yesterday, because it is, in its essentials, for ever.[1]

The book duly marked him out as a 'political scientist', at least in his own perception. Significantly, however, the assumption of this title appeared to close his options as a scholar in the subject of his lectureship – Modern History – which he then held at Wadham College. In a letter to his friend T.F. Tout, Professor of History at Manchester, who had urged him on after the success of his first venture, he wrote: 'I fear that whatever I do will not be in the domain of history. Nobody would take me seriously if I wrote history after having given myself as a writer in political science.'[2] Not surprisingly, therefore, only a year later, we find Barker expressing considerable interest in the proposed new lectureship in Political Theory and

[1] E. Barker, *The Political Thought of Plato and Aristotle* (London, 1906; New York, 1959), 15–16.
[2] Barker to Tout, 10 December 1908, Tout Papers, The John Rylands University Library of Manchester, 1/55/1.

Institutions at Oxford, which was to become the Gladstone Chair in that subject in 1912.[3] He was not, however, eligible for the post because of the desire of the Trustees of the University Endowment Fund that the successful candidate would be 'some able man from outside with practical experience'.[4] In rough accordance with this requirement, the appointment went to W.G.S. Adams, a Greats scholar who had branched out first into economics as a lecturer at the University of Manchester and then into superintending 'statistics and intelligence' at the Irish Department of Agriculture and Technical Instruction.[5] Yet notwithstanding his dashed hopes of securing the lectureship – which he shared with Graham Wallas[6] – Barker's remark to Tout raises a number of questions. First, how committed was he to the discipline of politics after the publication of *Plato and Aristotle*? Was he merely resigned to the professional identity he had now fatefully adopted? Why did he perceive history and political science as incompatible subjects, given their close proximity in the work of Sir John Seeley, E.R. Freeman, and other exponents of 'the comparative method' in the late-nineteenth century? What precisely constituted the study of politics for Barker as he embarked upon his career as a practitioner of that subject, albeit within a Faculty of Modern History? These questions will be addressed in this chapter, requiring some attention to the complex links which political science had forged with law at the turn of the century. But first it is necessary to consider the main ideas of *Plato and Aristotle*; for the substantive claims of political theory he advanced in that work held major implications for his conception of the place which the analysis of political life occupied in 'humane studies'.

THE SOUNDING BOARD OF GREEK POLITICAL THOUGHT

At least four prominent themes emerged in *The Political Thought of Plato and Aristotle*: a studied cautiousness in the use of political concepts and metaphors; a concern that the grip of the state should not be pulled too tightly around the individual and society; an emphasis upon the moral nature of the state; and a simultaneous

[3] According to A.E. Zimmern, Barker would 'love to have' the new post. Zimmern to Graham Wallas, 21 May 1909, Wallas Papers, British Library of Political and Economic Science, 1/42/49.

[4] *The Oxford Magazine* (20 May 1909), 309.

[5] *Dictionary of National Biography, 1961–70* (Oxford, 1981).

[6] See, for example, Sydney Ball's expression of regret to Wallas on his unsuccessful candidature in his letter dated 6 March 1910, Wallas Papers, 1/46/1.

emphasis upon its legal side as well. In these ways, Barker attempted to construct a fine balancing-act between holism and individualism in political theory. It was one which would accord with the 'moderate' temper of the English mind, the primordial English value of personal liberty, and yet at the same time accommodate the pressures in English society for greater social cohesion.

Barker's preoccupation with the dangers of a too-literal use of political language was immersed in a characteristically Whig aversion to 'abstract' thought as the hallmark of continental intellectual traditions. For instance, he frequently berated Plato for carrying the organic conception of the state so far that the state became the 'sole organism, to whose majesty all other organisms must be sacrificed'.[7] But this vice was not confined to Plato; rather, it had resurfaced in the modern world in the work of Calvin and Rousseau. This prompted his reflection that 'there is something French in Plato's mind, something of that pushing of a principle to its logical extremes, which distinguished Calvin in theology and Rousseau in politics'.[8] The Reformation and the French Revolution both bore testimony to the perils which awaited such lack of intellectual restraint, with their wholesale destruction of the existing body politic. No doubt these events and the thinkers who stood behind them acquired an added resonance as Barker nervously surveyed the revival of the organic analogy in contemporary political thought for which Social Darwinism was largely responsible.[9] The hard-worked concepts of biology in recent years heightened his fear for individual freedom; as he was to remark of the idea of the social organism in Spencer's work in his *Political Thought in England from Herbert Spencer to the Present Day* (1915), it obscured the sense in which 'a parallel between the State and the individual is not an explanation of their relation'. The state could not be identified with the individual without compromising the 'self-determining' nature of the latter.[10]

It was not that Barker denied all truth to the model of the state as an organism. He stressed the great merit of organicism in combating the 'instrumentalism' which had become attached to the state in modern times; no mere contract between self-interested individuals, the state instead sustained a 'common weal'. Moreover, in good

[7] E. Barker, *Plato and Aristotle*, 159. [8] Ibid., 162.

[9] See G. Jones, *Social Darwinism and English Thought: The Interaction between Biological and Social Theory* (Brighton, 1980).

[10] E. Barker, *Political Thought in England from Herbert Spencer to the Present Day* (London, 1915), 108.

Idealist fashion, Barker rated Plato's organicism above that of modern theorists like Spencer because it built a moral *telos* into the state as 'an entity *consciously* self-directed towards a conception of the Good'.[11] Ultimately, however, he emphasised the strict limits against which the organic analogy came up, specifically those posed by the members of the state having a 'will of their own' and the existence of other organisations besides the state. It was Aristotle who best appreciated these limits. 'The Aristotelian doctrine', maintained Barker, 'stops short of being fully organic: it does not lose the individual's life in that of the State, though it fully recognises the necessity of the State to the individual's life'.[12] To this extent, Aristotle warranted perhaps Barker's highest accolade, that of possessing 'an English spirit of compromise . . . Where Plato turned Radical under the compulsion of the Idea, Aristotle has much sound Conservatism: he respects property; he sees good in the family. He recognises the general "laxity" of actual life, the impossibility of concluding man wholly within the pales of any scheme.'[13]

His identification with Aristotle was further strengthened by another sense of organicism in the writings of the latter, besides that which denoted a harmonious union of parts: the idea that societies develop 'naturally' in accordance with their inner principle of life. He discerned a strong parallel with Burke here, although significantly he showed a marked preference for Aristotle over Burke. Aristotle, unlike Burke, did not push his developmentalism into a 'conservative antipathy to human interference' but instead regarded political science as a 'practical and remedial thing'. It was an odd conclusion to draw from Burke's writings, particularly as the latter had been strongly associated in the nineteenth century with the principle of gradual reform. This suggests that perhaps Burkeanism had overtaken Burke himself by the end of the nineteenth century, a development which has been reversed in recent decades, as will be seen in the Conclusion.[14] The favour which Aristotle found over Burke here most probably reflects the early impact of Green's Idealism on Barker, with its firm commitment to social improvement through the action of the state. There is also the fact that Aristotle was more of a 'philosopher' than Burke, and had captured the imagination of most of his philosophy teachers at Balliol.[15] On the other hand, he had to admit

[11] E. Barker, *Plato and Aristotle*, 158. [12] Ibid., 281. [13] Ibid., 162.
[14] See below p. 216.
[15] E. Barker, *Age and Youth: Memories of Three Universities and Father of the Man* (Oxford, 1953) 318–9.

that Aristotle too had his blind spots, most notably in his defence of slavery. This was analogous to Burke's support of rotten boroughs, leading Barker to conclude that: 'the sense of the State as a living system due to development tends to over-conservatism, as the sense of the State as a mechanism created by contract leads to excessive innovation'.[16]

The second major theme of *Plato and Aristotle* is contained within the first but nevertheless warrants separate discussion. This is Barker's concern lest individuals be 'engulfed' by the groups to which they belong, not least the state. Thinkers like Plato, he believed, became slaves to their categories precisely because of their penchant for 'the Republic, one and indivisible'. Plato had been consumed by his zeal for the state, hence his embrace of communism. It is no exaggeration to say that the stark uniformity of the latter, the abolition of all differences between individuals, the dissolution of all social ties except that of the state, haunted Barker. He was too much the child of the era of Mill, Maine, and Spencer – who saw individuality as the crowning achievement of the modern world – to swallow Plato's Idealism whole. For relief he turned once again to Aristotle, and it was in one of his many passages in praise of the latter that he pressed home the cardinal lesson of evolutionary social theory, an idiom which he otherwise regarded with considerable scepticism and suspicion. 'Undifferentiated unity', he maintained, 'belongs to a lower scale of evolution: it is the lowest type of animal which is composed of like and similar parts. Heterogeneous unity belongs to the highest; and it is man who is composed of unlike and dissimilar organs.'[17] Aristotle's thought was in full sympathy with this principle: the claims of the Aristotelian state upon the individual were 'not unto the last surrender of every vestige of self'.[18]

Barker also admired what he perceived as the 'pluralist' character of Aristotle's political philosophy. Pluralism was to become an important ingredient in his own thought, as will be made clear in the following chapter. In this respect he saw Aristotle as having made a significant modification to Plato's thought by insisting that the state was not 'the one association and the sole end of man . . . but the supreme association and the dominant end'. The state, so conceived, did not 'negate' but 'embraced' other associations.[19] Barker made a similar point when he praised Aristotle's notion that, while the state is

[16] E. Barker, *Plato and Aristotle*, 281, f/n. 1.

[17] Ibid., 404. [18] Ibid., 232. [19] Ibid., 228.

certainly 'a product of mind – that it is mind concrete in an external organisation: it is not true that the unity of the State is as the unity of a single mind, or that mind must be concrete in a single organisation'.[20]

A third theme of *Plato* and *Aristotle* – and one which is distinctively Idealist – is an emphasis upon the moral nature of the state. This has been touched upon in discussing Barker's cautious approach to the organic analogy. He went along with the latter in so far as it challenged the notion that the state exists simply to promote the 'natural rights' of individuals. Against this fundamental error in Roman law and, later, social contract theory, Barker echoed Plato and Aristotle in their battle with the Sophists, maintaining that the state was an association of human beings for 'the best object that they can attain'.[21] However, following Green (and Bosanquet) to the letter, he underlined a signal difference beween the relationship of state and morality in the ancient and modern worlds. While in the ancient world the state was charged with the positive inculcation of moral goodness, in the modern world it took the more indirect, 'preventive' route to the righteousness of its citizens; its role was merely to 'remove hindrances' to the moral life. Subordinated since the Middle Ages to the church and afterwards separated from it, the modern state left the education of the moral will to other agencies. Lacking the moral intensity of the *polis* that went with its limited size and homogeneity, modern society typically experienced the state as an unwarranted intrusion.[22]

Yet Barker had no doubts about the superiority of the modern over the ancient world in this regard. Having fully imbibed Green, he set a high premium upon 'moral spontaneity', on account of which he distanced himself from *both* Plato and Aristotle. While Aristotle had softened the harsh edges of Plato's political theory, nevertheless he too saw the virtue of the state as the virtue of individuals writ large; hence he regarded the state as having a duty to 'habituate' its members in the ways of goodness as a condition of its own righteousness.[23] Modern thinkers, by contrast, did not confuse the state with the individual in this way; their motto was '[b]etter the half of a good act done from within, than the whole enforced from without'.[24] But it was a lesson which had only been learnt through bitter experience; in England, it had been most forcibly drawn during the Commonwealth after attempts to make men good 'raised up in one generation a crop of

[20] Ibid., 157. [21] Ibid., 292. [22] Ibid., 8. [23] Ibid., 291–2. [24] Ibid., 7–8.

imitative hypocrites, and in the next a crew of reactionary debauchees'.[25] Such instances of moral tyranny (the terms of which show Barker far more on his guard against abuses of political power and Puritan rectitude than Green) were not only rooted in a false equation between the state and the individual; they were also nourished by an equally false fusion between society and the state. On this ground again, both Plato and Aristotle stood condemned. Where the modern world scored considerably over the ancient world was in the establishment of a 'mediating authority' between society and the state, preserving the independence of both spheres but also facilitating mutually beneficial interaction.

The Hegelian influence behind Barker's reference here to the importance of a 'mediating authority' is unmistakable. It primarily spelt, in his eyes, the legal rules and procedures through which the state acted. This constitutes the fourth theme of *Plato and Aristotle*: the notion that the state is rooted in law as well as morality. For Barker, the philosophers of ancient Greece were constantly groping their way towards such a conception; however, while much alive to 'the conception of the common good as the aim of every political group, [they] never attained a full conception of the right organ for securing that common good'.[26] The idea of an impersonal but flexible system of law as the cornerstone of the state was quite foreign to their way of thinking. Plato, in particular, clung tenaciously to the ideal of 'knowledge' in defining politics, despising the rigidity of law but not minding the rigidity of a principle. In the *Politicus* (or *Statesman*) this led him to disregard entirely the 'will of the people or its representatives' as the benchmark of good government. Instead, he favoured the personal rule of an Absolute Monarch, who would respond in accordance with the principle of 'reason' to the '*nuance*' of each case.[27]

It is true, remarked Barker, that Plato abandoned this visionary conception of the state, with its roots in *The Republic* in his last work, the *Laws*. Here, he resigned himself to a state that was merely 'sub-ideal'. Communism was abandoned, and the rule of 'philosopher-kings' along with it. In their place he put the principles of the 'sovereignty of law' and the 'mixed constitution' – the combined forces of monarchy and democracy. This introduced a gulf in Plato's *oeuvre*: 'on the one side is the "guardian" unfettered by law: on the other, the "guardian of the law", who is its "servant"' and even its "slave"'.[28] It is at this

[25] Ibid., 246. [26] Ibid., 12. [27] Ibid., 170. [28] Ibid., 184.

point that Aristotle's debt to Plato was greatest. Barker suggested that Aristotle's distinctive 'naturalism' or 'realism', his instinct for 'practical compromise', and his conception of law as 'dispassionate reason' all derived from the *Laws*. Reflection upon this debt brought Magna Carta to Barker's mind, revealing his embryonic preoccupation with the 'law-state' and the incremental way in which it had developed in England, images of the English state which resonated in Whig history. For, just as there was little that was absolutely new in Magna Carta, he claimed, so the same applied to Aristotle's *Politics*: 'Neither is meant to be new: both are meant to codify previous development. But Magna Carta remains the great document of English history; and the *Politics* remains the great document of Greek political thought – as Plato remains the great political thinker of Greece.'[29]

Yet Barker detected serious shortcomings in the Greek conception of the law-state, arising from the considerable continuity that remained between *The Republic* and the *Laws*. First, he evidently disagreed with both Plato and Aristotle that it *was* second best to some higher but unattainable ideal. Second, the law-state in Plato's *Laws* was seriously compromised by the return at the end of the book to the rule of superior intelligence in the form of a 'nocturnal council'.[30] Finally, the Greeks took the rigidity of the law all too literally; they had little of 'that sense of law as a progressive development which is universally felt today'. They were, in this respect, pre-eminently medieval, law being for them 'a formed body of precepts rather than a living growth'.[31]

There can be little surprise that these matters weighed heavily with Barker; underlying his emphasis upon the legal nature of the state was the same commitment to 'limited politics' which contained his enthusiasm for Idealism. It would be obvious and correct to point to the influence of Whiggism in shaping this preoccupation with the legal limits of the state. Certainly, when Barker referred in a passage quoted above to Plato's indifference to the 'will of the people *or its representatives*' in effecting legal change, the Whig veneration of democratic institutions like parliament and local self-government can be heard above other exponents of popular sovereignty, most notably Rousseau. Whiggism is also audible in his assertion that reform was quite compatible with the preservation of 'ancient law', something

[29] Ibid., 185. [30] Ibid., 201. [31] Ibid., 171.

which was beyond Plato's comprehension.[32] But in addition, Whiggism had acquired a new dimension at the end of the nineteenth century. This was a sense that English liberties were rooted in English law and the legal profession as much, if not more, than political institutions. Because of an ingrained prejudice against the presumed 'theoretical' character of the legal mind on the part of the Whig historians of the middle of the nineteenth century – Stubbs and Freeman, for example – the English constitution had been detached from its legal base.[33] The recovery of the latter was to become an increasingly prominent influence on Barker's own work, and formed the basis of his interest in the English state. Some examination of this shift within Whiggism is necessary if we are to understand the parameters of Barker's early political thought and his identification with political science at the outset of his career.

POLITICS AND 'THE RULE OF LAW' IN ENGLAND

The development in question was primarily associated with A.V. Dicey. Dicey's sympathies are not usually thought to extend beyond a resolute Austinianism combined with Benthamite individualism. But, as Stefan Collini has argued, the 'diffused Burkeanism' of the nineteenth century affected Dicey no less than other Victorian intellectuals.[34] Nonetheless, Dicey consciously rewrote the terms of the success story which Whiggism told of English history. This is most apparent in his comment upon Macaulay when writing an obituary for F.W. Maitland in 1907. Acknowledging Macaulay as an historian of 'rare legal capacity', Dicey expressed astonishment of how 'small a part law was made to play in the development of the English nation' prior to Maitland.[35] Dicey's Burkeanism was fully in tune with the leading characteristic of that intellectual current in the latter half of

32 Ibid., 171.

33 J.W. Burrow, *A Liberal Descent: Victorian Historians and the English Past* (Cambridge, 1981), 133–4.

34 S. Collini, *Public Moralists: Political Thought and Intellectual Life in Britain, 1850–1930* (Oxford, 1991), 293. For example, extolling that quintessentially English virtue celebrated by Burke – the ability to tread a fine path between radicalism and conservatism – Dicey wrote: 'The occasional outbreak of revolution has among Frenchmen been unfavourable to that habit of constantly and gradually amending the law, which has become natural to Englishmen, whilst admiration for American institutions and a certain general satisfaction with things as they are, have in the United States created a remarkable kind of legal conservatism.' *Lectures on the Relation between Law and Public Opinion in England during the Nineteenth Century* (London, 1905, repr. 1940), 8.

35 *Cambridge University Reporter*, 12 July 1907, quoted in H.A.L. Fisher, *F.W. Maitland: A Biography* (Cambridge, 1910), p. 175.

the nineteenth century – a belief that unconscious institutional mutation rather than design lay behind the achievements of English polity. But he was inclined to attribute those successes to the lawyers, particularly the judges, rather than the political departments of state.[36]

Thus, Dicey put law firmly on the map of English national identity. This is best illustrated by his concept of 'the rule of law', one of three principles he attributed to the English constitution in his widely read *Law of the Constitution* of 1885. For example, he there referred to 'that rule of equal and settled law which is the true basis of English civilization'.[37] He might well have added, 'and English civilization alone' for, in true Burkean style, he cast an acerbic eye over what passed for legal systems in neighbouring countries. He also sustained the rhetoric of liberty that was central to Burkean Whiggism, although giving greater emphasis than in that tradition hitherto to the sense in which the constitution secured personal as well as collective political freedom.

These changes and continuities within the Whig tradition are evident in the three meanings which Dicey attached to the 'rule of law'. First, with undisguised pride and a heightened sense of national consciousness, he announced that 'Englishmen are ruled by the law, and by the law alone; a man may with us be punished for a breach of the law, but he can be punished for nothing else'.[38] Dicey threw this meaning into sharp relief by the graphic example of the Bastille at the dawn of the French Revolution; it was 'the outward and visible sign of lawless power', the fall of which was thought to 'herald in the rest of Europe that rule of law which already existed in England'. To some extent this promise had been fulfilled, although Dicey could not resist adding that in 'every continental community' the executive still enjoyed 'far wider discretionary authority in the matter of arrest, of temporary imprisonment, and the like' than its British counterpart. Continuing in this strongly celebratory vein that abandoned the lofty objectivity he had deemed appropriate to, but hitherto lacking in the study of the constitution,[39] he elaborated the second meaning of the 'rule of law': that it applies equally to all, including officials. It is characteristic of 'our country', he argued, that 'here every man,

[36] Collini, *Public Moralists*, 295.
[37] A.V. Dicey, *Introduction to the Study of the Law of the Constitution* (1885, London, 1962), 18.
[38] Unless indicated otherwise, all of the following quotations from *Law of the Constitution* are from ch. 4, 'The rule of law: its nature and general application.'
[39] Dicey, *Law of the Constitution*, 3–4.

whatever be his rank or condition, is subject to the ordinary law of the realm and amenable to the jurisdiction of the ordinary tribunals'. Again, turning the spotlight upon France as the 'type of a continental state' to provide a negative contrast, Dicey pointed to the French official's subjection 'only to official law administered by official bodies', and even then, just in 'certain respects'. Finally, Dicey extolled the extent to which the 'rule of law' pervaded the English constitution because the latter was part of the 'ordinary law of the land' rather than determined by a separate branch of constitutional law. Scarcely able to conceal his delight, he noted in the English constitution 'an absence of those declarations or definitions of rights so dear to foreign constitutionalists'. Instead, the courts had concentrated on securing 'the rights of private persons in particular cases brought before [them]', providing an altogether more effective set of liberties than those eloquently set down in constitutions that had been created by legislative acts. It was all very reminiscent of the Burkean crusade against 'paper constitutions' in the nineteenth century, as when Dicey insisted: 'The Habeas Corpus Acts declare no principle and define no rights, but they are for practical purposes worth a hundred constitutional articles guaranteeing individual liberty.'

Dicey was by no means alone in tying Englishness to law in the late-nineteenth century. The growth of law as an academic discipline consequent upon changes in legal education after the middle of the century had alerted its practitioners to the pivotal national importance of the subject.[40] For example, Frederick Pollock – who became Corpus Professor of Jurisprudence at Oxford in 1883 – wrote in the same vein as Dicey in a popular lecture delivered in the late 1870s. Though it was entitled 'The history of English law as a branch of politics', a reversal of these terms would more accurately describe its argument. For Pollock made high claims for the formative role which law had played in English national development. While legal institutions had originally been created to facilitate political rule – such as the establishment of circuit judges after the Norman Conquest – they soon acquired an independent existence and indeed had become a 'rallying-point' for politics. Even the would-be tyrants in English history had been obliged to make 'a show of legality', he claimed. Hence, the 'forms of legal institutions, conception, and claims of strictly legal right, even the fictions of legal speculation,

[40] On the mid-century changes in legal education which introduced greater professional rigour into the law, see. R.J. Cocks, *Foundations of the Modern Bar* (London, 1983), chs. 2–3.

have entered into the very bones and marrow of the history of our country'. Pollock too drew the only (Burkean) moral that seemed possible in accounts of English history in this period: that 'law and the machinery of law, like all other human institutions, grow and cannot be made to order'. He concluded that the English race was pre-eminently a 'law-abiding' race, a characteristic of 'great political importance'.[41]

Clearly, both Dicey and Pollock entertained large intellectual as well as cultural ambitions for law, both political science and political institutions being subsumed by their legal equivalents in the work of these two scholars. Indeed, there was a strong tendency at Oxford at the end of the nineteenth century to identify political science with law. One observer, at any rate, casually remarked that the eminent members of the Faculty of Law – which included Dicey, Pollock, T.E. Holland, James Bryce, Sir William Anson, and Sir William Markby – 'deal largely with political science'.[42]

This was a competing association to that which was being sealed simultaneously between politics and moral philosophy by the combined forces of Greats and Idealism. It derived much of its impetus from an identification among Oxford lawyers with the analytical jurisprudence of Hobbes, Bentham, and Austin, a tradition which Pollock regarded as the quintessence of 'English political science'. This was distinguished from continental political science – in his view – by the assignment of 'separate fields to political ethics, constitutional politics, and positive law'. Unlike its continental counterpart, English political science concentrated on law 'as it exists', rather than law as it ought to be (and indeed law as it *was*, as Pollock glanced dismissively at the Historical School of Law associated with Savigny). In possessing this quality the English school was the closest heir to Aristotle, in whose political writings Pollock managed to discern the same 'capital advance'.[43]

Pollock's hostility to ethics for leading the science of politics astray was presumably only directed towards 'non-scientific' accounts of the former. Pollock himself was part of a prominent coterie of late-Victorian intellectuals who had great hopes that Darwinism would

[41] F. Pollock, 'The history of English law as a branch of politics', in A.L. Goodhart (eds.), *Jurisprudence and Legal Essays* (London, 1961).

[42] D.G. Ritchie, 'Political science at Oxford', *Annals of the American Academy of Political Science*, 2 (1891), 89.

[43] F. Pollock, *An Introduction to the History of the Science of Politics* (1890; London, 1935), 123, 15.

give ethics a secure scientific footing.[44] Nevertheless, Social Darwinism's hold over moral philosophy in the late-nineteenth century was limited. Hence the question of the authentic territory of politics became much contested – by rival theorists of ethics, on the one hand, and by exponents of law, on the other. Only D.G. Ritchie seemed to straddle the boundaries of law, politics, and ethics – considered in both a 'Continental' Hegelian and the recent Darwinian sense – with any degree of ease.[45] Barker came a close second to Ritchie, in the early years of his career at least, although without making any concessions to Darwinism. Thus, he applauded Aristotle's conception of political science as a 'trilogy': 'It is the theory of the State; but it is also a theory of morals and a theory of law. It contains two subjects, which have since been removed from its scope, and treated as separate spheres.'[46] But, as we shall see in chapter 6, he too harboured increasing doubts about the dominance of ethics in political inquiry, for which – unlike Pollock – he held *English* rather than continental political inquiry largely responsible. To appreciate the origins of his unease and the legal direction in which he attempted to take political science in later years, it is necessary to examine a yet further locus of that subject in the late-nineteenth century: that of legal history. This will bring us nearer to a solution of the problem posed at the beginning of this chapter as to why Barker felt that political science and history were incompatible professions; or rather, *which* kind of political science, exactly, he felt was in tension with history.

LEGAL HISTORY AND POLITICAL SCIENCE

The growing link between the disciplines of law and politics in the late-nineteenth century was nourished by an older one between law and history at both Oxford and Cambridge Universities. The product of a forced marriage intended to lend academic respectability to both subjects, it pleased the teachers of neither. Reflecting the inveterate nineteenth-century Whig antipathy against law, Edward Freeman argued in 1859 that: 'An examination in "Law and Modern History" is about as much an harmonious whole as would be an examination in Law and Hydrostatics, or in Phlebotomy and

[44] Jones, *Social Darwinism and English Thought*, 38–9.

[45] This is best reflected in his interest in the natural law tradition. See his *Natural Rights: A Criticism of Some Political and Ethical Conceptions* (1894; London, 1924), esp. ch. 2, 'On the history of the idea of "nature" in law and politics'.

[46] E. Barker, *Plato and Aristotle*, 7.

Modern History.'[47] However, no sooner had law and history won their institutional independence than new arguments emerged in favour of their complementarity. These were signalled in F.W. Maitland's inaugural lecture in 1888 as Downing Professor of the Laws of England at Cambridge, which undoubtedly inspired Dicey's obituary for Maitland mentioned previously. Here, Maitland bemoaned the lawyers' purely instrumental attitude towards the past in which successive interpretations of the law were seen as approaching the 'true intent and meaning of the old law'. The result was that legal history had become mixed up with legal dogma, and 'the subtle process whereby our common law had gradually accommodated itself to changed circumstances' had gone by the board. Similarly, it was Maitland's belief that legal history held the key to many other spheres of history, certainly in the Middle Ages and certainly in England.[48] Maitland resigned himself to the prospect of a law school at Cambridge whose teaching touched little upon legal history, such were the growing professional pressures on the curriculum. However, his elevation of legal history found a ready acceptance among historians, particularly historians at Oxford.[49] There, a tradition of 'historical jurisprudence' had flourished since Henry Maine's tenure of the Corpus Chair between 1869 and 1878.

It is true that only Maine and another of his successors to the Corpus Chair – Sir Paul Vinogradoff, who occupied it on the resignation of Pollock in 1904 – were devoted to the ambitious project of 'historical jurisprudence' as such: the construction of broad generalisations about legal change across widely divergent societies. Yet, in the view of several Oxford lawyers of the generation following Maine there was a clear association – or perhaps confusion, if Maitland's view is taken[50] – between 'historical jurisprudence' and the history of English law. They pursued the latter in both its common

[47] Quoted in P. Slee, *Learning and a Liberal Education: The Study of Modern History in the Universities of Oxford, Cambridge, and Manchester, 1800–1914* (Manchester, 1986), 87.

[48] F.W. Maitland, 'Why the history of English law remains unwritten', in *The Collected Papers of Frederic William Maitland*, ed. H.A.L. Fisher, 3 vols. (Cambridge, 1911), vol. I, 491–2, 486.

[49] The extent of Maitland's influence at Oxford can be gauged by those who attended the opening of the 'Maitland Library' at All Souls in 1908, just after his death. They included A.L. Smith, Maitland's first biographer; Paul Vinogradoff, first literary editor of the Selden Society which Maitland had founded to make available the rich legal sources of English history; H.A.L. Fisher, editor of his *Collected Papers*; and Barker, who continued Maitland's work of translating and interpreting the works of Otto Von Gierke for English audiences. H.A.L. Fisher, memoir of Paul Vinogradoff, *The Collected Papers of Paul Vinogradoff*, ed. H.A.L. Fisher, 2 vols. (Oxford, 1928), vol. I. 40.

[50] On Maitland's scepticism about historical jurisprudence, see Collini, *Public Moralists*, 303.

and constitutional guises, thus contributing a good deal to the fulfilment of Maitland's hopes for the subject he had founded.

According to Raymond Cocks, Dicey set the stage for this interpretation of Maine's legacy by selectively applying the latter's sociological principles to the English constitutional past.[51] In this sense, Dicey constructed a general contemporary stream of English legal scholarship embracing such diffuse authorities as Maine, Maitland, and himself. Significantly, he perceived further common ground between Maine and Maitland (and Blackstone as well) in their struggle to establish law as 'part of the literature of England', a cause for which Dicey himself fought hard.[52] Moreover, he not only attempted to draw historical jurisprudence into the general realm of legal history, particularly English legal history; he also saw no incompatibility between holding broad Austinian sympathies and cultivating historical inquiry as a fruitful avenue to legal understanding. For all Dicey's animadversions against 'mere antiquarianism', he shared a widespread ambition of the time for writing 'a history of England from the legal point of view', even if he accomplished little in the field himself.[53] The attenuation of the tension between historical and analytical modes of legal analysis had much to do with the raised profile of law in the study of English history. This intermingling of Austin, history, and Englishness is well illustrated in Pollock's remark that: 'In England the positive law of the land has for centuries been single, strong, and conspicuous in all public life, and therefore positive law presented itself as an adequate object for distinct scientific study.'[54]

The close link at Oxford between law, politics, and history was solidified in 1885 when 'Political Science' was introduced into the modern history syllabus. The subject was to share a paper with political economy in an effort to inject greater intellectual rigour into the School. Both areas were to be approached through the analysis of texts, unlike at Cambridge where 'inductivism' reigned under the auspices of Sir John Seeley. Political economy was illuminated by J.S.

[51] R.J. Cocks, *Sir Henry Maine: A Study in Victorian Jurisprudence* (Cambridge, 1988), 149.

[52] See Dicey's obituary for Maitland, quoted in Fisher, *F.W. Maitland*, 176. Once again, Dicey was somewhat optimistic about the closeness of Maitland's concerns to Maine's and his own. On the more popular tone of Maine's writings relative to those of Maitland, see Collini, *Public Moralists*, 303.

[53] P. Cosgrove, *The Rule of Law: Albert Venn Dicey, Victorian Jurist* (London, 1980), 149. This aspiration is best exemplified in F. Pollock and F.W. Maitland, *The History of English Law Before the Time of Edward I* (Cambridge, 1895).

[54] Pollock, *History of the Science of Politics*, 125.

Mill's *Principles of Political Economy*. Political Science was studied in three books: Aristotle's *Politics*, Maine's *Ancient Law*, and J.K. Bluntschli's *The Theory of the Modern State*.[55] The latter was a much laboured book by a German professor, hurriedly translated for the first cohort of students to take the revised syllabus. As the translators – of whom D.G. Ritchie was one – declared in the preface, Bluntschli's work was important as 'an attempt to do for the European State what Aristotle had accomplished for the Hellenic'.[56] But Bluntschli's tome had something else in its favour – something indeed by which the *Politics* was also recommended, to judge by Barker's tribute to the latter in *Plato and Aristotle* – which brought both books into line with Maine's work. This was its organisation around the theme of law, reflecting the general trend of political science in Germany towards *Allgemeines Staatsrecht* or public law. A further indication of why Bluntschli's work was keenly adopted at Oxford is given in another essay by Pollock. Bitterly hostile to the tradition of natural law which seemed to have consumed German legal thought, Pollock made an exception of Bluntschli and Holtzendorff. In their work, 'German philosophical ideas are tempered by history and knowledge of practical politics into a shape which need not frighten any fairly open-minded English reader.'[57]

The resort to Bluntschli for lack of any indigenous equivalent suggests a marked interest at Oxford in developing political science as a related although separate field to law. In the study of both constitutional law and history in the late-nineteenth century, there was a strong tendency to identify 'polity' with the constitution and various institutions in England, not as a 'coherent pattern of authority' standing apart from them.[58] For example, Dicey notoriously made public law a species of private law in England: his considered

[55] In an attempt to arouse enthusiasm among students for these books, the Professor of Modern History, C.R.L. Firth, wrote in a memorandum of 1886: '[They] sound formidable, but are really excessively interesting, and a certain amount of knowledge of them should form an ingredient in every liberal education.' Loose document in Box G.A. Oxon. B. 140, Bodleian Library, Oxford.

[56] J.K. Bluntschli, *The Theory of the Modern State*, translated by D.G. Ritchie, P.E. Matheson, and R. Lodge (Oxford, 1885), v.

[57] F. Pollock, 'The methods of jurisprudence' (1882), in *Oxford Lectures and Other Discourses* (London, 1890), 17.

[58] The words are Kenneth Dyson's, although he uses them in relation to English political theory rather than law and historiography. While his conception of the lack of a strong sense of the state in the 'British intellectual tradition' is largely correct, more needs to be said about the attempts of Maitland and Barker to develop this sense. See ch. 3 below. K. Dyson, *The State Tradition in Western Europe: A Study of an Idea and Institution* (Oxford, 1980), 199.

dislike of the system of *Droit administratif* in France led him to venerate the English common law which governed relations between citizens and citizens, and citizens and officials alike. In assimilating the state to private law, Dicey trod a well-worn path which had been mapped out by his eighteenth-century mentors, Paley and Blackstone. Of the latter's *Commentaries* Maitland had remarked that 'there is wonderfully little of the state',[59] a verdict which could apply equally to Dicey's *Law of the Constitution.*

THE POLITICS OF 'MODERN GREATS'

How much light does this background shed on Barker's remark, quoted at the outset of this chapter, that he would not be taken seriously as an historian after having published in the realm of political science? The chief butt of his comment seems to have been his fellow historians at Oxford who kept the Modern History School tightly bound to constitutional history at the expense of 'political and economic problems'. He could readily sympathise with this stance. Intoning the most sacred of Whig assumptions in a discussion paper addressed to the faculty in 1908, he declared that: 'our Constitution is our great achievement as a people. Our legal development, with its juries, its *Habeas Corpus*, and the like; our institutional growth, with its Parliament, Cabinet, and party system – these are as much our contribution to civilization as philosophy was the contribution of Greece, or a code of law that of Rome'. His solution was to fuse constitutional with political history and increase the number of papers devoted to political and economic theory to two instead of one, thereby acknowledging 'things, which, under our modern conditions and in the civilisation of to-day, [are] of vast importance'. There were good pragmatic as well as intellectual reasons for effecting this change: Oxford and Cambridge Universities – but especially Oxford – were experiencing mounting pressure to expand their curricula into the region of 'modern studies'.[60] Unless the Oxford History Faculty

[59] F.W. Maitland, 'The Crown as Corporation' (1901), in *The Collected Papers of Frederic William Maitland*, vol. III, 254.

[60] Here, substantial pressure was exerted by the Workers' Educational Association. It campaigned for an education which, on the one hand, did not require knowledge of Greek and Latin, and on the other, embraced subjects which related to contemporary society. See J. Stapleton, 'Academic political thought and the development of political studies in Britain, 1900–1950', D. Phil. thesis, University of Sussex, 1986, ch. 7; and N. Chester, *Economics, Politics, and Social Studies in Oxford, 1900–85* (London, 1986), ch. 2.

met this challenge, Barker predicted, it could expect a new Final Honours School of Politics and Economics to lure away its best students and tutors. On the question of whether separate papers should be assigned to the two subjects of political and economic theory, he replied in the negative: aversion to 'the austerity of economic theory' among students would be lessened if it was mixed with 'the humaner subject of political theory'. To illustrate the wise scope of his term 'theory', he imagined that the first paper would focus on questions of 'abstract political and economic theory' and the second on those of 'the working of the political and economic institutions of to-day'.[61]

Clearly in 1908 Barker worked with a concept of political science which was dominated by political philosophy, a reflection of the formative place which Idealism held in his Oxford education. The antipathy of his colleagues may have been as much a reaction to this strain of 'political science' as to the prospect of bringing the history syllabus up-to-date by concentrating on 'modern problems'. Certainly, there was a pronounced suspicion of the level of abstraction entailed by philosophies such as that of Idealism among the English historical community in the late-nineteenth and early-twentieth centuries. This is captured in the amusing spectacle of E.A. Freeman – Stubbs' successor as Regius Professor in 1884 – hurling his copy of Plato across the room;[62] in the recollection of Sir Charles Oman – Regius Professor of Modern History from 1905 to 1914 – of his 'irritation' with Plato while reading for Greats and, as a 'Conservative', and 'Churchman', his 'frank dislike' of 'modern philosophy and metaphysic';[63] and even in H.A.L. Fisher, whom we have encountered as a disciple of Green in chapter 1, confessing a higher, 'Philistine' regard for Mill and Spencer as an undergraduate than his Idealist tutors would have approved.[64] If Greats created the *lingua franca* of Oxford Scholarship before the First World War, as Barker claimed in his autobiography, this did not always extend to the dominant philosophical current within it.

By 1915, however, Barker had changed his tack. Faced with the mounting interest in developing a new school of 'modern studies'

[61] E. Barker, 'On the need for the redistribution of the work prescribed for the school of Modern History' (Oxford, 1908), in Balliol College Library, Oxford.

[62] J. Bryce, *Studies in Contemporary Biography* (London, 1903), 269; on Freeman's love of Athenian democracy, although not its philosophical expositors, see Burrow, *A Liberal Descent*, 175.

[63] C. Oman, *Memories of Victorian Oxford and of Some Earlier Years* (London, 1941), 92–3.

[64] H.A.L. Fisher, *An Unfinished Autobiography* (London, 1940), 50.

which he had predicted in 1908, he became involved in an attempt to establish a 'Master of Civil Sciences' programme embracing political economy, political science, and pubic law. This endeavour to launch a more systematic study of political science at Oxford – at postgraduate rather than undergraduate level – took law rather than philosophy as its mainstay. In addition to Barker, the committee which devised the scheme included W.G.S. Adams (Gladstone Professor of Political Science) and W.M. Geldart (Dicey's successor to the Vinerian Chair of English Law).[65] As well as an effort to develop political studies at Oxford on non-philosophical grounds, the proposal also grew out of the recent failure to create a diploma in commercial education at Oxford. This initiative had aroused the opposition of those who harboured considerable prejudices against the world of industry and trade. But the principle of providing advanced education in the subjects connected with contemporary social and political organisation remained alive, stimulating the search for a degree that would build 'modern' subjects upon solid academic foundations.[66]

There were three components of the proposed 'Master of Civil Sciences' syllabus: 'Political Economy', 'The History of Political and Economic Theory', and 'Political Science and Public Law'. The last rubric held the key to the whole degree. The accompanying description ran: '[t]hese two subjects, from the point of view of the course, are so closely related one to the other that it is desirable to group the subjects together'. It certainly adds weight to the suggestion made earlier in this chapter that there was some sense of the need to situate political science in the proximity of constitutional law at Oxford in the 1880s, although not to fuse the two subjects entirely. At any rate, the components of the conjunction 'Political Science and Public Law' attest to the recent strength of legal-political scholarship in England – especially at Oxford – which was associated with Dicey, Pollock, Maitland, and James Bryce:

(1) Jurisprudence and the Theory of the State.
(2) English Constitutional Law and Administration.
(3) Comparative Constitutional Law and Institutions.
(4) International Law and Diplomacy.[67]

The first coupling had acquired much topicality due to the recent

[65] Hebdomadal Council Papers (HCP), University of Oxford, 101, xxxv.
[66] See Chester, *Economics, Politics, and Social Studies in Oxford*, 21–4.
[67] Report of Committee on Proposed Degree in Economics, HCP, University of Oxford, 101, 10 June 1915, 217–21.

wave of Pluralist thought, a movement which will be examined in the next chapter and which principally emerged from Maitland's reflections on the nature of corporate life. The first subject had also been nourished by the work of James Bryce, whose *Studies in History and Jurisprudence* was published in 1901. The second item of study bore Dicey's clear imprint. The third suggested the comparative perspective which Maine, Maitland, Bryce and others had made central to the study of law and politics in the late-nineteenth century. And the fourth had acquired a new urgency with the outbreak of the First World War, as will become clear in chapter 4. Given, as we have seen, that history often supplied the disciplinary backdrop to such 'legal' forms of political science, it follows that the two subjects were not always so opposed as Barker intimated in his letter to Tout in 1908. It seems that this was only the case when politics was conceived in an abstract 'Hegelian' light. Indeed, it was within an historical framework that Barker subsequently constructed his agenda for English political theory and political studies conceived along juridical lines.

The history of political thought was crucial to this project. As we have seen, Barker identified with this aspect of political inquiry from an early stage of his career, the first-fruits of which were his books on *Plato and Aristotle* and *Political Thought in England from Herbert Spencer to the Present Day*. It was appropriate that the subject appeared alongside 'Political Science and Public Law' in the scheme for a 'Master of Civil Science'. For Barker could well have taken to heart Maitland's point that: 'political philosophy in its youth is apt to look like a sublimated jurisprudence, and, even when it has grown in vigour and stature, is often compelled or content to work with tools – a social contract for example – which have been sharpened, if not forged, in the legal smithy'.[68] The natural law tradition was to become the precise focus of Barker's work in the history of political thought – as it had done for Ritchie – a discourse which struck a chord with both his Idealist heritage and his consciousness of law as the pivotal force in English political life and thought.

In 1915, then, Barker was a key votary of the idea that political science lies in the interstices beween law, history, and political philosophy. His years in the Oxford History Faculty between 1899 and 1919 coincided with the presence at Oxford of many eminent figures who had carved out that intellectual niche and with whom he

[68] Otto Gierke, *Political Theories of the Middle Age*, translated with an introduction by F.W. Maitland (Cambridge, 1900), viii.

was also on personal terms. For example, he had worked for Bryce on a new edition of his *Holy Roman Empire* in 1904;[69] and he regularly consorted with Dicey and Vinogradoff in the Political Economy Club at Oxford.[70] But in elevating their approach in the struggle which developed over the form which 'modern studies' like politics should take in the Oxford curricula, some significant cracks began to appear in the broad edifice of his intellectual inheritance. Put briefly, his early Idealist conception of political science as moral and political philosophy was becoming overshadowed by a view of law as the cornerstone of political understanding.

This shift in his conception of the disciplinary locus of political science mirrored changes that were taking place in Barker's political thought more widely. Thus, in the new edition of his book on classical political thought published in 1918 Barker gave a much-extended and sympathetic analysis of Plato's last work, the *Laws*.[71] To some extent, this can be explained by the exclusive focus of the second edition on 'Plato and his Predecessors'.[72] But he had evidently found fresh meaning in the *Laws*, specifically drawing his readers' attention to the chapters which dealt with them in the Preface. It is significant that much of his analysis of Plato's late recognition of the 'sovereignty of Law' was couched in terms of Dicey's principle of the 'Rule of Law'. For example, describing the 'law-state' which Plato had embraced in the *Laws*, Barker wrote that in it, '[l]aw must come first as sole and supreme sovereign, and government must be constructed in the interest of law. But law is one and the same for all; and it follows that the government which is constructed in its interest must also be constructed in the interest of all.'[73] While Rousseau might also appear

[69] E. Barker, 'Lord Bryce', *English Historical Review*, 37 (April, 1922), 219–24. He clearly held this elder statesman of English political science in the highest esteem. Thus, he wrote to Bryce in 1915, thanking him for his favourable comments on a recent book. It ended: 'I have learned so much from you, for so many years past, that your encouragement means more than that of any other man.' Barker to Bryce, 1 June 1915, MS. Bryce 26, fol. 39, Bodleian Library. His reverence for Bryce is also evident in his review of the latter's swan song, *Modern Democracies*, 2 vols. (London, 1921) in *The Observer*, 24 April 1921.

[70] E. Barker, *Age and Youth*, 18.

[71] The significance of Barker's concentration on the *Laws* was not lost on reviewers. A.E. Taylor, for example, hoped that *Greek Political Theory* would put an end to 'the scandalous practice of keeping the Oxford Honours student, who is supposed to make Plato the foundation of his reading in ethics and politics, wholly ignorant of Plato's final and matured judgement on the deepest issues of practical philosophy'. A.E. Taylor, review of *Greek Political Theory*, *Mind*, 28 (1919), 347.

[72] He was to have published a second volume on 'Aristotle and his Successors'. The latter never materialised, not in this form at any rate. The closest Barker came to it was his edition of Aristotle's *Politics* published in 1946, which contained an extensive introduction.

[73] E. Barker, *Greek Political Theory: Plato and his Predecessors* (London, 1918; 1960), 352.

as the inspiration behind these remarks, nevertheless it was to Dicey that Barker explicitly turned in search of a modern comparison (and contrast) with Plato's ideal of law.[74] Moreover, it was probably Dicey's influence which attuned him at this time to the sense in which – for the Greeks – 'there is, as yet, no distinction between a science of politics and a science of jurisprudence'. This comment related to the Greek philosophers' belief that the search for an 'ideal' code of law went hand in hand with the search for an ideal state.[75] While this rationale was certainly foreign to that which had been made by Dicey and other lawyers of his generation, nevertheless Greek political theory seemed to prescribe the same legal direction for the study of politics which they had sought. That this 'legal' conception of political science to some extent rivalled that which was rooted in ethics is evident in Barker's anticipation of hostile reaction to *Plato and Aristotle* from his fellow historians. It was somewhat ironic, therefore, that the ground for shifting political science away from ethics was laid as early as that work. There was already in *Plato and Aristotle* an evident sensitivity to law as the institutional essence of the state, even if the ethical perspectives of ancient political thinkers formed the primary focus of the book's analysis.

While winning some initial approval, the proposal for a 'Master of Civil Science' was never implemented. The committee which had launched it remained in existence until 1920; but after 1918 the initiative came up against keen competition from various proponents of a new undergraduate School. In this new wave of interest in introducing modern studies at Oxford, Barker ranged himself with economists and historians against the philosophers. He joined a sub-committee of the Committee for Economics and Political Science (which ran the diploma in those subjects established in 1904) composed of himself, W.G.S. Adams, F.Y. Edgeworth, A.J. Carlyle, Edward Cannan, L.L. Price, and Henry Furniss. In contrast to the plan of the philosophers to make their subject the centre-piece of a new Honours School in Philosophy, Politics, and Economics, the sub-committee defended a scheme for one in politics and economics alone (albeit with a strong historical foundation, and a European one at that). Aside from the omission of philosophy as a central plank of the School, the proposal with which Barker was associated included the 'Elements of Jurisprudence and International Law' in the

[74] Ibid., 384. [75] Ibid., 343.

'Economic Theory and Political Philosophy' part of the course[76] (see appendix 1). By contrast, in the Idealist-inspired plan for a School of Philosophy and Politics – led by two of Green's other disciples, A.D. Lindsay and J.L. Stocks – political philosophy was securely bracketed with moral philosophy, and no concessions were made to the province of law[77] (see appendix 2). In the event, the latter proposal triumphed, largely due to the strength of the philosophers at Oxford. It formed the basis of 'Modern Greats' (philosophy, politics, economics) which was launched in 1920, with philosophy as the dominant partner in the enterprise.[78] Barker did not have to live with this result, leaving Oxford in 1920 to become Principal of King's College London. There can be no doubt, however, as one surveys his activities during the first two decades of the twentieth century at Oxford, that political science was more than just a label with which he found himself stuck after the publication of his book on *Plato and Aristotle*; rather, it was a profession with which he positively identified and for which he had high intellectual ambitions.

While Barker's designs for a political science that was associated with law may have failed at Oxford, he made them central to his manifesto when he took up the Chair at Cambridge in 1927. However, before turning to his later career, it is necessary to consider one final stone in the foundations of his political thought which were laid just before the First World War: that of Pluralism.

APPENDIX I

SCHEME FOR AN HONOURS SCHOOL OF ECONOMICS AND POLITICS, FEBRUARY 1920

I

Economic Theory and Political Philosophy, together with the elements of Jurisprudence and International Law

II

The History of Economic and Political Theory

[76] Draft Scheme for an Honours School in Economics and Politics, HCP, 115, 16 February 1920, 84.

[77] Report of Joint Committee on a School of Modern Humanities, HCP, 116, 8 May 1920, 89–92.

[78] See references in footnote 60, above.

Social Anthropology

The Economic History of Europe, the British Empire and the United States mainly from 1760

The History of the Political Institutions of Europe, the British Empire and the United States mainly from 1688

Economic Geography

III

The Structure and Problems of Modern Industry, Commerce, Finance and Currency

The Political Structure and Problems of Modern Europe, the British Empire and the United States

IV

Two Special Subjects to be selected by candidates from a list

Source: Hebdomadal Council Papers, University of Oxford 115 (January–March 1920), p. 84

The Draft Statute for a Final Honours School of Economics and Politics which was submitted to the Hebdomadal Council in May 1920 simplified the above proposal. Significantly, the inclusion of jurisprudence still stood. Parts of the Draft Statute are reproduced below.

The Examination in the Honour School of Economics and Politics shall always include:

(1) Economic Theory and Political Philosophy
(2) The History of Economic and Political Thought
(3) Modern Economic and Constitutional History
(4) The Economic and Political Organisation of Modern Society

Candidates will be expected to show such knowledge of Economic and Political Geography and Jurisprudence and Statistical Method as is necessary for the proper study of the subjects of this examination.

Suggested scheme of papers:

(1) and (2) Economic Theory, including the History of Economic Theory
(3) Modern Economic History from 1700
(4) Political Philosophy
(5) The History of Political Thought
(6) British Constitutional History, including that of the Dominions, from 1688
(7) The Economic Organisation of Modern Society
(8) The Political Organisation of Modern Society

(9) and (10) A Special Subject
Source: Hebdomadal Council Papers, University of Oxford 116 (April–June 1920), pp. 144–5

APPENDIX 2

Excerpts from the Draft Statute for an Honours School in Politics and Philosophy, May 1920

The subject of the Honours School of Philosophy and Politics shall be the study of the structure, and the philosophical, political and economic principles, of Modern Society.

The examination in this School shall always include:

(1) Moral and Political Philosophy
(2) British Political and Constitutional History from 1760
(3) British Social and Economic History from 1760
(4) The History of Philosophy from Descartes
(5) Political Economy
(6) Prescribed Books in any two of the following subjects
 (a) Metaphysics and Moral Philosophy
 (b) Political Philosophy
 (c) Political Economy
(7) A further subject in Philosophy or Politics or Political Economy
(8) Unprepared Translation from French, German, or Italian authors. Every candidate must satisfy the Examiners in two at least of these languages

Source: Hebdomadal Council Papers, University of Oxford, 116 (April–June 1920), pp. 89–92

CHAPTER 3

Society and the state in the English national past: the lure of Pluralism

THE CONTEXT AND CHALLENGE OF PLURALISM

We have seen how, in Barker's intellectually formative years, his political values and concerns were formulated on the extensive border between Whiggism and Idealism. In particular, it was there that he attempted to steer a middle path between individualism and collectivism in moral and political philosophy. This entailed acknowledging the extent to which individuals are products of a wider social mind, a notion which in contemporary parlance easily became the national mind, or character, or still more effusively, the national 'genius'. But for all the concessions to collective identity and purpose that the common ground between Whiggism and Idealism made possible, it also accommodated Barker's keen sense of the primacy of individual moral agency. This insistence stemmed largely from a Nonconformist upbringing in which individual conscience was deemed sacrosanct. Another influence in this respect was his principal Idealist mentor T.H. Green. For although Green was born and bred an Anglican, he held the greatest respect for Nonconformity, particularly the Congregationalism in which Barker had been raised. Nonconformism was also a contributory factor in Barker's deep appreciation of the political liberty that was celebrated in Whiggism. Like Green, he broke with the animosity towards 'tradition' which had previously polarised Nonconformist and Whig Liberalism – in the work of Herbert Spencer, for example. Finally, Nonconformity was significant in sensitising him to the Pluralist attack upon state sovereignty and the elevation of English voluntary societies, of which the Puritan Congregation was a prime example.

The Pluralist movement developed in the first decade of the twentieth century, mainly in response to the seemingly high-handed treatment of voluntary associations in the Taff Vale (1901) and Free Church of Scotland (1900–4) cases. It acquired further momentum between 1910 and 1914, against the backdrop of the militancy of labour, the suffragettes, and Irish Unionists. Then, as George Dangerfield argued in 1935, the world of nineteenth-century liberalism – with its strong foundation in the authority of parliament – came perilously close to collapse under these multiple pressures.[1] In this atmosphere Pluralism itself assumed a strident character, especially among younger protagonists such as Harold Laski and G.D.H. Cole. In their view, the recent unrest provided irrefutable evidence that the supremacy of the state was by no means assured. The outbreak of war fuelled their iconoclastic stance still further, shifting the basis of their criticism to the new and dangerous powers which the state could readily assume in times of crisis.[2] In these ways, Pluralism captured a wider cultural mood in England during the early years of the century, one in which – as Jose Harris has argued – civil society was seen as 'the highest sphere of human existence'.[3]

It was suggested above that for Barker the political and spiritual values of Nonconformity provided a vital connecting thread between Whiggism, Idealism, and Pluralism. But it was not the only link between these three political theories; and neither was it the only source of his interest in Pluralism. Indeed, Pluralism may be regarded as a direct offshoot of both Whiggism and Idealism themselves; as such, it proved attractive to those who had imbibed these two intellectual roots. For example, we saw in the first chapter that the British Idealists readily affirmed the pluralist basis of society, particularly English society. For Green and Bosanquet, the search for the common good in politics was quite compatible with, indeed was premised upon, the notion of difference and diversity.[4] Pluralism also derived considerable impetus from nineteenth-century Whiggism; its sense of the importance of spontaneously formed groups was analogous to the high premium which had been placed upon the English locality in the Whig historiography of Stubbs, Freeman, and Green. Just as local institutions in this view constituted the cornerstone of the English

[1] G. Dangerfield, *The Strange Death of Liberal England* (London, 1935).

[2] On Cole's Pluralism, see A.W. Wright, *G.D.H. Cole and Socialist Democracy* (Oxford, 1979), chs. 2–5. On Laski's Pluralism, see B. Zylstra, *From Pluralism to Collectivism: The Development of Harold Laski's Political Thought* (Assen, 1968). The most recent analyses of English Pluralism are A. Vincent, *Theories of the State* (Oxford, 1987), ch. 6; and P.Q. Hirst, *The Pluralist Theory of the State: Selected Writings of G.D.H. Cole, J.N. Figgis, and H.J. Laski* (London, 1989).

[3] J. Harris, 'Society and the state in twentieth-century Britain', in F.M.L. Thompson (ed.), *The Cambridge Social History of Britain, 1750–1950*, 3 vols., vol. III, *Social Agencies and Institutions* (Cambridge, 1990), 67.

[4] D. Nicholls, *The Pluralist State* (London, 1975), 77–8.

nation, so, in Pluralism, that role was extended to voluntary associations at large. As J.W. Burrow has perceptively observed, the Pluralism of Maitland, at any rate, represented the adaption of Whiggism to the 'more fluid conditions of commercial and industrial society'. English liberty was now symbolised in the flourishing group life that included, but also cut across, the boundaries of local self-government.[5]

Moved by both Idealism and Whiggism, in addition to Nonconformity, Barker was in some ways well disposed towards the new Pluralist ideas in Britain during the early years of the twentieth century. In a retrospective view of his work at the time of the First World War he confessed that he was then 'more inclined to what is called "pluralism" – an exaltation of the claim of groups *vis-à-vis* the State – than I was in later days and in my later writings'. He continued: 'I then felt strongly the tension between the *regnum* – the "sovereign" authority of the secular State – and the free play of the voluntary society (religious, economic, or whatever its basis might be), with its scope of liberty and ease for the unfolding of human worth and dignity; and my sympathy then ran towards the voluntary society.' He was quick to qualify this admission by emphasising that one of his main publications at the time, an article entitled 'The discredited state', ended with a recognition of 'the ultimate rights of the "sovereign" authority of the *regnum*', an unconscious prophecy – he believed – of the First World War.[6] Indeed, as if to underline the limited extent of his Pluralist sympathies when the article was published in 1915 – a year after it had been read to the Philosophical Society at Oxford – he appended the subtitle 'Thoughts on politics before the war'. These riders confirm his assertion in his autobiography that he was more 'curious' than 'convinced' by Pluralism. Certainly, to the extent that he regarded Pluralism as a theory which 'dissolves and divides the sovereignty of the State among a plurality of different groups and communities', he was right to disclaim any responsibility for its advance.[7] While he was receptive to the Pluralist attempt to counter the two 'Absolutes' which had dominated recent political

[5] J.W. Burrow, 'The Village community and the uses of history', in N. McKendrick (ed.), *Historical Perspectives: Studies in English Thought and Society in Honour of J.H. Plumb* (London, 1974), 281; and *Whigs and Liberals: Continuity and Change in English Political Thought* (Oxford, 1988), ch. 6.

[6] E. Barker, new preface to the American edition of *Church, State, and Study* (London, 1930), re-titled *Church, State, and Education* (Ann Arbor, 1957).

[7] E. Barker, *Age and Youth: Memories of Three Universities and Father of the Man* (Oxford, 1953), 76.

theory – that of the individual and the state – he was apprehensive about the possible emergence of a new 'Absolute' in their place: that of the group. In his view such a development endangered both individuality on the one hand, and the authority of the state on the other.

Yet, when he had stripped away what he evidently considered as the chaff in Pluralist ideas, Barker found much wheat of permanent political and cultural value. Consequently, he set about removing the sharp cutting edge of Pluralist thought, eliciting instead its full potential for cultural celebration. His task entailed emphasising the prominence of voluntary association in Britain, but a prominence for which the state could take equal credit with society. In this way, individual freedom had been preserved against the demands which groups made upon their members and upon society at large, while ensuring maximum social 'progress' through them. How did he take the sting out of Pluralism in this way? This chapter examines Barker's attempt to promote the state within Pluralist thought, an undertaking which was firmly rooted in his conception of English national development. This will become clear if we turn to the two main figures who influenced his Pluralism: F.W. Maitland and George Unwin. While he never knew Maitland personally, his intellectual debt to him was incalculable. As we have seen, Unwin was a Lancashire acquaintance, one with whom Barker shared a Nonconformist background and an education at Oxford in which Green's Idealism featured prominently.

ENGLISH CLUBS AND 'SOCIAL EXPERIMENTATION'

An appropriate place to begin unravelling the influence of Maitland upon Barker is the latter's eulogy to the great medievalist in 1936, on the occasion of his Presidential Address to the Sociological Society. Perhaps to legitimate his own title to this role while holding a Chair in political science rather than sociology, Barker focused upon his mentor's status as a sociologist. Quoting H.A.L. Fisher – Maitland's biographer – he emphasised that in Maitland's hands, the history of law became 'a contribution to the general history of human society'. But for Barker Maitland deserved a commanding place in the pantheon of sociologists primarily on account of his theory of groups.

This part of his address provides a vital clue to understanding Barker's admiration for Maitland, especially his contribution to Pluralist political theory. He was careful to stress that Maitland was not only moved to take up the cause of voluntary association as a result of the latter's political travails at the turn of the century – the skirmishes with the state over the group's so-called right to develop in its own manner in the celebrated Taff Vale Case and Scottish Free Church Appeals. Also, he claimed, Maitland's interest in corporations stretched wider than his absorption in the writings of Otto Von Gierke. The latter, part of whose *Das deutsche Genossenschaftsrecht* Maitland translated in 1900, defended the group's 'real personality' and 'inherent rights' against the fiction theory of the corporation, the notion that groups were born of the 'concession' of the state. This was not an argument to which Barker was receptive, as we shall see. Rather, in explaining the source of Maitland's enthusiasm for corporate life, Barker placed most emphasis on the nature of Maitland's professional interests: the history of English law and English legal institutions. He drew what he considered to be the most important conclusion from Maitland's work in this field: that, 'whatever else we may say about England, it has certainly been a paradise of groups'. Linking Maitland's Pluralism to the work of the Victorian antiquarian, Joshua Toulmin Smith, on the history of English guilds, he continued:

> They [i.e. groups] begin in old Anglo-Saxon frith-gilds (mutual insurance societies, as I should call them, for the safer commission and the surer compensation of cattle-raids), if they are not even earlier than the frith-gilds: they continue through mediaeval religious gilds, mediaeval societies of lawyers called Inns of Court, seventeenth-century Free Churches, seventeenth-century East India and other companies, down to modern groups such as Lloyd's, the stock-exchange, the Trade Union, the London club (such as the Athenaeum), and, as I am in private duty bound to mention, this Institute of Sociology which I am now addressing.[8]

This account of Maitland's Pluralism certainly struck the right note. Maitland's assertion of the 'real personality' of groups was the corollary of a more basic delight in the unrivalled capacity of the English nation for voluntary association, a talent which had flourished despite all the odds of Roman law that had been stacked against it. Group-life in England, Maitland maintained, was 'richer even than that which has come under Dr. Gierke's eyes'.[9] For this the English had their lawyers to thank. In a significant parallel with Dicey's

[8] E. Barker, 'Maitland as a sociologist', *The Sociological Review*, 29, no. 2 (April, 1937), 127.

[9] F.W. Maitland, Introduction to Otto Gierke, *Politial Theories of the Middle Age*, transl. F.W. Maitland (Cambridge, 1900), xxvii.

reverence for the legal profession as the touchstone of English liberty, Maitland celebrated the ingenuity of the bar and the bench in developing the concept of the 'trust'. In his view this device constituted 'the greatest and most distinctive achievement performed by Englishmen in the field of jurisprudence'.[10] Originating in fourteenth-century land-law as a means of bypassing restrictions upon testamentary succession, the trust was to yield much wider benefits as a means of bypassing the odious 'concession' route to incorporation.[11] The trust – developed in the Court of Chancery – created a wall or screen, within which groups found the liberty denied to them in Roman law. As Maitland claimed, 'the trust has given us a liberal substitute for a law about personified institutions. The trust has given us a liberal supplement for the necessarily meagre law of corporations.' The strongest protection of groups through the trust was provided by the lawyers themselves who belonged to an unincorporated body *par excellence* – the Inns of Court. So long as the latter continued to dwell thus in 'free fellowship', their common law rhetoric that it is 'a crime for men "to presume to act as a corporation"' proved innocuous.[12]

Maitland's pluralism, then, emphasised yet another 'peculiarity of the English'. He had none of the brash complacency of a Macaulay or Dickens' Mr Podsnap; but in a softer, more convivial manner, he too held the quirks of English culture with which he was concerned in high regard. In effect, Maitland extended a growing awareness of the strength of English associationism that had arisen on the basis of mutual self-help among the working class to other social groups, as well as building upon the importance of local identities in nineteenth-century accounts of Englishness.[13] Both he and his disciple J.N. Figgis projected an arresting image of English society as pervaded by the ties of voluntary association at all levels. As Figgis wrote in his seminal Pluralist book *Churches in the Modern State*, published in 1913:

> As a matter of fact, in England at least, it is these smaller associations which have always counted for most in the life of the individual. His school, or college, his parish or county, his union or regiment, his wife or family is the most vitally formative part in the life of most men; and in so far as England

[10] F.W. Maitland, 'The unincorporate body', in *The Collected Papers of Frederic William Maitland*, ed. by H.A.L. Fisher, vol. III (Cambridge, 1911), 272.

[11] F.W. Maitland, 'Trust and corporation', in *The Collected Papers of Frederic William Maitland*, vol. III, 332–6.

[12] Maitland, *Political Theories of the Middle Age*, xxxi.

[13] The key study of working-class associations at the end of the nineteenth century is J.M. Baernreither, *English Associations of Working Men*, translated by Alice Taylor (London, 1889).

has anything worthy in civic life to show to the world, it is the spectacle of individuals bred up or living within these small associations which mould the life of men more intimately than the great collectivity we call the state.[14]

The Pluralist onslaught upon political theories which projected the state as the highest form of social life is readily intelligible in this light; for such accounts of the state were perceived as alien to the richness and vitality of spontaneous association in England. The ideal of 'spontaneity' in human action and social organisation was widely upheld in mid-Victorian thought, finding exponents as diverse as J.S. Mill, Samuel Smiles, Toulmin Smith, E.R. Freeman, J.R. Green, and T.H. Green. But it is in the work of Pluralists like Maitland and Figgis that the deep-seated cultural practices in England which underpinned this affirmation became most explicit.

This is particularly apparent if we consider the dynamic framework of Maitland's Pluralism. No static 'snapshot' of politics and society, it contained a highly normative view about the character of historical change derived essentially from reflections upon English national development. The key to this historical interpretation lay in the notion of 'social experimentation' of which the trust was seen by Maitland as a 'powerful instrument'.[15] In the same vein he asserted that while the trust may have made English jurisprudence 'disorderly', nevertheless it 'gave to it something of the character of an experimental science'.[16]

As these quotations suggest, the word 'experiment' crops up regularly in Maitland's Pluralism. His meaning is best captured in his examples, such as that of the capacity of married women to hold property prior to the Married Women's Property Act of 1882. The law on this matter having become 'osseous' at an early stage, 'trusts of money or of invested funds became as usual as trusts of land'. All that was needed was a 'wall of trustees' whom the law could hold responsible. When the law was changed in 1882, this was no revolutionary move, no 'leap in the dark', but simply a bringing of 'our *eheliches Guterrecht* (matrimonial law)' into line with actual social and legal practice.[17]

To take another of Maitland's illustrations of how progress takes place through 'social experimentation', and one which especially

[14] J.N. Figgis, *Churches in the Modern State* (London, 1913), 47–8.
[15] F.W. Maitland, 'The unincorporate body', 278.
[16] F.W. Maitland, 'Trust and corporation', 376–7.
[17] Ibid., 355–6.

highlights the role of groups in the making of English liberty, he argued that '[a]ll we English people mean by "religious liberty" has been intimately connected with the making of trusts'. In the absence of trusts, Nonconformist sects would have been beholden to the state for incorporation, and hence subject to its control. Saved by the trust, all they had to do was to elicit a little toleration of the state, toleration which would have been meaningless if the state had been able to intervene in their affairs through stipulating the conditions of incorporation. With obvious satisfaction, Maitland stood back and observed the result, one of infinite religious diversity: 'And now we have in England Jewish synagogues and Catholic cathedrals and the churches and chapels of countless sects. They are owned by natural persons. They are owned by trustees.'[18]

Barker fully shared Maitland's admiration for the good work performed by the English trust. Moreover, he seized on the connection in Maitland's thought between innovation and society (rather than the state), making it especially pronounced. Thus, after noting that 'the concept of the trust has aided the progress of social experimentation', he added, with a flourish: 'That is a great thing, perhaps the greatest of all things, if you believe, as I do, that the process of social experimentation is prior to the State, is greater than the State, and must be served and preserved by the State.'[19] Indeed, he was even so bold as to suggest that in addition to illuminating 'British social development', perhaps Maitland had also discerned 'the normal growth of all peoples' and provided 'a light which should guide future growth'.[20] He had no difficulty in building a broad philosophy of history on the English foundations which Maitland had erected. But it was one which kept the contribution of the state sharply in focus, holding no truck with the tendency in parts of Maitland's work – and that of other English Pluralists – to disparage political authority unduly.

Barker's distance from Maitland in this respect is well illustrated by his defence of the Latin heritage of Western civilisation, against the vogue of Teutonism in Victorian Britain. It is well known that Maitland was an enthusiast of all things Germanic, thereby sustaining a keynote of Whiggism; and Germanicism was epitomised in his eyes in a high capacity for free association. For the opposing Latin principles of sovereignty – with its central characteristics of uniformity and compulsion – he held considerable disdain. By contrast, Barker

[18] Ibid., 364. [19] E. Barker, 'Maitland as a sociologist', 135. [20] Ibid., 135.

was keen to weigh Latin and Teutonic achievements more evenly. For example, at the same time as he entered the Pluralist controversy he wrote an article in praise of the Latin contribution to medieval political thought. The kingship that existed in medieval England and France was based on the principle of political sovereignty, in addition to that of 'feudal suzerainty' or *personal* relations between lord and vassal. The former element ensured that the ruler was a 'public officer, and politics a matter of impersonal law'. Barker went on to raise the rhetorical question, '[i]f you remove the Roman tradition of sovereignty, what would our kings have been but the leaders of war-bands like those of Hengest and Horsa?'[21]

Barker's attachment to Latin political culture is further evident in his response to the decision in the Free Church of Scotland case which had done much to provoke Pluralist thought in Britain. Maitland had sharply denounced the stance taken by the legal authorities (and implicitly the state) in this case, claiming that the 'dead hand' of the House of Lords had fallen 'with a resounding slap upon the living body [of the Church]'.[22] Barker certainly agreed with Maitland that the judges had operated with too restrictive a notion of group personality. Nevertheless, true to his Latin sympathies, and also with distinct echoes of Dicey, he could at least admire the way in which the House of Lords had applied the law 'equally and impartially'. He believed that it was some consolation that: 'Churches have suffered in the same way as trade unions: the Scottish Church case is very like the Osborne case. In both the restrictive force of some original act – statute or trust deed – in limiting the action of groups has been a cardinal feature of the judgement.'[23]

In this quotation, there is an implicit criticism of Pluralists that they could sometimes be too hard on the state. This was against the better judgement of Maitland, at least. For he had recognised that groups – whether incorporated or simply 'sheltering' under the trust – were rightly accountable for unlawful acts. He had also acknowledged that the key to the 'progressive' character of English history lay in permanent, controlled, and yet creative tension between state and society. For Barker, state and society under conditions of political sovereignty were not set on the ineluctable collision course that was

[21] E. Barker, 'The Roman heritage in the Middle Ages', *History*, 3, 2 (old series) (1914), 91, 95.

[22] F.W. Maitland, 'Moral personality and legal personality' (1903), in *The Collected Papers of Frederic William Maitland*, vol. III, 319.

[23] E. Barker, 'The rights and duties of trade unions', *Economic Review*, 21 (1911), 151.

sometimes suggested in the writings of Maitland, and certainly that of his younger followers like Laski and Cole. Such an analysis sprang from the mistaken assumption that groups – including the state – possessed 'real personalities' and 'real wills'. To the extent that Barker assigned personality to groups, it was a 'juristic' one, denoting their capacity for legal action but not action in general. The latter, he claimed – true to his 'anti-nominalist' self – was an attribute of individuals only.[24] Along with other Pluralists, he insisted in 'The discredited state' that group personality 'grows' rather than being artificially constructed by the state. However, drawing on Bosanquet's philosophy, he argued that groups cohere around certain 'organising ideas' which enter into, and are altered by the minds of a changing membership. De-personalised in this way, he argued, 'we cease to feel murder in the air' because of an 'internecine struggle between the real personality of the State and the real personality of groups'.[25]

The emollient strains of Idealism are further in evidence here, and still more so if we consider the distinct and ultimately sovereign status which Barker attributed to the state in rescuing it from the Pluralist attack. For he claimed that in a 'polyarchic' society, it was vital that groups be brought within the 'organising idea' of the state, this being the priority of 'law and order in the external converse of man with man'. The recent spate of social legislation, turning the state 'from a plain grocer's shop into a Whiteley's emporium' had not altered this essential foundation. A few years before his *Greek Political Theory* of 1918, we see a legal definition of the state taking centre-stage in his thought, couched in the Idealist imperative of maintaining the 'external' conditions of moral life. That this was nevertheless regarded by survivors of the Idealist avant-garde as overdoing the legal side of the state is clear from a remark which J.H. Muirhead made in 1924. Barker, he argued, had done less than justice to the 'credited' state by treating it too exclusively from the side of law and order. 'As the individual is more than his orderly habits so the state is more than the policeman and the courts.'[26] The starkness of the Idealist state in its guise as public 'right' in some ways invited this emphasis, especially to those like Barker who were keen students of

[24] E. Barker, *Political Thought in England*, 176. On his conception of nominalism, and distance from it, see note 59, chapter 1 above.

[25] E. Barker, 'The discredited state: thoughts on politics before the war', *Political Quarterly* (old series) 2 (February 1915), 113.

[26] J.H. Muirhead, 'Recent criticism of the Idealist theory of the General Will', *Mind*, 33 (1924), 240.

Dicey as well as Bosanquet. It certainly led him to neglect the vital accompanying sense in Idealist thought of citizens internalising the Idea of the state as supreme power in society and the embodiment of a 'complete way of life'. Overlooking this aspect, he claimed that the state was necessarily a 'forced and bare universal' because of the breadth of forces which it was charged with integrating.

Yet as he was quick to emphasise in his *Political Thought in England from Herbert Spencer to the Present Day* published in the same year as 'The discredited state', the state was nonetheless the linchpin of society. That insistence was prompted by Spencer's administrative nihilism; but it possessed a wider target in Barker's contemporaries who were apt – in his view – to underestimate the importance of the state in their enthusiasm for groups. Spencer had erroneously believed that society could be organised along voluntary lines more effectively than through the action of the state – the natural conclusion of a long historical process resulting in the triumph of 'industrialism' over 'militancy'. However, replied Barker, echoing Bosanquet, the complexity of modern industrial society as an intricate web of voluntary organisation depended upon the state's mechanism of 'adjustment'. What Spencer had failed to see was that 'voluntary co-operation is only made possible by the State, and, what is more, that the more there is of voluntary co-operation, the more need there is of the State'.[27]

Moreover, in Barker's view, the state's inability to construct more than an 'imperfect synthesis' was a cause for jubilation rather than consternation. In his words: 'The very attempt of factors which conceive themselves neglected to push themselves forward as absolute wholes on their own account may serve as an incentive to a truer synthesis.'[28] Put briefly, the Pluralist state was a 'progressive state' when characterised as existing in a condition of 'unstable equilibrium' with society. This line not only contrasts with the Pluralism of Laski and Cole which often conceived state and society as irreconcilable opposites; it is also marked off from the more pacific Pluralist vision of Figgis. The latter looked forward to the revival of the late-medieval notion of the state as a *communitas communitatum* in which 'the lion of the throne would lie down with the lamb of spiritual freedom'.[29]

[27] E. Barker, *Political Thought in England*, 118–9.
[28] E. Barker, 'The discredited state', 116.
[29] Figgis, *Churches in the Modern State*, 80–1.

SALVAGING THE IDEALIST STATE

In developing the potential in Maitland's Pluralism for a 'progressive' philosophy of history based on institutionalised conflict between state and society, Barker seems to have leant considerably on the work of his fellow Mancunian, George Unwin.[30] Though contemporaries at Oxford where they both read Literae Humaniores followed by modern history, the two men first met on their home ground during one of the vacations. They went on occasional walks together there; but it was after they had finished their degrees that they became best acquainted. Barker paid glowing tribute to Unwin in his autobiography and acknowledged the deep impact of his ideas.[31]

In the early years of the century, Unwin was hard at work on his broad outline of economic history in the West which especially highlighted the creative role of voluntary associations like the guilds. In this respect, he had evidently been influenced by the rising tide of Pluralist thought. He used the latter to embellish his belief – derived mainly from T.H. Green – in mankind's infinite capacity for spiritual progress. Given his Idealist sympathies, he was unlikely to adopt the negative posture towards the state of other Pluralist thinkers. This was despite his bitter opposition to imperialism, particularly after the Boer War. The state provided in Unwin's view an essential mechanism of 'order' against society's relentless pressure for 'progress'. It was true that if this delicate balance were tilted in favour of the former – as in the Roman Empire – then all mediating agencies between the individual and the state would be obliterated, bringing progress to a halt. But it was also true that if the forces of 'free fellowship' gained the upper hand, the result would be 'aimlessness' and 'anarchy'. It was a lesson he had learned from the Webbs' broadside against the spell which the idea of 'primitive democracy' cast upon early trade unions.[32] As he argued in his inaugural lecture when he became Professor of Economic History at Edinburgh in 1908, the happy compromise between the two extremes could be found in British history from its earliest stages:

We can there watch in all its successive phases that transformation of social forces into political forces which is an essential feature of what we call progress. We see class after class constituting itself a social force by the act of

[30] I have explored Unwin's ideas in 'Pluralism as English cultural definition: the social and political thought of George Unwin', *Journal of the History of Ideas*, 52 (1991), 665–84.
[31] E. Barker, *Age and Youth*, 294.
[32] G. Unwin, *The Gilds and Companies of London* (London, 1908), 6, 12.

self-organization. Then, as the new force gains political recognition, the voluntary association passes wholly or partly into an organ of public administration. As class power generates class privilege and exclusiveness, new social forces gather to a head and find expression in new voluntary associations, which tend, in their turn, to be transformed as they are drawn into the vortex of political activity.[33]

There is much to compare between this quotation and the last one in the previous section from Barker's essay 'The discredited state' where he emphasises the vital condition of 'unstable equilibrium' in state–society relations necessary for progress. This may be more than an affinity since Barker had absorbed Unwin's thoughts well, even before they were published. Thus in his *The Political Thought of Plato and Aristotle*, which appeared in 1906, he too had invoked the perils which befell the Roman Empire; particularly when the later Roman state had hardened into a 'repressive crust . . . as the *municipium* or *collegium* were rigorously regimented and controlled', thereby preventing the 'free growth of society'.[34] This comment appeared in the first chapter of the book, for which – in the Preface – he expressed his gratitude to Unwin for reading in draft. Moreover, Barker not only shared the Idealism on which Unwin's Pluralism rested; he also shared the Whiggism which constituted its other main pillar. Once again, the cross-currents between these two streams of late-nineteenth-century political thought become clear, finding an Archimedean point in Unwin and Barker's development of Maitland's thoughts on the relationship of state to society in England.

For example, while Unwin may have cast the distinction between state and society in the Comtean terms of 'order' and 'progress', his analysis was infused with the Whig account of English constitutional development. We have seen that his social theory was embedded in English history, and he was certainly well acquainted with the Whig interpretation of the latter.[35] The tension he highlighted between polity and society – polity responding to prior changes in society but never initiating change itself – was central to the Whig paradigm in the early-nineteenth century. As J.W. Burrow has remarked, that duality was an attempt to steer a Burkean path between 'Tory timidity and . . . radical rationalism and utopianism'. It entailed 'a

[33] G. Unwin, 'The aims of Economic History' (1908), in R.H. Tawney (ed.), *Studies in Economic History: The Collected Papers of George Unwin* (London, 1927), 35–6.

[34] E. Barker, *The Political Thought of Plato and Aristotle* (1906; New York, 1959), 11.

[35] Unwin confessed to a correspondent in 1916 that he had 'learnt all my history from [J.R.] Green and Macaulay'. *Studies in Economic History*, lxvii.

notion of constitutional adjustment, peacefully restoring the relation between polity and society which the progress of civil society might disturb'.[36] This theory is highly visible in Unwin's Pluralism; it would also seem to underlie Maitland's analysis of the strength and virtue of 'social experimentation' in England too. While such a notion was conceivably vitalised by other strands of mid-Victorian political thought – for example, the paean in Mill's liberalism to 'experiments in living' – its deeper roots in Whiggism are evident in its strong evocations of the English national past.

It was not only the Pluralists who warmed to this Whig recipe for combining change with stability and continuity through the good offices of the state; it appears to have made a similar impact upon the Idealist philosopher, Bernard Bosanquet, too. This is clear in his use of the term 'adjustment' to denote the primary function of the state. Thus in *The Philosophical Theory of the State* of 1899, he described the state as 'the operative criticism of all institutions – modification and adjustment by which they are capable of playing a rational part in the object of human will'.[37] He may have introduced some philosophical terms which were foreign to Whiggism; but he surely wrote in the same vein as both Whiggism – and Maitland's Pluralism – in his introduction to the second edition of the book in 1910 when he argued that: 'The work of the state is *de facto* for the most part "endorsement" or "taking over" – setting its *imprimatur*, the seal of its force, on what more flexible activities or the mere progress of life have wrought out in long years of adventurous experiment or silent growth.'[38] Furthermore, Bosanquet perhaps only articulated what Whiggism presumed in emphasising that society needed to be brought into harmony with polity, and thereby with itself: that the state possesses 'a working conception of life'.[39] In this way the tension that appeared between Whiggism and Idealism in the 1870s as the older political ideal of 'balancing interests' confronted the newer one of realising 'the General Will'[40] seemed to dissipate. At least, there was the potential for it to do so, as we shall see presently in considering Barker's minimalist interpretation of Bosanquet's concept of 'adjustment'. Bosanquet himself was apt to inflate the state's 'working conception of life' into something with much less of a 'rule of thumb' air about it.

Clearly, Whiggism stood in the background of both the Idealist

36 J.W. Burrow, *Whigs and Liberals*, 40–1.
37 B. Bosanquet, *The Philosophical Theory of the State* (London, 1899; 1923), 140.
38 Ibid., xxxviii. 39 Ibid., 141. 40 Burrow, *Whigs and Liberals*, 48.

revival in England and the Pluralist movement which followed in its wake. These three strands were most closely united in Unwin's social and political thought, providing Barker with an intellectual framework in which he could have his Pluralist cake and eat it – Idealist style – too. With its firm anchor in Whiggism, this synthesis counteracted the tendency within Idealism to absorb society into the state, against which Barker was permanently on his guard. It also acknowledged the positive role of conflict and tension in society – albeit when kept within bounds. By contrast, the English Idealists are often accused – not without foundation – of glossing over social fissures. Moreover, Unwin's synthesis gave Idealism a strong English twist by showing how political institutions in England exemplified the responsiveness implicit in the Idealist notion of 'adjustment.'

At the same time, Unwin's conjunction of Whiggism and Idealism gave to Maitland's thesis on the high English aptitude for 'social experimentation' a more pronounced recognition of the essential function of the state in 'receiving' new social influences into the universal, or political, domain. While Maitland appreciated the 'dark side' of groups like charitable institutions and the need for the state to supervise their resources to some degree,[41] nevertheless his concessions to the state were generally grudging. The real hero of his Pluralist theory and historiography was the trust, not the state, despite the latter's equally significant contribution in his account to the progress of English society through its work of consolidating change.

In supplementing the Pluralism of Maitland with that of Unwin, Barker went some way towards settling his profound unease with the elevation of groups. Recent developments in trade-union law and organisation made him particularly anxious. He was worried by the compulsory levy, the 'energy', 'closed character', and 'multifarious activities' of trade unions. He concluded that unions were no longer voluntary associations in the true sense of the word; since sealing their alliance with the newly formed Labour Party, they posed 'a danger to the State'. The exercise of political influence upon the state by 'loose voluntary organisations' was one thing; it was quite another when a putative voluntary society entered upon 'a career of general political activity'.[42] It was a suspicion of Labour politics that he never lost, prompting his stinging attack upon the Attlee government of 1949, for example.[43]

[41] Maitland, 'The unincorporate body', 283.
[42] E. Barker, 'The rights and duties of trade unions', 139.
[43] See below, ch. 7.

Barker's concern just before the First World War with what seemed like the deification of groups was further provoked by a widespread defiance of the state at this time. As he tetchily remarked in 1915,

[a]ll this groping after guild socialism or syndicalism, federalism or Home Rule, rights of churches or disestablishment of churches, belongs to a general trend of opinion which perhaps found its first expression in France, and in the economic field, but which has since spread to England and into wider fields . . . We see the State invited to retreat before the advance of the guild, the national group, the Church.[44]

This agitation seemed symptomatic of the recent cult of 'irrationalism' in philosophy and social psychology. He was much heartened by the publication of Graham Wallas' book *The Great Society* in 1914. There, Wallas distanced himself from the challenge to the 'intellectualist' assumptions of political science which he made in his *Human Nature in Politics* (1908).[45] In the latter work, he had underlined the extent to which political behaviour and institutions are ruled by irrational human forces, quite out of step with the deliberative capacities which early democratic thinkers like Bentham had assumed in individuals. But he now looked to human thought – as an 'original and independent' disposition – for salvation in a society whose scale and complexity had grown to an unprecedented degree. In doing so, Wallas seemed to be offering a much-needed fillip to Idealism – and the Idealist state. This, at least, was Barker's interpretation. He still held reservations about Wallas' psychological starting-point, his tendency to 'explain . . . social behaviour as inheritied survival from primitive woods'. But he was grateful to his friend for

admitting intellect back again into court. What you say of the instinct to think – what you say of the need to consider a rational purpose . . . is splendid service against the psychological Pan who is invading, as Bosanquet puts it, the rational Olympus . . . I am glad to see you going this way. Your *Human Nature* encouraged, I have found, my advanced syndicalist pupils in contempt for politics, for representation, for the rational state . . . I shall now quote the *Great Society* at them when they quote *Human Nature in Politics* at me.[46]

Wallas was perhaps not quite as far back on the straight and narrow as Barker would have liked; for he took the opportunity of his

[44] E. Barker, *Political Thought in England*, 182–3.

[45] On Wallas, see M.J. Wiener, *Between Two Worlds: The Political Thought of Graham Wallas* (Oxford, 1971); and T. Qualter, *Graham Wallas and the Great Society* (London, 1980).

[46] Barker to Wallas, 15 July 1914, Wallas Papers, British Library of Political and Economic Science, 1/57, 2, 111.

review of Barker's *Political Thought in England* to deliver a characteristic blow against 'Oxford Political Science' for its lack of 'political realism' and over-fondness of 'the pure instance'.[47] However, if Barker forced Wallas rather too much into the Idealist mould, he also recognised Wallas' distance from Hegel; indeed, Barker delighted in this, praising Wallas, in the closing remarks of his letter, for allowing him to look at 'life (*real* life, not Hegelian abstraction)'. This was consistent with his scepticism in 'The discredited state' of the full-blooded Hegelian state which lifts all social differences into a higher ethical unity:

When Hegel tells me that 'the being of the State (on its objective side) is the in-and-for itself universal', and that yet 'the State, as self-knowing and self-acting, is pure subjectivity and *one* individual'; when I hear that I, 'seeking to be a centre for myself, am brought by the State back into the life of the universal substance' – I throw up my hands.[48]

It is important to recognise that if Barker shunned the anti-statist tendency in Pluralism, nevertheless he welcomed the reproach it delivered to Hegel at the same time. It was not just the obscurity of Hegel's language which repelled him; it was also the monolithic image of the state suggested by Hegel and which moved Barker to accentuate the phrase '*one* individual' in the above passage.

Nevertheless, it was still a form of the Hegelian state which he raised against Pluralists and other critics of the sovereign state, if an attenuated one. This is best illustrated in his defence of the state's role of 'mediation' in society. It is clear from his views about the relationship between society and the state that he regarded the

[47] G. Wallas, 'Oxford and political thought', *The Nation*, 17, 15 May 1915, 227–8. Wallas returned to the attack on 'Oxford Political Science' in 1928 in his inaugural address to the Institute of Public Administration. See his 'The British Civil Service', in *Men and Ideas: Essays by Graham Wallas*, ed. May Wallas (London, 1940), 118–9. He wrote in the same vein in a letter to Harold Laski in 1921: 'I still think that there is room for a non-Hegelian political science. The worst of the metaphysical approach is that it is apt to have the same effect as the old "final causes", first in making existing facts seem sacrosanct because they are part of an intended scheme, and next in distorting one's conception of the facts by making them seem more harmonious . . . than they are. As long as medicine . . . [was] approached from the metaphysical angle one saw the same effects – I say this without wanting to belittle the interest and importance of the metaphysical problems as such – One may be deeply interested in the question whether there is any truth, and, if so, what truth in the statement "There is a God", and yet think that it is dangerous to appreciate the relation between the lungs and the heart or beween the citizens and the state, primarily from the point of view (as did the medieval thinkers) of the will of God.' Wallas to Laski, 19 April 1921, Laski Papers, International Institute of Social History, Amsterdam.

[48] E. Barker, 'The discredited state', 116–7.

'particular' elements of the former as never wholly integrated in the latter; in this sense, he would surely have fought shy of some of Bosanquet's statements on the all-subsuming character of the state.[49] Yet he emphasised that there had to be a 'general and embracing scheme of life' (significantly, not 'all-embracing') to which the diverse forces of society must be tuned:

> The state must necessarily adjust the relations of associations to itself, to other associations, and to their own members – to itself, in order to maintain the integrity of its own scheme; to other associations, in order to preserve the equality of associations before the law; and to their members, in order to preserve the individual from the possible tyranny of the group.[50]

This was evidently his interpretation of the 'rational state' to which he referred in his letter to Wallas, one which fitted the contours of 'the law-state' which he was also developing at this time. It was a looser understanding of the state than he found among the more ambitious Idealist thinkers, one which was in close sympathy with R.M. MacIver's criticism in 1911 of recent 'Hellenistic writers', such as 'Hobhouse and Bosanquet': they were oblivious to the fact that 'the [modern] state stands for an area of common good, not for the whole of common good'.[51] In the context of Pluralism, Barker's defence of a modified Hegelian state answered his difficulties with the notion of 'group rights', a wariness which was to become all too painfully confirmed for him in the interwar period with the militant upsurge of national, racial, and economic groups in Europe.

SEARCHING FOR THE ENGLISH STATE

However, it was not only a concern to defend a weak theory of the Hegelian state which prompted Barker's engagement with the Pluralist champions of group autonomy. Rather, he was equally anxious to show that, historically, the English state had not measured up to the omnipotent, all-encompassing institution which the Pluralists had vilified. So easily does he begin 'The discredited state' with a discussion of this issue that one is inclined to miss its significance. For

[49] For example, that while the state might appear to be leaving such spheres as Art and Religion alone, 'it is none the less dealing with them. It only lets them alone in a certain way and on certain terms, conceived in the interest of the best life.' Bosanquet to R.M. MacIver, 19 June 1911, in R.M. MacIver, *Politics and Society*, ed. D. Spitz (New York, 1969), 242–3.

[50] E. Barker, *Political Thought in England*, 178–9.

[51] R.M. MacIver, 'Society and the state', *Philosophical Review*, 20 (1911), 40–1.

his guiding questions seem to have been not 'What is the state?' but 'What is the nature of the English state?', not 'How should the state be perceived?' but 'How is the English state perceived, and should be perceived by Englishmen?' This is especially apparent if we read 'The discredited state' in conjunction with a piece he wrote concurrently on 'The rule of law'. In doing so, we can see a further dimension of English political debate with which Pluralism – and Idealism – linked up: that of the structure and norms of public authority in England.

The first section of the 'The discredited state' advanced the claim that the English state was quite accustomed to discredit. Those two praetorian guards of legal positivism in England – Hobbes and Austin – were not so much indicative of a general cultural enthusiasm for the sovereign state but exceptions to the rule of an entrenched dislike of it. The doctrine of *majestas* which they fervently upheld was culturally foreign, 'French in its immediate and perhaps papal in its ultimate origin'.[52] Hobbes and Austin aside, the state in England had always been at a discount. Witness, argued Barker, the revolts of 1215 and 1688 by disgruntled property-owners – the 'good syndicalists' – in defence of their class-privileges. Of greatest significance, however, for the English state's lack of esteem among its citizens was Nonconformity. Reckoning this influence to be the 'noblest', Barker hailed the leaders of Congregationalism for protesting vigorously in the seventeenth century against the intrusion of the state into the inward affairs of conscience. The other 'distinctively English product in the sphere of the mind' – political economy – was equally hostile to the state. Indeed, in at least one notable case, that of Herbert Spencer, the latter influence had been substantially nourished by the former.[53]

Not only were English attitudes, from an early date, firmly fixed against the action of the state; the state itself had never attempted to 'magnif[y] its own office, or exalt . . . its own dignity'.[54] Here Barker drew directly upon Maitland to emphasise the weakness of the English state against the exaggerated concept of state sovereignty in much Pluralist thought, including that of Maitland himself. On its executive side, the English state was simply a 'bundle of officials, . . . only united by a mysterious Crown'.[55]

Intrigued by the English state – or lack of one – Maitland had traced its eclipse to Coke, who had classified the King with the Parson as a 'Corporation Sole'. The result was that the larger world of state,

[52] E. Barker, 'The discredited state', 109. [53] Ibid., 104–5. [54] Ibid., 106.
[55] Ibid., 101.

commonwealth, or nation had become concentrated in the monarch's person, suffering demise and re-birth with each reign. The alternative and far more appropriate conception of the 'Corporation Aggregate' gained some ground with the reign of Elizabeth I, when official business was despatched in the name of the 'Commonwealth of England'. Before long, however, the term plunged into a long period of disuse as 'Republic' or 'Commonwealth' implied kinglessness and hence treason. The ill-fated Corporation Sole stuck; the word 'State' only appeared after 1600 and was generally confined to political thought, taking much longer to reach the law-books.[56]

In the meantime, the Corporation Sole was extended to other offices of state – like the Postmaster-General and the Solicitor to the Treasury – with disastrous results. For the natural person and the corporation were never clearly distinguished, thus offering no safeguard against the misuse of office by the incumbent, nor any remedy for crimes committed against the office when it was between incumbents.[57] Maitland welcomed the recent return to the statute-books of the concept of the 'Commonwealth' with the federation of the white colonies. This seemed to point the way out of the 'mess' into which the personification of the king had led, allowing 'continuous life to the state'.[58] By personifying the king – not even the Crown – early modern lawyers had ignored 'the personality of the greatest body corporate and politic that has ever existed'. If they had not been led astray by the 'foolish parson', the English state – like the American state – would have been perceived as a corporation at an early date.[59]

Given Maitland's Pluralist predilections, it may seem odd to find him despairing of the English state's lack of corporate existence. Would he not have rejoiced in a fractured state that was periodically paralysed by the death of its ancestral heads and that of its key office-holders? There were three reasons why Maitland looked favourably upon the incorporation of the state in England. First, he regarded acceptance of the corporate personality of the state as the essential condition of the same quality being recognised in the group. He saw a glimmer of hope in this direction with the recent Idealist attribution of a 'real will' to the state. As he argued in his introduction

[56] F.W. Maitland, 'The Crown as corporation' (1901), in *Collected Papers*, vol. III, 254.

[57] F.W. Maitland, 'The Corporation Sole' (1900), in *Collected Papers*, vol. III, 242; 'The Crown as Corporation', 269.

[58] F.W. Maitland, Introduction to Gierke, *Political Theories of the Middle Age*, xxxvii; 'The Crown as Corporation', 266–7.

[59] Maitland, 'The Crown as Corporation', 268 and 266.

to Gierke, 'it must occur to us to ask whether what is thus affirmed in the case of the State can be denied in the case of other organised groups'.[60] Second, the English state's development into a Corporation Aggregate would heighten its legal profile as an entity which could sue and be sued. This too was a pre-eminent Pluralist concern; the state's lack of a centre of gravity was as unwelcome as its claim to unlimited sovereignty. So long as there were 'holes' in the state through which official misdemeanours or crimes against it could slip, so long as the state lacked legal coherence, the Pluralist ideal of partnership between state and society was a remote possibility. Finally, for Maitland, the latter ideal was obstructed by another consequence of the English state's legal indeterminateness: that is, the absence of an institutional focus for the English nation, of the identity of which he was acutely conscious. By invoking 'the English people' as a body corporate which should find ultimate expression in the state, Maitland echoed Matthew Arnold's earlier strictures on the lack of any well-developed sense of 'statehood' in England corresponding to 'our collective best self'. As Arnold complained in *Culture and Anarchy*, published in 1869, '[e]veryone of us has the idea of country, as a sentiment; hardly any one of us has the idea of the *State*, as a working power'.[61]

As we have seen, Barker was unsympathetic to the view that groups – whether the state or voluntary associations – possessed 'real personalities' and 'real wills'. But he certainly went along with the conclusion which Maitland drew from this assumption: that groups – not least the state – are legally accountable. He also found the third of Maitland's arguments for personifying the English state compelling; during the First World War he discerned positive steps in this direction, heartened by the permeation of the idea of the 'Commonwealth' throughout English society as it acquired a new sense of common purpose. Significantly (and, as ever, optimistically), he believed that this was manifested in a new consciousness of 'station' among Englishmen, and the fulfilment of the duties accompanying it. Such a Bradleyan gloss would probably not have appealed to Maitland's lighter philosophical instincts.[62] Before the war, however,

60 F.W. Maitland, Introduction to Gierke, *Political Theories of the Middle Age*, xi.

61 M. Arnold, *Culture and Anarchy: An Essay in Political and Social Criticism* (1869; Cambridge, 1960), 58, 55.

62 E. Barker, 'Social relations of men after the war', in L. Gardner (ed.), *The Hope for Society: Essays on 'Social Reconstruction after the War' by Various Writers* (London, 1917), 208–13.

the absence of such a sense of moral solidarity contributed to the English state's failure to measure up to its generic type, at least as conceptualised by Hegel in his more moderate passages. As Barker argued at the outset of 'The discredited state', '[a] sovereign and majestic State, a single and undivided imperium, lifted above the conflicts of society, neutral, mediatory, impartial, such as Hegel conceived and such as German theorists still postulate – this we have not known'.[63] In Maitland he found a cogent explanation as to why the English state fell short of this limited Hegelian ideal, and also – paradoxically, in the light of such a Pluralist source – a prescription for change in the required Hegelian direction.

But there was a further twist to this complex intellectual formula which Barker adopted, one which obscured the boundaries between the multifarious concerns in English political thought during the early-twentieth century still further. For in his eyes the same conclusion as to the English state's need for incorporation seemed to follow from Dicey's reflections upon the English Rule of Law. From a very different legal starting-point, Dicey too had emphasised the obliqueness of the English state, an insight which Barker was quick to marshall in support of his thesis on 'The discredited [English] state'. In England, argued Barker, paraphrasing Dicey, officials were subject to the 'ordinary courts . . . and the ordinary rules of the common law'.[64] Nothing distinguished the officer of state from his 'civic brethren'. This was the essential meaning of the 'Rule of Law', one which separated the Anglo-Saxon state from its continental counterpart. As he wrote in 'The rule of law', '[n]ot our Parliament, or our parties, or our Cabinet, but the rule of our judicature constitutes our form of State a different species'.[65] Dicey of course was well satisfied with this arrangement whereby the acts of public authorities and those of private citizens were subject to the same law. Spared the bias of administrative law in favour of officials, Englishmen enjoyed a legal system that alone among its European counterparts constituted the *sine qua non* of political liberty.

However, in Barker's view, the outlines of the English state were so faint that it easily escaped 'the Rule of Law'. Writing as the business of government rapidly expanded following the social legislation of the early-twentieth century, he expressed concern at the lack of redress available to those who suffered as a result of wrongful acts committed

[63] E. Barker, 'The discredited state', 101. [64] Ibid., 106.
[65] E. Barker, 'The rule of law', *Political Quarterly*, 1 (May, 1914), 118.

by the agents of the state. The state not being taken for the 'great company' it was, an aggrieved party held little hope of recompense from the small private means of officials. This was the price that was paid for the 'highly individualistic' manner in which such action was currently conceived and treated. The full operation of the Rule of Law required that the state be legally called to account as a 'juristic person, with its responsibilities and liabilities'.[66] Moreover, to satisfy all the implications of this demand for legal incorporation, it was necessary to institute adminstrative courts alongside the existing courts of justice. In view of the technical nature of administrative disputes, 'the accumulated experience of the executive official is a necessary guide'.[67] Anxious, however, not to capitulate entirely to French adminstrative law, he proposed a supplementary quasi-judicial system of 'referees and umpires' drawn from outside government departments to arbitrate in disputes. There would also be an appeal to a final Court of State in the guise of the Judicial Committee of the Privy Council. Such structures, running concurrently with the ordinary courts, would not diminish the scope of the Rule of Law but would extend it. It is of no small significance that Barker took the administrative law of Prussia as his model here, a country whose strong state tradition had inspired his political theory from an early age. A year later, and all things Prussian were to plummet in this intellectual esteem.[68]

Pluralism, therefore, provided a nodal point around which several of the concerns in Barker's early political thought converged. Or rather, it assumed this place when carefully adapted to his foundational beliefs. First, it appealed to his keen Aristotelian sense of the diversity of society. Second, the notion which he derived from Maitland that the state was a legal corporation with rights and liabilities like other public bodies gave scope for further development of Dicey's thoughts on the English Rule of Law. Third, Pluralist sensitivity to the welter of groups in modern society seemed to strengthen rather than weaken the case for the Idealist state as a centre of 'adjustment'. Fourth, Pluralism contained an underlying 'progressive' model of state–society relations which translated into new terms an older Whig (and more recently, Idealist) dualism between social innovation, on the one hand, and political order, on the other. Fifth, Maitland – at least

[66] Ibid., 121. [67] Ibid., 126. [68] See ch. 4 below.

– developed his Pluralist theory of state and society with specific reference to English development. Barker had always been alert to this English national backdrop of political inquiry, Maitland's Pluralist reflections heightening his responsiveness still further.

In short, Barker underlined what he considered to be the Latin presuppositions of Pluralist thought, toning down its strong Teutonic bias. In part his goal was to emphasise the credit which the English state could properly claim for the vitality of corporate life in England; in part, too, he aimed at suggesting ways in which the English state could sustain its effectiveness as an instrument of social co-ordination in the changed legislative climate of the early-twentieth century. The development of a degree of self-consciousness in the state through legal incorporation seemed the most promising route forwards, ensuring that the relationship of creative tension with civil society which had yielded such rich associational fruits in the past would continue long into the future.

CHAPTER 4

Statehood, nationhood, and internationalism: English political theory and the First World War

THE ISSUES OF THE WAR

By the outbreak of the First World War, then, Pluralism had served to sharpen Barker's conception of the state and to reinforce his commitment to it. No denigrator of the state, his intention in taking up Pluralist issues was to bring the state back into credit by the logic of Pluralist thought itself. At the end of his book *Political Thought in England from Herbert Spencer to the Present Day* (1915), he conceded the case for a new, 'federalistic' theory of the state to match recent developments in Irish Home Rule, Welsh disestablishment, trade-union rights following the Trades Disputes Act of 1906, and growing denominationalism in education. But he warned against undermining the state too much: 'The State and its institutions are with us and we must make the best of them.'[1]

Arguments in favour of the sovereign state had become especially compelling for him with the outbreak of the First World War. We have seen that 'The discredited state' concluded with the confident prediction that in times of crisis, the sense of citizenship would override all other loyalities and identities. This was certainly true of himself. Whatever – slight – misgivings he may have felt towards the state prior to the First World War, they quickly dissolved in the wave of patriotism which swept English public life in 1914. Even in 1916, with the introduction of conscription, he remained steadfast in his commitment to the principle of state sovereignty. While many liberals withdrew their previous goodwill towards the state with the rapid erosion of civil liberties, Barker wrote eloquently to *The Times* that: 'There are many paradoxes in human affairs. It is perhaps one of them that liberty cannot be saved by liberty. And the saving of

[1] E. Barker, *Political Thought in England from Herbert Spencer to the Present Day* (London, 1915), 251.

liberty – on that we all agree – is the great dominating issue of the hour.' Nor did he think that there was anything 'un-English' about conscription. Always ready with an historical illustration or precedent, he emphasised that the Nonconformists – now the most vocal of opponents to compulsory military service – had embraced the latter when fighting for their liberties in the seventeenth century. Half the New Model Army, he maintained, were 'pressed men' during the first six years of its existence.[2]

At the outset of the war Barker, along with most British academics, rallied to the national cause, mounting a vigorous propaganda war against Germany and particularly German thought.[3] The distinctiveness and superiority of English political traditions relative to those of Germany became central to this attack. Not only did the English scholarly community lose no time in distancing itself from the world of German learning, which had influenced much of its best work in recent decades; in addition, it quickly forgot the large contribution which German thinkers had made to English self-understanding since the middle of the nineteenth century.[4] There is the further irony that the English intellectuals' leap to the defence of their state was much inspired by the philosophy of citizenship in German Idealism which many of its members had internalised in the previous quarter of a century.

Yet if the war restored the fortunes of the English state at the level of instinctive patriotism, it also exposed a fundamental weakness in its claim to legitimacy. This related to the issue of national self-determination. In so far as the Allied cause was wedded to the defence of small nations against their stronger neighbours, supporters of Britain's participation in the war were inevitably drawn to embrace some form of the doctrine of national rights. Yet this forced attention upon the diverse nationalities which composed the English state. If there was a right to national self-determination, did not the English state stand condemned as an oppressor along with the German state?

The war prompted fresh reflection upon the meaning of nationality

[2] E. Barker, letter to *The Times*, 8 January 1916. On the erosion of liberal sympathy for the state in the First World War, see M. Freeden, *Liberalism Divided: A Study in British Political Thought, 1914–1939* (Oxford, 1986), ch. 2.

[3] S. Wallace, *War and the Image of Germany: British Academics, 1914–1918* (Edinburgh, 1988); also S. Hynes, *A War Imagined: The First World War and English Culture* (New York, 1991).

[4] An example is the portrayal of 'local self-government' as axiomatic to English identity by the Prussian historian Rudolf Von Gneist. I have explored his influence in 'Localism versus centralism in the Webbs' political thought', *History of Political Thought*, 12 (Spring 1991), 147–65.

and the political framework it required. A key task for political theorists like Barker was to articulate a conditional right of nationhood, one which would not only leave the eclectic national mix of the English state – and indeed the Commonwealth – intact, but would valorise them at the same time. Yet this concern was not simply an exercise in crude special pleading on behalf of the English state. While certainly laced with considerable self-congratulation on the English state's apparent ability to transcend national and ethnic division, Barker's pragmatic approach to nationalism was also rooted in his firm internationalist convictions. The First World War moved these to a central position in his political thought where they remained for the rest of his life. His attempt to implant the multinational state and the nation-state within a world of states entailed some revision of the terms of his Idealist heritage: not just the elevation of Green's notion of 'human brotherhood' against the greater significance which Bosanquet attached to state boundaries; but also a further accentuation of the legal side of the state which was visible in his work as early as *The Political Thought of Plato and Aristotle*.

THE VIRTUES OF MULTINATIONALISM

Barker was one of the first academics to enter the intellectual fray by participating in the collective statement of the Oxford History Faculty entitled *Why We Are At War: Great Britain's Case* (1914). While the book claimed to review recent events leading up to the First World War in the light of impartial historical science, it actually launched a savage attack upon the political system and ideas of Germany. Its putative objectivity was also compromised by a strong self-righteous tone, capitalising on recent associations – explored in the previous chapter – between Englishness and law-abidingness. This is especially evident in the final chapter of the book which castigated 'The new German theory of the state'. Against the stress which recent German thinkers like Treitschke and Bernhardi had placed upon the 'Absolute Sovereignty' of the state and contrary as well to their 'glorification of war', England had remained true to her historic 'legal cause'. Significantly, however, this late-nineteenth-century conception of Englishness as rooted in law, and which had been well focused in Dicey's work, now acquired a Gladstonian gloss. Thus the chapter claimed that England 'stands for the idea of a public law of Europe, and for the small nations which it protects'.[5] Given the clear showing of this aspect of Gladstonianism in his writings during the First World War, Barker would seem to have played an instrumental role in the book's conclusion.

His Gladstonian allegiances are evident, for example, in his *Political Thought in England from Herbert Spencer to the Present Day.* Here, Barker pointed to the identification of 'England' abroad with 'sympathetic intervention in favour of Liberal and national causes', credit for which belonged to Gladstone. Employing the language of Mazzini, this constituted – he asserted – England's 'national mission'. He contrasted it with the more 'exclusive' brand of nationalism which sought aggressive territorial expansion. Such a mood had of late possessed England (almost certainly a reference to the Boer War); now, however, it gripped Germany. Germany was filled with the conceit that its national civilisation represented civilisation at large.[6]

Barker expanded upon the current mood in Germany in his more popular wartime tracts. For example, in his contribution to the series of 'Oxford Pamphlets', in 1914, *Nietzsche and Treitschke: The Worship of Power in Modern Germany*, he attempted to show how two leading German thinkers, working from very different intellectual foundations, had turned their backs upon the 'European comity of nations'. Treitschke the virulent nationalist had preached the 'finality' and 'absolute' value of the state which sustained an exclusively German culture. The corollary of nationalism in Treitschke's thought was thus militarism and a disdain for international law. Nietzsche held no truck for nationalism, but he nevertheless fanned its flames by 'his gospel of power'. Good European though he was, his vision of a United States of Europe was marred by its aristocratic prejudices.[7]

Barker's propaganda war against Germany continued unabated in the following year. He wrote a series of articles in the spring of 1915 for *The Times* which sang the praises of France as loudly as those of England. This consolidated his growing Francophilia which broke the classic Whig hostility towards all things French and to which he

[5] E. Barker, C.R.L. Fletcher, L.G. Wickham Legg, H.W.C. Davis, Arthur Hassall, and F. Morgan, *Why We Are At War: Great Britain's Case* (Oxford, 1914), 116–7.

[6] E. Barker, *Political Thought in England*, 22, 238–9.

[7] E. Barker, *Nietzsche and Treitschke: The Worship of Power in Modern Germany*, Oxford Pamphlets no. 20 (Oxford, 1914), 15.

himself had subscribed in *The Political Thought of Plato and Aristotle*.[8] The grounds on which he now elevated England's historic enemy were precisely those for which France had been reviled in Whig quarters during the previous century: the revolutionary battle-cries of Liberty, Equality, and Fraternity. When placed beside the aggrandisement and authoritarianism of German political culture, these French watchwords seemed striking for their generosity of spirit. Pressing Mazzini into service once again, Barker attempted to distinguish the empire-building of the French from that of the Germans: 'Even under her Caesars France never forgot, what under her Kaisers Germany has never learned, that a great State has a mission to discharge not unto itself alone, but to the general cause and in the general service of humanity.'[9]

He resumed this theme in *The Submerged Nationalities of the German Empire*, also published in 1915, a full and damning account of Germany's policy of 'compulsory nationalisation' in neighbouring territories. The pamphlet was produced by Wellington House, a clandestine arm of government propaganda which was primed by leading 'men of letters' and academics.[10] The organisation aimed at influencing public opinion in neutral countries, particularly America. But as Barker wrote to Bryce, who had congratulated him on the efficacy of *The Submerged Nationalities*, he also hoped that the book might 'trickle' to Ireland as well.[11] This was because it was partially designed to refute German claims that Britain itself contained 'subject nationalities', chief amongst which was the Irish. Such a suggestion was far from the mark, retorted Barker, emphasising the long association between England and Ireland as against the relatively recent one between Prussia and Poland, for example. Moreover, the 'sins' of England towards Ireland were committed in the age of

[8] It was not only the wartime alliance between Britain and France which elicited his goodwill towards the latter country; his friendship with the French historian, Elie Halévy, which began around 1908, must also have been an important influence. Certainly, Barker dedicated his *Essays on Government* to Halévy's memory in 1945. Parts of the book focused on the 'parallels, the differences, and the general relations between England and France'. It therefore seemed appropriate to invoke 'a great French scholar whose knowledge and judgement and friendships bridged and spanned the Channel', p.vii. Halévy's influence on Barker is explored further in ch. 5 below.

[9] E. Barker, *Mothers and Sons in War Time: And Other Pieces Reprinted from The Times* (London, 1915), 55.

[10] On the origins of Wellington House and its downfall in 1917, see D.G. Wright, 'The Great War, government propaganda and English "men of letters" 1914–18', *Literature and History*, 7 (1978), 70–100.

[11] Barker to Bryce, 1 June 1915, MS. Bryce 26, fol. 39, Bodleian Library, Oxford.

Cromwell whereas the barbarous treatment of the Poles by the Germans had taken place in the 'full light of the twentieth century'.[12] Finally, any parallels between the European nationalities of the German Empire and the Irish under English rule dissolved in the face of recent economic and cultural policy in Ireland. While Poles were being expropriated from their land to make way for German settlement, the Irish peasants had regained their birthright with the Irish Land Act of 1870. And while native languages had been proscribed in Polish, Danish, and French territories of the German Empire,[13] a Gaelic League flourished freely in Ireland.

That Barker endorsed the principle of national self-determination during the war is evident in at least one of his wartime pieces. In his 1915 pamphlet on *Great Britain's Reasons for Going to War* he proclaimed that 'England stands for the right of each national group to enjoy the form of government to which it aspires'.[14] In the case of Ireland, however, he simply did not believe that the nationalists represented the will of the Irish people. A fervent Home Ruler, he dismissed the Easter rebellion of 1916 as the work of 'extremists' – provoked by Germany, on the one hand, and Irish-American 'irreconcilables', on the other.[15] He believed that the main injustices that Ireland had suffered at the hands of the English were now largely rectified. Writing in 1917, he staked out Ireland's future firmly within the fold of the British Commonwealth, consolidating seven centuries of 'common history'.[16] He had high hopes that Ulster would soon be included in a Home Rule settlement for the whole of Ireland. But any more ambitious proposal for Irish independence, even the attainment of dominion status, met with stiff resistance on his part. As he wrote to A.D. Lindsay in 1921, in response to just such a suggestion, 'I believe in the state rather than the nation, and I think the state which embraces several nations is all the better for its width.'[17]

However blinkered Barker's vision of Irish public opinion may have been at this time, his ideal of the multinational state was at any rate eminently consistent with his political thought before the war. Proclamations of sovereignty on behalf of all groups, nations included, had always made him shudder. The war gave him the opportunity to

[12] E. Barker, *The Submerged Nationalities of the German Empire* (London, 1915), 5.
[13] E. Barker, *Linguistic Oppression in the German Empire* (London, 1918), 5.
[14] E. Barker, *Great Britain's Reasons for Going to War* (London, 1915), 10.
[15] E. Barker, *Ireland in the last Fifty Years, 1866–1918*, 2nd and enlarged edition (Oxford, 1919), 113.
[16] E. Barker, *Ireland in the last Fifty Years, 1866–1916* (Oxford, 1917), 104.
[17] Barker to Lindsay, 16 June 1921, Lindsay Papers, Keele University Library, L156.

develop a flexible version of the nationality principle, one which would not rock the foundations of every state regardless of its worth. Typically, his formula was permeated with a broad nineteenth-century concern, deriving largely from Mazzini, for strengthening moral character and personality through the free expression of national character. This was the criterion by which nations should be judged free or oppressed. As he wrote in 1915:

> When we speak of the right of a nationality to enjoy its own form of government, we mean that a number of persons, whose development is being stunted by their submission to an alien government, have a relative rightness in enforcing by war their demand, that they shall be allowed to live under political conditions which will make the development of their worth and their character more readily possible.

Of course, this begged the question of what constituted the 'stunting' of national development. Revealingly, Barker gave as an example of a nation which satisfied his criterion of 'oppression' that of Mazzini's Italy in 1830. The domination of Bourbons and Austrians at that time had impeded 'the free development of Italian worth and Italian character – of the worth and character of each Italian'.[18] But other cases were much less clear-cut in his view. In the turmoil created by nationalism during and after the First World War he could not afford to equate statehood with nationhood, as some of his Idealist mentors and indeed Mazzini had tended to do. In their eyes, each state was, or should be, the embodiment of a single nation as the focus of the 'common good'. In loosening the Idealist connection between particular national minds, on the one hand, and sovereign states, on the other, he looked to the multinational state as the best hope for most nations of the world in the twentieth century.

Barker appears to have substituted Lord Acton for the Idealists and other proponents of state nationalism on this score. His concerns about the principle of national self-determination echoed Acton's famous essay on 'Nationality' which was published in 1862. In the name of nationalism, Acton declared, 'governments must be subverted in whose title there is no flaw, and whose policy is beneficent and equitable, and subjects must be compelled to transfer their allegiance to an authority for which they have no attachment, and which may be practically a foreign domination'. This was the French approach

[18] E. Barker, *Nationalism and Internationalism*, Christian Social Union Pamphlet no. 45 (London, 1915), 16.

to nationality. Far superior, in Acton's view, was the English alternative, which regarded nationality as an 'essential, but not a supreme element in determining the forms of State . . . tend[ing] to diversity and not to uniformity, to harmony and not to unity'.[19]

In reviewing a cluster of recent books on nationalism which appeared in 1919, Barker extolled Acton's belief that the 'universal' character of the state is fatally undermined by the doctrine of 'national rights'. Grounded in 'neighbourliness', the multinational state transcended the narrow cultural limits of the nation-state, invariably cemented by the bonds of enmity towards outsiders. Ever concerned about the explosive potential of inward-looking groups, he emphasised the superiority of 'contiguity' over 'kinship' as the basis of political organisation: '[a]fter all, it is in some ways better – better and easier – to love one's neighbour than to love one's kinsman or fellow-national. Neighbourliness is a quiet virtue – quiet but deep and permeating.'[20]

Moreover, in his view, multinationalism represented a tried and tested formula for internationalism as well as statehood, especially when nurtured by imperial ties. His conception of the British Empire as the English multinational state writ large is evident in a comment he made in 1917: 'Whatever the sins of the British Commonwealth, exclusive nationalism is not one of those sins. The Commonwealth has not sought to proselytize all its peoples into acceptance of a single culture . . . It flourishes on diversity.'[21]

THE PROSPECTS OF INTERNATIONALISM

The international ideal was implicit in Barker's attack upon 'exclusive nationalism', or what he perceived as the German variety of nationalism. It underpinned his enthusiasm for Mazzini's alternative construction of nationalism along ecumenical lines; and also the analogous blend of nationalism and supra-nationalism in Gladstone's

[19] Lord Acton, 'Nationality' (1862), in J.N. Figgis (ed.), *The History of Freedom and Other Essays* (London, 1907), 288–9.

[20] E. Barker, 'Nationality', *History* (new series), 4 (October 1919), 144. The article prompted Harold Laski to remark that 'there's a good deal of the Victorian fragrance about [Barker] still'. Laski to A.E. Zimmern, 29 September 1919, MS. Zimmern 16, fol. 72, Bodleian Library.

[21] E. Barker, *Ireland in the Last Fifty Years*, 2nd edn (1919) 147. This should be contrasted with Bosanquet's scepticism about the empire expressed in 1917. Including, as it did, 'dependencies on a lower level of culture', the empire was for Bosanquet too diverse to sustain a viable polity. Quoted in P.P. Nicholson, *The Political Philosophy of The British Idealists: Selected Studies* (Cambridge, 1990), 226.

idea of 'Public Right' in Europe.[22] Barker's broadsides against extreme forms of nationalism were further fuelled by the economist Sir Norman Angell, who promoted the 'International Polity Movement' in British universities.[23] Following in the tradition of Manchester liberalism, Angell embraced an ideal of internationalism in which divisive political frontiers had been broken down by wider ties of economic interest under a regime of free trade. War was now simply umprofitable and hence the state had become obsolete. In fact, it was from Angell that Barker derived the notion of 'contiguity' as frequently, at any rate, the best foundation of political life. He could not of course, go all the way with Angell in attacking patriotism, and hence the state itself; for Barker, political relations could never be supplanted entirely by economic relations, or indeed determined by them. But he admired the internationalism towards which Angell's crusade against nationalism was directed, a cause – he argued – which could ill afford to reject any ally.[24]

However, perhaps the most important influence on Barker's internationalism was T.H. Green. This attempt to capitalise on the potential within Idealism for international pacification during the First World War has been unduly neglected in existing accounts of that philosophy's fate. Here, attention has mainly focused upon the widespread vilification of Idealism because of the high premium it accorded to the state as the ultimate source of morality and authority, the alleged root of all Prussian evil.[25] By contrast, in his account of Green's Idealism in *Political Thought in England from Herbert Spencer to the Present Day*, Barker praised Green's departure from Hegel in insisting that there is no finality to the state. *Sittlichkeit* was by no means confined to each individual state but extended across the states of Western Europe and America, at least. This was the 'comity of nations' which he accused Germany of wilfully flouting. Evidence of its existence was to be found in 'the common body of moral opinion in Christendom'. This in turn, had been built upon the sense of the individual's 'right to life' in Roman law, giving rise to a strong conception of 'universal brotherhood' in Western thought. Such a notion laid clear moral responsibilities on the state, making war only

[22] The centrality of this conjunction to Gladstonian Liberalism has been emphasised by C. Harvie, 'Gladstonianism, the provinces, and popular political culture, 1860–1906', R. Bellamy (ed.), *Victorian Liberalism: Nineteenth-Century Political Thought and Practice* (London, 1990).

[23] Wallace, *War and the Image of Germany*, 15.

[24] E. Barker, *Political Thought in England*, 247.

[25] J. Morrow, 'British Idealism, "German philosophy" and the First World War', *The Australian Journal of Politics and History*, 28 (1982), 380–90.

a 'relative' and not an absolute right. Barker reiterated Green's argument that war is only an attribute of the imperfect state, the incidence of which would decline as states became 'better organised'.

While it has recently come to light that Bosanquet often took a similar line to Green on the issue of war, Barker followed many of his contemporaries in interpreting Bosanquet as a more orthodox Hegelian.[26] On the other hand, the distinction which Barker drew between Green and Bosanquet on the question of international morality possessed some cogency. The difference turned upon the extent to which the two leading thinkers in English Idealism recognised the existence of an international society necessary to support the notion of moral obligation between states. While Green (and Barker) found ample supports for such a duty in the classical and Christian heritage of Europe, Bosanquet set more exacting requirements. Writing in 1917, he maintained that an international community required 'a very high degree of common experience, tradition, and aspiration', a condition which existed nowhere at that time except in the nation-state.[27] It is true that Bosanquet gave his blessing to the League of Nations after the war; but as Nicholson argues, he did so on the understanding that the war itself had brought the nations of the world into the same moral sphere.[28] The notion that a 'comity' had previously existed between European nations, at least, would have been problematic for him in a way that it had not been for Green and Barker. Ironically, it was his identification with Green on issues associated with internationalism which drew Barker closer to Plato during the First World War. In the preface to his *Greek Political Theory*, published in 1918, he declared that 'Plato has come to mean more for the writer, on many points, than he would have meant if war had not stirred the deeps.' These points included his elevation of 'right' over 'might'; his condemnation of militarism; and his sensitivity to the existence of a Greek world – beyond individual city-states – as a 'single society, with a civility or comity of its own'.[29] Once again, such sympathies suggest that Barker's receptiveness to Bosanquet's political philsophy stopped short of his more ambitious claims for the state: for example, that it constituted 'the guardian of a whole moral world';

[26] E. Barker, *Political Thought in England*, 78–80. For a revised view of Bosanquet on international questions, see Nicholson, *The Political Philosophy of the British Idealists*, 227.

[27] B. Bosanquet, 'The function of the state in promoting the unity of mankind', in *Social and International Ideals: Being Studies in Patriotism* (London, 1917), 294.

[28] Nicholson, *The Political Philosophy of the British Idealists*, 227.

[29] E. Barker, *Greek Political Theory: Plato and his Predecessors* (London, 1918; 1960), vi, 308.

and 'the ark in which the whole treasure of the individual citizen's head and heart is preserved and guarded within a world which may be disorderly and hostile'.[30]

There was certainly an element of nostalgia in Barker's writings during the First World War for the 'internationalism' of medieval Christendom based on shared spiritual values among the nations of Europe. Having lectured regularly on medieval history at Oxford, he had acquired a deep sense of Europe's cultural homogeneity in that period. Therefore, when asked to participate in a 'Unity' Summer School at Birmingham in 1915 organised by one of the few remaining positivists in Britain – F.S. Marvin – he enthusiastically accepted. The project was based upon the belief of its contributors that while Britain's action in the war was wholly just, it was 'not inopportune to reflect on those common and ineradicable elements in the civilization of the West which tend to form a real commonwealth of nations and will survive even the most shattering of conflicts'.[31] Barker's paper was entitled 'The unity of medieval civilization', and it projected a world in which the advent of nations had not yet shattered a fundamental unity of outlook in the West, rooted in the Christian faith. Already in this article, he invoked Dante's sense of culture, or 'civility', as 'the common possession of Christian humanity',[32] a theme of which he was to make much in the aftermath of the Second World War. Just as his writings on the Greek *polis* at the outset of his career were intended to illuminate his own society by the method of comparison and contrast, so his reflections upon the medieval world during the First World War were designed to throw the modern world into sharp relief. He was most struck by the inversion of the medieval relationship between culture and economics in the modern world. For whereas the unity of the Middle Ages was rooted in a shared culture, that of the modern world derived from international finance. In the medieval world, economic life was endlessly fragmented, this being the sad state of culture in contemporary Europe. The war impressed upon him the heavy 'spiritual' price which economic integration had exacted, progress which – paradoxically – had proceeded from the splintering

30 B. Bosanquet, 'Patriotism in the perfect state', in E.M. Sidgwick (ed.), *The International Crisis in its Ethical and Psychological Dimensions* (London, 1915), 134. The dualism in Bosanquet's theory of the state – between 'community', on the one hand, and 'public power', on the other – has been illuminated by James Meadowcroft, 'Conceptions of the state in British political thought, 1880–1914', ch. 4, unpublished D.Phil. thesis, University of Oxford, 1990.

31 F.S. Marvin (ed.), *The Unity of Western Civilization* (Oxford, 1915), Preface.

32 E. Barker, 'Mediaeval civilization', in *Church, State, and Study* (London, 1930), 63–4.

rise of nations and the national economy. There was a tendency in his essay to see Christianity and nationality as somewhat in tension with each other, a view which he corrected when he returned to the subject in the 1920s.[33] But at the height of the war, he momentarily let nationalism slip from his vision of salvation, even the outward-looking, Mazzinian variety. This was despite a recognition that the world of medieval Christendom was now lost for good.

Barker's patience with the nationalist ideal was indeed much tested during the First World War. An indication of this is his response to a letter from Marvin in connection with the 'Unity' lectures. Marvin had written to Alfred Zimmern – author of the much-acclaimed study of fifth-century Athens, *The Greek Commonwealth* (1911) – seeking his participation in the series. Zimmern declined in a characteristically pugnacious style, stating that his focus on the *polis* and the meaning of citizenship would be at odds with the course's main theme: that of human unity. What seems to have upset Zimmern was Marvin's suggestion that 'unity' inhered in European civilisation. Of German-Jewish descent, Zimmern – from the beginning of the war – had denounced the actions of his native country. Swept along in the patriotic fervour of the times, he pinned his hopes on the British Commonwealth as the most promising route towards greater internationalism.[34] 'The fact is', he wrote, 'that in my political philosophy the bond between London and Nigeria is closer than the bond between London and Dusseldorf.'[35]

[33] See his Burge Memorial Lecture for 1927 entitled 'Christianity and nationality' (Oxford, 1927). This is also reprinted in *Church, State, and Study*. In reviewing the 'inconsistencies' in his thought across the divide of the First World War, Barker admitted in the preface that 'changing times' had produced 'changes' between this essay and *The Unity of Mediaeval Civilization*.

[34] Zimmern was a leading instigator of a project among British academics at the outset of the war to apprise the British working class of foreign affairs, on which their knowledge was deemed inadequate. His concluding essay contained a rousing defence of the Commonwealth's mission: the spread of free institutions and the 'rule of law'. This was the 'great, the supreme task of politics and statesmanship', he proclaimed; it contrasted with the narrower, purely national, and in any case spurious goals of German foreign policy which were centred upon *Kultur*. A.E. Zimmern, 'German culture and the British Commonwealth', in R.W. Seton-Watson, E. Percy, J. Dover Wilson, Alfred E. Zimmern, and Arthur Greenwood, *The War and Democracy* (London, 1914), 371.

[35] A.E. Zimmern to F.S. Marvin, 9 April 1915, MS. Marvin, Eng. Lett. d. 263, fol. 50, Bodleian Library. Yet there were cracks in Zimmern's strong patriotic façade. He wrote to Walter Lippmann a few months later that 'I have never felt less English than since the war began.' He added that 'the old Emperor's portrait still hangs in our house at home, and Goethe and Schiller still adorn our shelves'. Zimmern to Lippmann, 13 June 1915, Walter Lippmann Papers, Manuscripts and Archives, Yale University Library. I am indebted to Christopher Collins for this reference.

These remarks saddened Barker, eliciting his deep expression of regret to Marvin that 'so good a man' as Zimmern had become 'such a definite nationalist'. He added, poignantly, 'if that is what the city-state means I am glad it perished'.[36] Ironically, Zimmern shared Barker's agreement with Acton that nationalism was – or at least, should be – a 'cultural' or 'psychological' rather than a political force, giving no entitlement to separate statehood.[37] But his rather aggressive defence of the English (and the Jews) for rising above this primitive nationalist mentality was opposed to the magnanimous, Actonian spirit by which it was inspired.

In general, it was this spirit rather than one which was hostile to nationalism *per se* which Barker invoked to smooth troubled international waters during the First World War; and he thought the English people were especially well placed to receive his message. He commended the cosmopolitan outlook to his fellow countrymen in an article of 1917, maintaining that it had always accompanied their renowned insularity. He praised the hospitality which England had traditionally given to foreigners, particularly traders, and on the same note he pointed to 'our policy of free trade' as further corroboration of the large English capacity for cosmopolitanism. He saw the war as another boost to the fortunes of English cosmopolitanism, and correspondingly another nail in the coffin of 'our [old] exclusive, Anglo-Saxondom'.[38]

Probably this optimism was helped along by Barker's recent association with two groups which actively campaigned to raise the general level of awareness of foreign affairs in England, particularly among the working class. The first was the Round Table movement led by Lionel Curtis, which focused upon the empire;[39] the second was the short-lived 'New Europe' society formed in 1916 around the claims to independence of East European nations and soon to evolve into the journal *The New Europe* edited by R.W. Seton-Watson.[40]

[36] E. Barker to F.S. Marvin, 18 April 1915, MS. Marvin, Eng.Lett.d.263, fol. 52, Bodleian Library.

[37] A.E. Zimmern, 'True and false nationalism', in *Nationality and Government: And Other War-Time Essays* (London, 1917).

[38] E. Barker, 'Social relations of men after the war', in L. Gardner (ed.), *The Hope for Society: Essays on 'Social Reconstruction after the War' by Various Writers* (London, 1917), 208–11.

[39] Barker offered to give talks for *The Round Table*. This was taken up by Philip Ker in his letter to Barker, 15 July 1918, MS. Round Table, Eng.Hist.c.831, fol. 105, Bodleian Library.

[40] See E. Barker, *Age and Youth: Memories of Three Universities and Father of the Man* (London, 1953), 109. On the evolution of the 'New Europe' see H. Hanak, *Great Britain and Austria–Hungary During the First World War: A Study in the Formation of Public Opinion* (London, 1962); and H. and C. Seton-Watson, *The Making of a New Europe: R.W. Seton-Watson and the*

Certainly, he thought that while German influences upon English life were unlikely to recover their old ground after the war, new centres of cultural interest would develop in their place, both in the West and in the East. In the West, Englishmen would discover – or rediscover – their kinship with the Romance peoples, a bond which had been close in the sixteenth century when there was great familiarity in England with 'the language and thoughts of France and Italy'. In the East, the war had opened English eyes to the Slavonic nations and Russia itself, bringing nearer the prospect of 'closer intercourse' and a more intimate knowledge of Russian literature, music, and religion. Finally, he anticipated a 'British Commonwealth which belongs to a common system of Europe', assisting – in this way – to 'guarantee the peace of all the world'.[41] Of course, there was a good deal of wishful thinking about all of these predictions, reflecting, as they did, Barker's own shifting cultural sympathies and Mazzinian ambitions for English culture. A recent study of English attitudes and values in the First World War has underlined the swift retreat from a developing 'cosmopolitan awareness of Europe' in previous years, particularly in the arts.[42] However, his keen aspirations for world harmony – centred upon England – are notable, as is his identification of internationalism with free contact between cultures at all levels. This was the most secure basis of internationalism in his eyes, and internationalism was the vital condition of a tempered form of nationalism.

It was a traditional liberal formula for reconciling the particular and universal contexts of organised human life. But for Barker, the state was vital as a framework in which the two dimensions could be harmonised. Acton aside, liberal nationalists in the late-eighteenth and nineteenth centuries had either set little store by the state, or treated it unproblematically as the instrument of individual national purposes. While Herder well illustrates the former tendency, Mazzini

Last Years of Austria-Hungary (London, 1981). Barker was approached by R.W. Seton-Watson to become Secretary of the New Europe Society, but he declined because of pressure of work at Oxford. However, Seton-Watson's attempt to persuade him to think again reveals much about contemporary perceptions of Barker: 'We believe that your name would give the Society the kind of *cachet* which it requires – that of a sane thinker, not committed to fads, and with a reputation for progressive views such as would inspire confidence both among academics and (still more important) working-class people.' Quoted in H. and C. Seton-Watson, *The Making of a New Europe*, 226. Barker's link with the 'New Europe' was to become an important stepping-stone to his post as Principal of King's College London, and to his increasing interests in the dispossessed nations of Eastern Europe. See ch. 5 below.

41 E. Barker, 'Social relations of men after the war', 208–13.

42 Hynes, *A War Imagined*, 67.

provides the best example of the latter. Either way, the state was marginalised in their visions of international unity. Yet what kind of state did Barker hang in this balance between the national (or multinational) and international levels of society? An analysis of his writings during the First World War reveals a bifurcation in his ideal of the state that would perform this intermediary role: between the 'law-state', on the one hand, and the 'culture-state', on the other.

THE LAW-STATE AND THE CULTURE-STATE

The law-state constituted a crucial vehicle of internationalism in Barker's view. He certainly found the most promising avenue of internationalism in 'legal development', reflecting the ascendancy of the idea of the law-state in his political thought during recent years. This 'legal development' involved the extension of treaties along the lines of the Hague Convention, which in turn would be rooted in a sense of 'right inherent in . . . the common conscience of the civilised world'. The widening of economic ties, as espoused by Angell, would not in itself evolve an adequate form of international political structure.[43] Nor was Barker among those – such as Bertrand Russell and to a lesser degree G.D.H. Cole – who reacted to the 'finality' of the Hegelian state by envisaging a new international order built upon resistance to the state as such.[44] Instead, he moved outwards from the law-state to the international law-state, a process in which nations played a secondary role. Having established this principle, he went on, in the interwar years, to elaborate the precise meaning of that 'common conscience' which transcended national differences and formed the basis of the *Sittlichkeit* on which the legal integration of the 'civilised' world would depend.[45]

What were the characteristics of the law-state in its national setting which would provide the basis of this movement towards greater internationalism? First, Barker's understanding of the law-state entailed firm legislative limits. In a letter to his friend and fellow-historian, T.F. Tout, during the war he wrote that 'I always was an individualist, in my own view, and I get more of one.' The remark was made in relation to Herbert Spencer, Tout – no doubt – having referred to Barker's recent book on English political thought in which

[43] E. Barker, *Political Thought in England*, 247.

[44] Wallace, *War and the Image of Germany*, 55–6.

[45] See below, ch. 6.

Spencer had featured prominently.[46] It can only have been in a political sense – as an opponent of large-scale government intervention – that Barker described himself as an individualist. For his Idealist roots would not have permitted him to embrace the atomistic and egoistic view of society which accompanied some forms of classical liberalism.[47] Indeed, this interpretation of his remark is confirmed by his enthusiasm for a book which was published in 1893 by C.H. Pearson entitled *National Life and Character*. In sombre tones, it predicted the drying up of the springs of individualism as the state – under democratic pressure – pervaded ever more areas of 'private' life: the family, religion, art, education, and so forth. The grim consequence would be the decay of the European nations and the surrender of their supremacy to the races of Asia; the substitution of the nobility of intellect and character founded upon the reign of the higher classes for the slavish materialism associated with the universal triumph of the lower orders.[48] Pearson's prognosis sent shivers up the spines of the generation of academic liberals by whom Barker had been influenced: Bryce, Dicey, and Goldwin Smith, for example.[49] Barker himself described *National Life and Character* as 'one of the great books in my life'.[50] He was too much of an optimist ever to be won over by its gloomy conclusions. But it was nevertheless a crucial force behind his cautiousness towards all proposals to extend the state, and also his interest in the study of English national character.

But where exactly did he draw the lines of the interventionary state? He was not, in the style of Spencer, an advocate of the minimal state, a state which protected property and contractual rights only. Instead he followed many of the Idealists in supporting the state's participation in social and cultural projects which would enhance the rational powers of its citizens. Significantly, when he referred in 'The discredited state' to the recent transformation of the state from a grocer's shop into a 'Whiteley's emporium' (at the end of the period of

[46] Barker to Tout, undated but from New College, Oxford, which he joined in 1913. Tout Papers, The John Rylands University Library of Manchester, 1/55/10.

[47] A. Vincent, 'Classical liberalism and its crisis of identity', *History of Political Thought*, II, no. 1 (Spring 1990), 143–61.

[48] C.H. Pearson, *National Life and Character: A Forecast* (London, 1893). Pearson's association of materialism with the ascendancy of the 'inferior races' and the popular will provides an English echo of the French aristocrat Arthur de Gobineau, whose *Essay on the Inequality of the Human Races* was published in 1853.

[49] C. Harvie, *The Lights of Liberalism: University Liberals and the Challenge of Democracy, 1860–1886* (London, 1976), 232–4.

[50] E. Barker, *The Values of Life: Essays on the Circles and Centres of Duty* (London, 1939) 19.

the Liberal Reforms), he saw this shift in 'cultural' rather than economic terms.[51] Indeed, at this level he readily endorsed state action, both during the First World War and subsequently. Education ranked particularly high on his political agenda. This was another area in which he found fresh meaning in Plato's thought after the war, providing a parallel with the rehabilitation of Rousseau among English thinkers on the same score.[52] As we shall see in chapter 5, he followed through this belief in the 1920s by playing a leading role in the Hadow Report on *The Education of the Adolescent.*

In contrast, Barker regarded the state's assumption of an 'economic' role with distinctly less enthusiasm. An instance of his hostility towards 'economic' legislation is the stance he took over the issue of worker's participation in industry during the war, one which had attracted considerable public attention since the worsening of industrial relations with the rise of syndicalism and guild socialism. In 1916 he began work for the newly formed Ministry of Labour, visiting factory committees in the north of England. He brought to this experience a determined opposition to the three forms of industrial organisation which were then being mooted as possible systems of the future: scientific management, guild socialism, and state socialism. He saw much scope for reconciling the priorities of the first two in the establishment of joint industrial councils of workers and employers, after the fashion of those which had been recommended by the Whitley Committee in 1917. It is typical of his inveterate hatred of conflict that the Whitley proposals should have secured his warm endorsement. So enamoured of the Whitley scheme was he that he urged its extension to international relations, reinforcing his tendency to assimilate the structure of national and international society during the First World War. The best hope for a League of Nations, he wrote in 1918, lay in its assumption of a Whitley form, the nations of the world gathering together around a common table for the purpose of 'discussion': 'discussion, which is the elixir of mental life

51 E. Barker, 'The discredited state: thoughts on politics before the war', *Political Quarterly* (old series), 2 (February 1915), 118.

52 Both thinkers seemed eminently down to earth in their educational proposals. For Barker, it was possible to find in Plato 'the scope of a true national education'. E. Barker, *Greek Political Theory*, vi. For H.A.L. Fisher, another educational reformer and soon to become Secretary of the Board of Education, Rousseau was also in tune with the English times: 'It is worth noting that Emile receives little or no instruction which might not be given in a modern elementary school.' H.A.L. Fisher, 'The political writings of Rousseau', *Edinburgh Review*, 224 (July–October 1916), 54.

and the mother of mutual understanding – discussion, which ends disputes by ending the frame of mind, closed, suspicious, dour, which engenders all disputes'.[53] The same high expectations of the method of 'discussion' informed his vision of industrial peace, of 'each man ha[ving] a station, knowing that he had a station, and cheerfully performing the duty of his station because it was also his duty to society'. It was a vision which made few concessions to the state regulation of industry, although it did embrace the limited interventionism of T.H. Green – that the state should protect workers from 'sweated employment'.[54] Indeed, one of the grounds upon which he commended the policy of industrial co-operation was the escape it offered from 'the bugbear . . . of increased state control'. In order to distinguish this position from mere negative antistatism, he hastily added that voluntary co-operation between the two sides of industry would liberate the state to attend its 'proper work of education, of control of foreign relations, of settlement of imperial problems and all those problems other than the industrial problem . . . that await solution in the days of peace'.[55]

These concerns suggest the coherence of Barker's simultaneous embrace of both the law-state and the culture-state.[56] For, in his eyes, some degree of *Sittlichkeit* was necessary for the maintenance of an effective 'rule of law' at both a domestic and an international level. He followed R.B. Haldane here, a second-generation Idealist who became Secretary of State for War in 1905 and then Lord Chancellor in 1912. In 1913, Haldane delivered an address to the American Bar Association entitled 'Higher nationality' and significantly subtitled

53 E. Barker, *A Confederation of the Nations: Its Power and Constitution* (Oxford, 1918), 34.

54 E. Barker, *A Confederation of the Nations*, 30. In a very Greenian passage, he wrote: 'The Law of England makes me a free citizen; without the law I should be a shivering savage; and the more the law frees me from the liberty of being ignorant of the alphabet, or of working in a sweated employment, the more I gain true liberty.'

55 E. Barker, 'Industrial co-operation and Works Committees' (1917), 32, unpublished pamphlet for the Clarendon Press in the Barker Papers, Peterhouse, Cambridge, Box III. Curiously, his views were echoed by G.D.H. Cole, who also endorsed the Whitley scheme as an alternative to state intervention in industrial matters. J.M. Winter, *Socialism and the Challenge of War: Ideas and Politics in Britain, 1912–1918* (London, 1974), 137. The best account of the Whitley proposals is still E. Halévy, *The Era of Tyrannies: Essays on Socialism and War* (1938; London, 1967).

56 In this sense, Barker's political thought mirrored the 'state-to-nation' route towards nationalism in Western Europe. As A.D. Smith has argued, the territorial state – initially soldered by the ties of law and legal institutions – historically found it necessary to become a 'cultural community'. This involved, in particular, the development of the 'mass educational state'. A.D. Smith, *The Ethnic Origins of Nations* (London, 1986), esp. ch. 6.

'A study in law and ethics.' There, he linked three causes that were dear to Barker's heart: the distinctive spirit and traditions of English law, the Anglo-Saxon community, and the international legal order to which it gave rise.[57] Social and economic equality was not implied in the ideal of *Sittlichkeit* which formed the necessary basis of this order in Haldane's eyes; more important was a 'common inheritance' and sense of common identity. In the case of the United States, Canada, and England, evidence of such a sense of cohesion was nowhere more apparent than in the region of jurisprudence. In a similar way, Barker made adroitness in 'the rule of law' central to his hopes for a wider British Commonwealth and international society at large, strengthening in its turn the *Sittlichkeit* which had nurtured it. There were evident English biases in this formula for world peace and harmony, born especially of the prominence which law had assumed in accounts of the national character at the end of the nineteenth century.

Once again, then, we see the philosophy of Idealism translated into the historical experience of specifically English society, this time in its external relations. Idealism in this realm provided a language and vision which would make the sense of 'Englishness' as 'legal-mindedness' more secure by overcoming its traditional associations with insularity. The British Commonwealth was to become the focus of much of Barker's work during his retirement after 1939. In the intervening two decades after he left Oxford in 1920, his thoughts turned to Europe as the most developed sphere of internationalism hitherto – and also the most threatened.

[57] Viscount Haldane, 'Higher nationality: a study in law and ethics' (1913), in *The Conduct of Life and Other Addresses* (London, 1914), 99–136.

CHAPTER 5

Education and national character: the milieu of King's College London

FROM SCHOLARSHIP TO ADMINISTRATION

We have seen in the previous chapters that the foundation of Barker's thought had been laid by the end of the First World War. It was a workable, if somewhat fragile balance between a range of ideas about society and the state in British political thought at the turn of the century. Moreover, it was ensconced within a broader framework of English cultural values, attitudes, and images. His intellectual efforts hitherto were rewarded with invitations to visit colleges in the United States in 1920 and 1929; and the award of a Doctor of Laws degree from Edinburgh in 1921, a Doctor of Letters from Oxford in the following year, and a Doctor of Laws from Harvard when he visited America in 1929. The latter especially pleased him as it constituted – in his mind – 'the greatest honour the USA can do to an Englishman'. Also, by attaining it, he followed in the footsteps of a political scientist whom he much admired, Lord Bryce.[1]

But despite this recognition, his work was yet to be consolidated more fully; it existed in broad outlines only, with much elaboration and integration still to come from the 1930s onwards. It was not until after 1927 – when he secured the Chair of Political Science at Cambridge – that he turned to this task. In the years between 1920 and 1928, he was distracted from his vocation as a teacher and writer by a brief administrative career as the Principal of King's College London. His decision to take up the post at King's left him with mixed feelings. On the one hand, he was excited by the prospect of satisfying an enthusiasm for university 'business' which had grown during the First World War when teaching was in short supply; but on the other,

[1] Barker to Elisabeth Barker (his daughter), 17 May 1929, Barker Papers, Peterhouse Library, Cambridge, Box X.

as he confessed to his old tutor A.L. Smith, he was 'somewhat depressed at the thought of losing all the roots I have struck into the soil during 27 years in Oxford'.[2] The move was indeed a wrench, and his years at King's were not an easy time. In particular, he was faced with steering the college through several crises and transitions. But the rigours of academic leadership aside, he looked back on the experience as, by and large, a profitable one; and while his opportunities for teaching and publishing were curtailed by his administrative burdens, nevertheless his ideas continued to gestate and acquire new dimensions within the ambience of King's.

The overall effect of his new environment was to soften somewhat the provincial strains in his thought as he entered circles which were culturally and politically central. For example, he joined the Athenaeum, dined with the leaders of London's elite institutions in a society called the 'Confreres', experienced the world of officialdom at the Board of Education, and was entertained at Lambeth Palace. The last was perhaps the most significant indicator of his change of milieu. While religious tests for members of staff had been abolished at King's at the turn of the century, and while Barker's predecessor – R.W. Burrows – had become the first lay principal, nevertheless the College remained steeped in the Anglicanism in which it had been born. Certainly, it can have been no coincidence that Barker converted to Anglicanism just before he left Oxford.[3] Thereafter, he became a passionate advocate of an Established Church, rehearsing the arguments of Burke in diverse forums.[4] This seems to have entailed only a minor shift on doctrinal grounds and no renunciation of the great store which he set by the Nonconformist background in which he had been brought up. Indeed, never losing his attachment to the 'periphery' of English culture which the Congregational chapel essentially embodied in Establishment views of Englishness, his cultural thought after his sojourn at King's was notable for its attempt to counter this marginalisation of Nonconformity. It was yet another exercise in synthesis on his part, and one which employed the same intellectual currents which he had adopted earlier in the century. This chapter

[2] Barker to Smith, 22 July 1920, A.L. Smith Papers, Balliol College, Oxford. He expressed the same feeling to Graham Wallas in a letter dated 15 July 1920. Wallas Papers, 1/64 (2), British Library of Political and Economic Science.

[3] See his evidence to *Church and State: Report of the Archbishops' Commission on the Relations between Church and State*, 2 vols. (London, 1935), vol. 1, 75.

[4] For example, *Church and State*, vol. 1, 64–78; 'The Reformation and Nationality', in *The Modern Churchman*, 22 (1932), 329–43; and 'Address', *Evangelical Christendom* (1938), 123–6.

examines these and other concerns which preoccupied him during perhaps his least-productive period as a thinker and scholar. As will become clear in later chapters, they played a vital role in shaping his understanding of his role, audience, and message as a political scientist subsequently.

EUROPEAN PERSPECTIVES AND ACADEMIC FREEDOM

An aspect of King's College which was to leave a particularly lasting mark on Barker's political theory was its strong European interests in the fields of history and politics. This had largely developed through Burrows, a friend of the Greek Prime Minister Venizelos, whose Philhellenism extended to a strong sympathy with the Balkan nations of Eastern Europe. The outbreak of the First World War brought this region to public attention. Burrows had arrived at the college in 1913, determined to advance the study of the culture and history of Eastern European countries. Accordingly, in close co-operation with R.W. Seton-Watson, he established the School of Slavonic Studies at King's in 1915. This was part of a wider project, mentioned in chapter 4, to inform public opinion on the Eastern and Russian part of the European continent through the journal, *The New Europe*.

We have seen that Barker had come into contact with the group in London which launched *The New Europe* in 1916, and it was most likely this connection which brought him the office of Principal in 1920 following Burrows' early death in the previous year. Barker inherited from Burrows an institution which was rapidly becoming an intellectual focus of many European nationalities. Not only did the College promote General Lectures which often touched upon European themes, were delivered by speakers from the Continent, and were attended by delegations from European embassies in London; his predecessor had also encouraged links with governments abroad through their endowment of Chairs at King's in Greek, Portuguese, and Spanish.

Barker sustained both of these developments; but they were not always without attendant problems. The financing of academic posts by external sources, particularly foreign governments and communities, was to prove troublesome in the extreme in the case of the Koraes Chair in Modern Greek, named after one of the leaders of the Greek independence movement who was a great classical scholar. This had been established in 1918 by the Greek government in conjunction with a number of Greek donors who formed a Subscribers' Committee. The latter had received the blessing of Burrows, who negotiated the arrangements from the start shortly before his death; but its existence was concealed from Arnold Toynbee on his appointment as first incumbent. Most importantly, the conditions of Toynbee's appointment made no mention of the powers which the University of London's Senate had conferred upon this committee in response to the latter's demands. These were the right to request programmes of teaching, a triennial report, and – perhaps most controversially – to make 'criticisms and suggestions thereon'. In effect then, the Professor was answerable to the Committee of Subscribers.[5]

Toynbee – and Barker – remained oblivious of these terms until 1923, by which time Toynbee had fallen considerably out of sympathy with the Greek line which the subscribers clearly expected the occupant of the chair to toe. On leave amidst the Anatolian crisis in 1921, Toynbee wrote for the *Manchester Guardian* of the Greek atrocities which he had witnessed in occupied territories. Adding insult to injury, he concluded his *The Western Question in Greece and Turkey* published in the following year with the assertion that the Greeks had evinced 'the same unfitness as the Turks for governing a mixed population'.[6] Called to account by the Subscribers' Committee, Toynbee came under increasing pressure to resign, which he did in 1923. The ensuing furore introduced clear divisions in the college, with Barker ranged against Seton-Watson on the issue of the control which outside bodies should exert on posts which they had underwritten. While Seton-Watson thought that the conditions attached to the Chair were neither unreasonable, nor onerous, Barker vigorously defended the cause of academic freedom.[7] At the same time, he was concerned to preserve the dignity of Burrows' memory, without whose efforts the Chair would not have been founded. He was also mindful of the college's heavy dependence upon foreign disbursements like that which had made the Koraes Chair possible. Nonetheless, Barker supported Toynbee to the hilt, and whilst reluctantly accepting the latter's resignation, he was of the view that the Subscribers' Committee should withdraw the terms which they had initially

[5] R. Clogg, 'Politics and the academy: Arnold Toynbee and the Koraes chair', *Middle Eastern Studies*, 21, 4, special issue (October 1985), 40, 81.

[6] Clogg, 'Politics and the academy', 58. On the deeper intellectual roots of Toynbee's exposure of Greek atrocities, see William H. McNeill, *Arnold Toynbee: A Life* (Oxford, 1989), ch. 5.

[7] Clogg, 'Politics and the academy', 76–9.

attached to the Chair. The crisis ended in 1925 with the replacement of the Subscribers' Committee with a university committee. The latter would oversee the Chair on the same terms as other Chairs in the university, albeit with co-opted members from the Greek body it superseded.

Barker made no mention of the affair in his autobiography: shunning controversy of all kinds (as we saw in the Introduction) it was evidently an episode which he preferred to forget. But it steeled his belief in the virtue of untrammelled intellectual freedom, and he took the opportunity of his Presidential Address to the Education Section of the British Association in Toronto in 1924 to dwell on this theme. He maintained that the tradition of private benefaction in the two ancient universities was a valuable and noble one; however, in 'modern democratic communities' it was dangerous for universities to become over-reliant upon it. Private patronage could subvert the place of universities within the 'general commonwealth', transforming them into sectarian institutions. The correct attitude towards private funding was: 'To take benefaction if it comes, but not to go out to seek it; to look even a gift-horse in the mouth with a modest and discreet inquiry; to be sure that no endowment contravenes by one jot or tittle freedom of inquiry or freedom of expression.' With the sobering experience of the Koraes Chair no doubt fresh in his mind, and in the spirit of his general political theory, he continued: 'it is always possible that private benefactions may have their tacit implications – a form of capitalism; a particular kind of nationalism; some brand of confessionalism – which may make them enemies of academic freedom.'[8]

But such difficulties as those which were generated by the Koraes Chair aside, Barker seems to have been much stimulated by the European world which his time at King's opened up. It yielded invitations to many foreign embassies in London, and also the acquaintance of leading political figures and scholars in Europe. These included Thomas Masaryk, President of Czechoslovakia after the First World War, whom Barker revered as a 'scholar-statesman' in the same mould as English statesmen like Burke, Gladstone, and Bryce. Masaryk had been a lecturer in the School of Slavonic Studies while exiled in London during the war. The strong link of King's College with Czechoslovakia earned Barker the 'Order of the White

[8] E. Barker, 'Academic freedom', in *Church, State, and Study: Essays* (London, 1930), 239–40.

Lion' from the government of Czechoslovakia in 1927. He was quick to attribute the award – with typical modesty – to the initiative of his predecessor in securing Masaryk's post at the School. However, his own role in negotiating the Czechoslovakian government's endowment of the Chair in Central European History in 1923 – named after Masaryk – must have been equally influential.[9] Barker also forged close ties with Eduard Beneš, Masaryk's foreign minister, and Demetrios Caclamanos, the foreign minister of Greece, both of whom combined gifts of diplomacy with erudition in a way which could not fail to elicit his admiration.[10]

Perhaps the most important of the continental scholars with whom he came into contact at King's was Ernst Troeltsch, whose interest in the impact of Christianity and natural law on European political thought helped to inspire Barker's own in the following decade.[11] Troeltsch was to have delivered three lectures at King's in 1923 but his death intervened. The lectures were revised and translated, partly by Barker, and published in the same year.[12] As a result of these and many similar contacts, he later claimed that the knowledge of Europe which he had gained at King's, 'however slight, was a permanent acquisition. I think it made me a better professor in later days; and anyhow it made me a better European.' It was indeed, as he continued, a vital foundation for his work during the Second World War with the Conference of Allied Ministers of Education.[13]

STATE EDUCATION AND THE ENGLISH CHARACTER

Two of Barker's further concerns while he was Principal of King's College in the 1920s were public secondary education, on the one hand, and the idea of 'national character', on the other. These became firm and closely intertwined fixtures in his thought thereafter. While

[9] Minutes of the Delegacy, King's College London Archives, vol. VI, 26 April 1927, KA/C/M19; vol. IV, 25 September 1923, KA/C/M18.

[10] For example, he praised Thomas Masaryk and Eduard Beneš in the same terms as he praised British statesmen. 'They were men who brought to politics a large and liberal spirit – men, we may even say, who brought a conscious philosophy to the making and working of Czechoslovak government.' Preface to F. Táborský, *Czechoslovak Democracy at Work* (London, 1945), 6.

[11] He included Troeltsch's lecture on 'The ideas of natural law and humanity' (1922) as an appendix to his translation of Gierke's *Natural Law and the Theory of Society, 1500 to 1800* (Cambridge, 1934).

[12] E. Troeltsch, *Christian Thought: Its History and Application*, transl. Baron F. Von Hugel (London, 1923).

[13] E. Barker, *Age and Youth*, 145.

not exclusively associated with Idealism, the latter was nonetheless influential in underlining their importance and interconnections for him.

Barker's sustained commitment to Idealism in the 1920s can be seen in his remark at the 1922 Liberal Summer Schools Committee that the way out of the Liberal Party's current doldrums lay in a revival of the philosophy of T.H. Green.[14] This held the key to social and political unity which Barker then perceived as an urgent political goal. His main hopes for social integration lay with educational policy, being a member of the Board of Education's Consultative Committee throughout his period of residence in London. Other members of the committee who shared the Idealist roots of his educational interests were Sir. W.H. Hadow (chairman), R.H. Tawney, and Albert Mansbridge. Barker played a prominent role in changing the terms of the committee's function, securing the Minister of Education's agreement in 1923 to the committee suggesting a topic for consideration rather than pursuing one which originated in the Board of Education itself. The area of need which the committee identified – that of post-primary education outside of the existing secondary-school system – was of exceptional national importance in Barker's view. He became Chairman of the Drafting Sub-Committee of what later became the Hadow Report on *The Education of the Adolescent*, published in 1927. The essence of the report was a recommendation that the school-leaving age should be raised to fifteen, with a diversification of education beyond the primary level. The report, in fact, marked the origins of the two-tier system of secondary education in Britain; between the grammar schools leading to university, and secondary 'modern' schools, whose pupils would primarily enter industry and commerce. The modern schools would have a 'practical' and 'realistic' orientation; but the committee was anxious that they should include the literary and scientific curriculum of their academic counterparts – English, history, geography, a modern language, mathematics, and natural science – albeit related more closely to 'the living texture of industrial or commercial or rural life'. The thinking behind this proposal – at least from the point of view of the Drafting Sub-Committee's chairman – is well set out in an address which Barker delivered in Manchester in 1925. Touching upon a theme of which Bosanquet had made much, he asserted that: 'Our English genius is towards action and practice rather than speculation and knowledge. We should

[14] Quoted in J. Harris, *William Beveridge: A Biography* (London, 1977), 312.

stultify our genius, and we might stultify our children, if we failed to recognise this practical bias . . . [But] *it is a mirage and a delusion to think that you may not have a liberal education in practical things*.'[15]

The keynote of the Hadow Report, then, was provision for the different needs of pupils, and the maintenance of a minimal level of intellectual education in all schools, while at the same time working with the 'practical' grain of Englishness. Of course, this analysis left a sizeable element of the school population outside of the national type – those who attended the grammar schools. Their general aptitude was considered by the committee to be 'academic' as opposed to 'practical', in the sense of those children who – in the rather donnish words of the report – 'think with their hands'. But as Barker was later to write of and praise the 'amateur', non-specialist nature of English scholarship which had issued from the grammar and public schools, the distance between the two sides of the binary educational line which he recommended in the 1920s would not have seemed a large one.[16]

This appeal to the 'practical' bent of the English nation was crucial given that Barker and his colleagues commended their report on the grounds that fresh educational provision was necessary in order to strengthen character, both 'individual' and 'national'. Indeed, the two dimensions of character were indissolubly linked in their eyes. This connection sheds further light upon their conception of 'practice', and provides another bridge between the two streams of secondary education – grammar and 'modern' – which they proposed. For the association between individual and national character primarily reflected the broad Idealist consensus on the committee, transcending the ideological divisions between – for example – Tawney's staunch Labour sympathies and the liberal affiliations of Hadow and Barker.[17] This particular form of Idealist influence can readily be seen in the Report's precise defence of secondary education with a 'practical'

[15] E. Barker, *Social Ideas and Educational Systems*, an address to the Co-operative Union Ltd (Manchester, 1925), 11. (My italics.)

[16] E. Barker (ed.), *The Character of England* (Oxford, 1947), 366.

[17] On the contradictions in Tawney's position caused by his endorsement of a dual system of secondary education, see P. Gordon and J. White, *Philosophers as Educational Reformers: The Influence of Idealism on British Educational Thought and Practice* (London, 1979), 162–3. The Idealist influence on the Hadow Report provides a good illustration of Jose Harris' recent claim that, in public administration, 'the Idealist frame of reference became even more powerful and all-encompassing in the period *after* the First World War, when for a time at least the traditions of positivism and empiricism virtually faded out of large areas of the vocabulary of social science'. 'Political thought and the welfare state 1870–1940: an intellectual framework for British social policy', *Past and Present*, 135 (1992), 123.

slant; the latter was not to be construed in a narrow, 'utilitarian' sense but rather as the condition of 'a better and more skilled service of the community in all its multiple business and complex affairs'. Translated into educational policy for this 'highly industrialised' society, the concern for national and individual 'character' entailed the 'awakening and guiding of the practical intelligence', on the one hand, and the 'training of tastes which will fill and dignify leisure', on the other. The educational system implied by these two goals – the state closing the gaps in existing private and public provision at the secondary level – would serve to 'elevate' the nation.[18]

Clearly, in the view of its authors, the report provided a blueprint for capitalising on a key strength of English national character – that of an assumed greater capacity for 'action' than 'thought' – thereby sustaining the distinctiveness and standing of Britain in a competitive world environment. However, it is equally evident from the above quotations that this apparent concession to the priorities of industry was no simple attempt to boost the fortunes of capitalism. First, the needs of industry were framed in the Idealist language of the wider 'common good', an ethical rather than an economic construct and one whose spirit was to infuse grammar and secondary modern education alike. Second, recognition of industrial needs was balanced in the report by the importance of 'uplifting' leisure pursuits which could only be secured through a measure of liberal education at all secondary levels. This emphasis was underpinned by a critique of industrialism which was reminiscent of William Morris' attack upon the dehumanising effects of work in modern society, although the antidote prescribed by the Hadow Committee focused as much upon the acquisition of intellectual interests as that of artistic and manual skills. This became a recurrent argument in Barker's thought during the interwar period, one which will re-emerge in chapter 7 below. Here, it is necessary to note that the sharp divide between the grammar and secondary modern schools which subsequently became entrenched in British education reflected a failure of policy following the Hadow Report rather than the intention of its authors.[19] They had insisted upon the need for parity between the two streams, the 'modern' stream differing only in 'kind' and not being 'inferior in its promise or quality' to its traditional counterpart.[20]

[18] Board of Education, *The Education of the Adolescent: Report of the Consultative Committee* (London, 1927), xxiii–iv. [19] Gordon and White, *Philosophers as Educational Reformers*, 163.
[20] Board of Education, *The Education of the Adolescent*, xx.

THE QUIETNESS OF ENGLISH NATIONALISM

Thus, for Barker, education and national character were two sides of the same coin, constituting the dominant and mutually reinforcing themes of his work in the 1920s. When he turned to writing his lectures on *National Character* for the Stevenson Foundation in Glasgow in 1925, the basis already existed in his work for the Hadow Committee. The lectures – which became the only book to emerge from his period at King's – supplied the theory behind the practice of *The Education of the Adolescent*. Education there took its place beside law and government, religion, language, and literature as one of the key 'factors' – if not potentially *the* key factor – in determining national development. Its essence was 'a common system of training, which unites the minds of the members of a nation . . . serving not merely to imbue intelligences with a common content of ideas, but also to quicken characters towards the pursuit of common ideals'.[21] One of the few things which Barker regretted about the historical evolution of England was the delay of a century in establishing a public system of education following the Industrial Revolution. The direction of education towards the creation of the 'full man' – wholly in touch with the riches and breadth of the national tradition and whose mind had undergone a 'general development' – was not initiated until the Education Act of 1870.[22] In his view, voluntary provision did not nearly suffice to bring workers out of the narrow cultural limits of their occupational specialisation. This condition, combined with forced 'aggregation' into towns, acted to constrain political loyalties and undermine 'self-reliance'. It was not that he ignored the vibrant nineteenth-century tradition of working-class self-help here; rather, his animus was directed against the strength of collective identities – of whatever hue – in urban-industrial society, threatening as they did to overshadow the sense of individual selfhood.[23]

Barker's ennobled conception of the purpose of education was Idealist through and through, as was the understanding of 'national character' which it supported. The substance of the latter was inherently 'mental', he argued, instantly dismissing the French

[21] E. Barker, *National Character and the Factors in its Formation* (1927; London, 1928), 4.
[22] E. Barker, *National Character*, 242–3, 250.
[23] These qualms emerge in the final chapter of *National Character*, entitled 'The signs of the times'.

penchant for explaining it in terms of natural forces such as climate.[24] Lest there be any doubt as to his source here, he openly acknowledged the influence of Bosanquet, to whom he professed himself indebted 'in almost everything I have written on social matters'. Significantly, he invoked Bosanquet's support for a strictly individualistic view of the nation against recent – mainly continental – attempts to endow it with personality beyond that of its individual members. Rejecting suggestions that nations embodied a 'group mind' or 'folk soul', he insisted instead that: 'A nation is nothing more, and nothing less, than a body of men who are united and made one body in virtue of having in their minds . . . a common substance or content of ideas, which has been in the minds of men now dead and gone, as it will be in the minds of men unborn and still to come.'[25]

Suggesting, as it did, the notion of an 'eternal contract' between past and present, the passage is a peculiarly Burkean gloss upon Bosanquet. But Barker did not have to take too many liberties in his interpretation of Idealism here, Bosanquet himself being quite susceptible to the Burkean–Whig paradigm.[26] Bosanquet was certainly a valuable ally in dismissing not only holistic but also racial theories of the nation. Wedded to the Idealist conviction that the nation is an inherently 'spiritual' fact which emerges most vitally in the historical traditions of a society, any 'natural', 'organic' theory of the nation appeared untenable to Barker. Nations were 'artificial' in the sense that there was no 'physical' reason for their existence, nor any assigned 'destiny'; their character was not cast in stone but rather endlessly modified by the vicissitudes of history. But they were nevertheless grounded in 'rational' processes. This was in virtue of the organised transmission of the common thoughts and feelings which lay at their core, particularly in the era of universal public education to which cause Barker was strongly committed. While 'instinct' and 'habit' might play their role in these processes, they were themselves activated by a strong undercurrent of 'reason'. This was the case when the nation existed at both a conscious and an unconscious level.

[24] E. Barker, *National Character*, 77–8. His immediate target seems to have been Emile Boutmy's *The English People: A Study of their Political Psychology*, translated by E. English (London, 1904). This began with the claim that '[a]mong the influences which mould a nation, natural phenomena have most weight and efficacy', 3. Nonetheless, Barker was intrigued by the French interest in 'England', for which Boutmy's young colleague at the Ecole Libre des Sciences Politiques – Elie Halévy – rendered distinguished service. For Halévy's influence on Barker, see below p. 126. [25] E. Barker, *National Character*, 136. [26] See ch. 1, pp. 39–40.

To take the abstract edge off of this theory, Barker proceeded to illustrate it – predictably – by observing 'the making of England and the English type'. His crucial model in this undertaking was C.H. Pearson's *National Life and Character* (1893). We have seen in a previous chapter that this work constituted a landmark for Barker in his early intellectual development.[27] His general disposition, however, was much less gloomy than that of Pearson. Shored up by the optimism of English Whiggism – especially – Barker eluded his mentor's anxiety for the English stock and English traditions in the collectivist age. Despite some muffled grumbles about what the shire might mean nowadays to 'men who think in terms of their union, or Parliament to those who prefer the general congress of unions', he was not too perturbed by the loss of authority suffered by established institutions in some quarters. This is the more remarkable given that he was writing in the aftermath of the General Strike, an event which – as one historian has remarked recently – induced the same sense of foreboding in English cultural thought as the First World War had done a decade earlier.[28] For example, Barker remarked of the present 'industrial movement' (as expressed in the Labour party) that:

> If it is founded on the basis of working-class organizations, it is not by any means wholly identified with a single class, and it is more and more drawing into its ranks the representatives of other classes . . . The Trade Unions, on which it is mainly based, are legal associations, which have been regulated by law throughout their history; and save in rare moments of excitement they have always acted within the domain in law.

He was further reassured by the – again, strikingly optimistic – belief that the working-class movement in Britain was 'imbued with the same habit of discussion, and the same temper of compromise, which has been shown by the nation at large'.[29] But what he calmly interpreted as the continued supremacy of law in the face of working-class pressure for social change was the most important indicator for him that the English national character had retained its traditional vigour, despite the recent political crisis. In his chapter on 'Law and government', Barker even went so far as to suggest that 'the greatest product of the English nation in the sphere of social organization is perhaps not Parliament, but the Common Law'. It had created 'a common spirit of law-abidingness, pervading all

[27] See ch. 4, p. 107.
[28] S. Hynes, *A War Imagined: The First World War and English Culture* (New York, 1991), ch. 20.
[29] E. Barker, *National Character*, 176.

classes equally'. Within the common framework of law, 'the nation [had] acquire[d] a fundamental unity'.[30]

This was, of course, a clear echo of Dicey, especially given Barker's added comment that the 'sovereignty of Parliament' had proved the natural corollary of 'the rule of law'. I suggested earlier in this study that his Diceyan sympathies were instrumental in his view of the state as an 'impartial and impersonal structure', a 'scheme of organisation', and a 'political and legal fact'.[31] But by defining the state in this way, he was not only able to link the quintessence of statehood generally to Englishness, English judges having 'burned law-abidingness into the spirit of the nation';[32] he could also separate the principle of statehood from that of nationhood. During the First World War he had emphatically rejected the idea of a 'right' to national self-determination, instead promoting the virtues of multinationalism emanating from common political institutions. In this matter, as in most others, it was the example of England/Britain which he invoked to support his stance, one to which he continued to adhere after the First World War and indeed for the rest of his life. Thus, in *National Character*, he described English nationalism as 'never reflective, because it is so simply and obviously a fact'. That fact was the embodiment of the nation in an 'external political order of life'. The political structure in England was secure to such an extent, he maintained, that it could withstand the political leadership of a Scotsman, Welshman, and Jew; the Irish satires of a Swift or a Shaw; and the military leadership of an Irishman like Wellington. If it seems that he was denying to other nations that which had produced so felicitous a climate in his own country, he would have retorted that in England, the organisation of polity had preceded the development of what little national consciousness existed, and provided perhaps the only focus for the latter – fortunately. At any rate, he believed fervently that the only stimulus to national awareness in England was the occasional contemplation of its uniquely successful political system – the sense among citizens that 'the English constitution might be worse, and England, after all, is not a bad country'.[33] The so-called 'right' to national self-determination constituted in his mind a spurious demand for the political order to be (re)shaped in accordance with the sense of nationality itself, often one that was alarmingly impassioned. His argument here was fully consistent with his

[30] Ibid., 152, 155. [31] Ibid., 128. [32] Ibid., 156. [33] Ibid., 194.

rejection of the view of nations as essentially pre-political and pre-historic, instead being 'spiritual' entities shaped by common ideas, traditions, and institutions.

It is significant that what seemed to Barker as the unconscious, taken-for-granted character of English nationalism had caused much relief to Liberals of a previous generation; indeed, paradoxically, it constituted the root of their national pride. Acton's views on this score were mentioned in the previous chapter. Dicey likewise castigated the 'narrow spirit of nationalism' which prevailed on much of the continent. 'Happy', he proclaimed, 'from the Benthamite point of view, is the nation which is not haunted by the dream or nightmare of past or traditional glory. The singular absence in England of all popular traditions causes some natural regret to poets and even to patriots. Yet it has assuredly favoured the growth and the preservation of English freedom.'[34] For Barker, the muted tones of English national identity were a direct result of the multinational political environment in which it had developed. Shifting the emphasis to 'British national character', he extolled the way in which the state in 'our island' had managed to be simultaneously 'multi-national and a single nation, . . . teach[ing] its citizens at one and the same time to glory both in the name of Scotsmen or Welshmen or Englishmen and in the name of Britons'.[35] In this respect, it afforded a sobering contrast with Austria-Hungary before the First World War, a state which had proved incapable of forging any basis of unity among its several component nations while leaving their separate cultures intact.[36]

The lack of any clouds on Barker's horizon here is typical; resistant to all suggestions of a dissonant world, especially a dissonant 'English' world, he somewhat glibly assumed an instant Scottish and Welsh identification with 'Britishness'. He was brought up sharply by one of his reviewers in this respect – the historian Richard Lodge – who questioned whether the Act of Union between Scotland and England in 1707 had indeed successfully bound the two nations together, as well as healing internal divisions in Scotland itself as Barker suggested. Rather, the Act had effectively widened the gap between the prosperous Lowlands and the undeveloped Highlands.[37] Yet Barker's ideal of nationalism could be detached from his unsullied view of English nationalism, striking a sympathetic chord with other

[34] A.V. Dicey, *Lectures on the Relation between Law and Public Opinion in England during the Nineteenth Century* (London, 1905, 2nd edn 1914), 463. [35] E. Barker, *National Character*, 17.
[36] Ibid., 131. [37] R. Lodge, *History*, 13 (April, 1928), 37–9.

contemporaries. For example, it was warmly received by Leonard Woolf, who was to find one of Barker's later books – on the British Empire – exasperatingly smug.[38] Woolf commended *National Character* as a 'sober antidote to chauvinistic nationalism'. He was particularly persuaded by Barker's denunciation of the 'self-conscious' nation which had risen to prominence in European politics after the French Revolution and the Napoleonic Wars. He wrote that 'the self-conscious nation is indeed rather terrifying; it swallows the race and it swallows the State, and it even sometimes tries to swallow other races, States, and nations'.[39]

The 'historic state' was thus in Barker's eyes a decisive force in shaping national character at large, an argument which was reminiscent of J.S. Mill.[40] The national differences between France and England provided Barker with ample illustration of this theory. Certainly, the early unity of the English state and nation around judicial power above all else was responsible for the prevalence of 'localism and civil liberty' in England, a fact which possibly explained the strength of 'individualism' there as well. By contrast, the greater Romanisation of French life and political culture had produced a nation dominated by 'centralization and officialism' and also 'sociability', this latter factor being a legacy of the 'sociable town life' of the Roman state.[41] Barker had indeed read his Stubbs with singular profit, drawing out the full Diceyan potential in the latter's *Constitutional History of England* where these comparative themes assumed pride of place.

Barker elevated law to so prominent a place in English history that he projected the Revolution of 1688 – the *annus mirabilis* in the Whig calendar – as 'a revolution by legal process' more than the achievement of parliament. The parliamentary revolution belonged to his own times, and it essentially concerned 'social [by which he meant class] relations'. With characteristic good cheer, he predicted its success. This prophecy emerged from the close and anxious watch he kept on the recent conflagration between labour and capital, his optimism – as usual – enabling him to extract as much hope as possible that the tensions and conflicts of the economic world would be peacefully resolved. The 'parliamentary revolution' would complete a trilogy of beneficial disruptions in the nonetheless 'long and

[38] See below, ch. 8. [39] L. Woolf, *Nation and Athenaeum*, 41 (11 June 1927), 339.

[40] S. Collini, D. Winch, and J. Burrow, *That Noble Science of Politics: A Study in Nineteenth-Century Intellectual History* (Cambridge, 1983), 151. [41] E. Barker, *National Character*, 146–8.

unbroken course of English history', the first one being the Puritan Revolution and the Civil War. The three revolutions would all be of the same piece since even the Puritans, he argued with clear echoes of Green, had 'clung to tradition and precedent'. It was important for him to set the Puritans alongside the Whigs in the same positive light since they were a vital part of his religious and philosophical heritage. Still loyal to their legacy, despite his recent conversion to Anglicanism, he remarked that Nonconformity in both its Puritan and Wesleyan forms constituted 'the most peculiar, yet most effective, of all the elements of English character'; because of its influence upon economic life, the founding of colonies, and in generally 'steel[ing] our qualities, and accentuat[ing] our angularities', it accounted for much in the 'aspect we have presented to the world, and the judgement which the world has passed upon us'.[42] Whether or not this eulogy to Nonconformity was a direct response to Matthew Arnold's dismissal of the dissenting tradition as culturally marginal in Britain, it is certainly significant as a far more positive appraisal of the latter's position in the national culture. Furthermore, it was enunciated against an appropriate backdrop of declining denominational conflict after the First World War, a reconciliation which was nonetheless to rebound to the advantage of Baldwinite conservatism and the Conservative Party rather than the liberalism which Barker so highly prized.[43]

Barker's endeavour to bring Puritanism in from the cold was much assisted by Elie Halévy's recent studies in nineteenth-century English history, a writer whom he had known since 1908. Halévy's central thesis that Nonconformity – particularly, but not exclusively Methodism – had averted the revolutionary convulsions of the European continent at the end of the eighteenth century was one in which Barker exulted.[44] He also appreciated the force of Halévy's conception of the way in which Nonconformist thought had exerted a mellowing influence upon Benthamism, to which it often became allied. In his obituary for Halévy in 1938, Barker wrote that: 'Few, if any, have understood as well as he did the genius of English Nonconformity . . . or its profound importance in the history of English national life . . .

[42] Ibid., 202.

[43] See P. Williamson, 'The doctrinal politics of Stanley Baldwin', in M. Bentley (ed.), *Public and Private Doctrine* (Cambridge, 1993), 205–6.

[44] For an illuminating discussion of the 'Halévy thesis', see M. Chase, *Elie Halévy: An Intellectual Biography* (New York, 1980), ch. 3.

Here was a principle of spiritual order which held England together.'[45] In the same vein, Barker dissolved the oppositional image of Nonconformity in nineteenth-century social criticism by claiming that Puritanism 'perhaps owed something to earlier legal doctrines of the rights and liberties of the subject'. Puritanism was certainly imbued with the same spirit of 'individual autonomy' which pervaded English law, politics, and all other aspects of national life.[46]

The transformation of the Puritans from cultural outcasts to heroes in this way brought them within the pale of Whig history (from which they had been excluded by Macaulay, at least[47]) particularly when reconstituted along Diceyan lines. It formed a vital part of Barker's strategy as a cultural theorist and policy-maker to heal the rifts in English society by emphasising the basic 'congruity' among all the various factors which had shaped the nation. This explains his attraction to Halévy's work on English Nonconformity. But whilst he may have welded together Idealism and Whiggism on the plane of English historical interpretation and the theory of 'national character', he was soon to push them apart as theories of the state. In this realm, his preference shifted clearly to Whiggism.

[45] E. Barker, 'Elie Halévy', *English Historical Review*, 53 (January 1938), 83–4.
[46] E. Barker, *National Character*, 235.
[47] H.A.L. Fisher, 'The Whig historians', Raleigh lecture on history, *Proceedings of the British Academy* (1928), 317.

CHAPTER 6

'Continental' political science and the Cambridge Chair

PROFESSOR OF POLITICAL SCIENCE

How long Barker would have stayed at King's College London had a new Chair of Political Science not been founded at Cambridge in 1927 is an open question. He had certainly grown tired of the constant pressure of affairs by that time and desired a return to the quieter life of scholarship. It does not seem, however, that he was particularly anxious to secure the Cambridge Chair which was funded by the Laura Spelman Rockefeller Memorial of New York.[1] In his statement to the Council of King's College on his resignation he emphasised that he had (at first?) refused to be a candidate for the Chair although he had been pressed to allow his name to go forward. When offered the Chair, he felt it was his duty to accept.[2] By explaining his resignation in this way, he was evidently concerned to avoid offending those with whom he had worked closely in the college. Nonetheless, there was an ambivalence in his attitude to the post which made his hesitation in applying a very real one. His doubts about the Chair must have centred especially on its title; whilst he had readily envisaged himself as a Professor of Political Theory and Institutions at Oxford two decades earlier, the role of Professor of Political Science was less appealing. This emerged in his inaugural lecture, where he expressed considerable scepticism about the scientific status of his subject. Disliking the suggestion of 'exactitude' in the idea of a science of politics, he preferred to think of his profession in terms of a 'theoretical' or 'speculative' pursuit, after the fashion of Aristotle. This signified the nature of political inquiry as 'concerned with the moral phenomena of human behaviour in political societies'.[3] As he

[1] On the background to the Chair, see M. Bulmer, 'Sociology and political science at Cambridge in the 1920s: an opportunity missed and an opportunity taken', *The Cambridge Review*, 27 April 1981, 156–9.

[2] Minutes of Council, King's College London Archives, 5 July 1927, KA/C/M19.

[3] E. Barker, 'The study of political science', in *Church, State, and Study: Essays* (London, 1930), 194.

unfurled this essentially Idealist banner, informed members of his audience might well have wondered what had become of the positivist goals of the Rockefeller Trust.[4] Indeed, Barker's unhappy experience of external endowments at King's may have been another factor in his initial lack of enthusiasm for the Chair.[5]

Nor were the years he spent as Cambridge's first Professor of Political Science particularly memorable for fresh intellectual stimulus and camaraderie. Attached to the Faculty of History in whose degree he assumed charge of two political science papers, Barker was sensitive to his position as an 'outsider'. He remained somewhat marginal in the faculty, first as one who had spent his formative years at Oxford, and second as professor of a subject of whose obliqueness he was only too aware. As he emphasised in his inaugural lecture, the terrain which he now occupied 'is certainly nebulous, probably dubious, and possibly disputatious'.[6] He doubted whether political inquiry existed outside of the spheres of history and philosophy where it had traditionally been cultivated. This ambiguity would have been regarded as a virtue at his home university. He certainly missed the cross-fertilisation between academic disciplines which had played so formative a part in his own intellectual development at Oxford earlier in the century. But lacking the distinct and secure identity of his immediate colleagues, he felt 'somehow outside the circle as a nondescript sort of creature who hovered on the confines of different studies without any fixed or certain allegiance'.[7] As will be seen later in this chapter, he attempted to create his own institutional niche

[4] The purpose of the Rockefeller Foundation was to set the study of society on natural scientific lines. This meant a bias against theory in favour of empirical and applied research. The foundation was successful in promoting this end at the London School of Economics in the 1920s, where its ideas were much in tune with those of the director, William Beveridge. See Donald Fisher, 'Philanthropy and the social sciences in Britain, 1919–1939: the reproduction of a conservative ideology', *The Sociological Review*, 28, 2 (1980), 277–315; and J. Harris, *William Beveridge: A Biography* (London, 1977), ch. 12.

[5] In the event, the Board of Electors to the Chair was composed of men who were either historians or political theorists in the same mould as Barker himself. The historians included H.W.C. Davis, J.H. Clapham, Harold Temperley, and J.R.M. Butler. The political theorists were W.R. Sorley, A.D. Lindsay, and G. Lowes Dickinson. Cambridge University Archives (O.XIV.54), Cambridge University Library.

[6] E. Barker, 'The study of political science', 192.

[7] E. Barker, *Age and Youth: Memories of Three Universities and Father of the Man* (London, 1953), 158. Nevertheless, he ardently defended the place of political studies in the tripos against those in the faculty who would have preferred it to be an avenue of specialist historical study. Whilst playing down this conflict, he invoked the need for 'education for citizenship' as well as academic training in universities. See his article on 'The History Tripos', in Sir Philip Hartog (ed.), *The Purposes of Examinations: A Symposium* (London, 1938).

through launching a new tripos in 'Social and Political Studies', although without success.

The intrusion which Barker sensed that he represented in the faculty must have become especially apparent to him on his attempt to change the titles of the two 'Political Science' papers shortly after his arrival. His suggestion that 'Political Science B' should be renamed 'The Theory of the Modern State' raised no objections. However, in proposing to substitute the 'History of Political Thought' for 'Comparative Politics' in 'Political Science A', he encountered considerable hostility. Eventually he brought the Faculty Board round, arguing that the study of political institutions fell within the province of other subjects in Part I of the tripos and that the two political science papers would acquire greater coherence under his scheme. But according to the Faculty Board minutes, the loss of comparative politics caused some 'regret'. This was despite the gradual reduction in the empirical content of the paper that had taken place since its late-nineteenth-century inception under Sir John Seeley's auspices by the inclusion of issues relating to the history of political thought.[8] Indeed, 'regret' might well have been a polite expression for keenly felt resentment.[9]

Still, despite his isolation in the Cambridge Faculty of History, Barker never questioned the wisdom of his move from London in January 1928, 'claustrophobic' as that metropolitan experience had become.[10] Primarily, the Cambridge Chair gave him time and opportunity to develop his existing stock of ideas which he reaped to the full during a prolific retirement after 1939. In particular, he began to engage more closely with continental traditions of political science and philosophy. However, it was an interest which intensified the strains between his various intellectual loyalties.

IDEALIST HESITATIONS

The first signs of a retreat from the Idealist manifesto for political science which Barker had developed in 1928 came in a review he

[8] S. Collini, D. Winch, and J. Burrow, *That Noble Science of Politics: A Study in Nineteenth-Century Intellectual History* (Cambridge, 1983), 350.

[9] Minutes of the Board of the Faculty of History, 15 May 1928. Barker's proposals were first introduced at this session. Initially, the report of the discussion concluded that '[n]o strong opposition to the proposals showed itself'. However, this was crossed out by the chairman, Z.N. Brooke. Other relevant minutes are 13 November 1928 and 29 January 1929.

[10] E. Barker to M.B. Reckitt, 18 August 1957, Reckitt Papers, University of Sussex Library, 13/1.

wrote two years later of A.D. Lindsay's *The Essentials of Democracy* (1929). As mentioned in chapter 1, Lindsay was also an intellectual descendant of T.H. Green. Taking the concept of democracy as the distillation of all Idealist values, he argued that the modern democratic state embodied the 'common life of society'. Legislation and government action, he further maintained – in clear Idealist tones – were concerned not only with 'the satisfaction of individual demand but with moral issues, with upholding a certain standard and manner of life'.[11] Drawn to Idealism by way of Presbyterianism, Lindsay understood the 'General Will' at the heart of the state by analogy with 'the sense of the meeting' in Puritan congregations. To achieve the latter at a national level was, he believed, the vital end of democratic institutions. Moreover, he made no attempt to detach the ideal of democracy from its religious basis in seeking 'the will of God'. Indeed, one recent commentator has wondered 'how large a place politics actually occupied in Lindsay's thought, and how far his political system was the mundane launching point for the soul's flights to a higher realm'.[12]

The conduct of political discourse in these pointedly moral and implicitly religious terms elicited all the unease towards such an approach which had simmered in Barker's mind over the previous three decades. Struggling to find some definite point of disagreement while recognising his own sympathy with Lindsay's anti-utilitarian stance, he began by emphasising the pluralist foundations of the latter. It seemed to him that in projecting society's 'general will' as somehow 'focused' in the first instance by voluntary societies like presbyteries, Lindsay had allowed the notion of 'citizenship' as a distinct and overriding identity to slide into the background. In this sense he showed himself a better Idealist than Lindsay by salvaging political life from the morass of groups, deep in their partial communions.

In another sense, though, Barker showed himself much less of an Idealist than his contemporary. This emerged, paradoxically, from his invocation of a standard Idealist belief that the state was not directly concerned with 'moral issues, but only with the one issue of providing that legal framework of life within which all moral issues

[11] A.D. Lindsay, *The Essentials of Democracy* (1929; London, 1935), 74.

[12] G. Maddox, 'The Christian democracy of A.D. Lindsay', *Political Studies*, 34, 3 (1986), 455; see also H.A. Holloway, 'A.D. Lindsay and the problems of mass democracy', in *Western Political Quarterly*, 16, 4 (1963), 798–813.

must be freely settled by individuals for themselves'. It may seem a purely pedantic objection to have levelled against a writer who would not have thought otherwise. However, the point was perhaps worth raising given that Barker's purpose in doing so was to emphasise the purely formal nature of the 'common life' as achieved through the state, its sole purpose being to 'guarantee the rights of persons'. In this, he may be seen as part of a general, 'centrist' trend in liberal thought during the interwar period which marked a retreat from the earlier, New Liberal assignment of ethical ends to the state, at least those which were defined in communal terms.[13] As we shall see presently, he was apt to adopt a more orthodox Idealist position on the nature of society, seeing greater possibilities for *Gemeinschaft* there than in the state. In 1930 Barker evidently sensed, and sensed correctly, that Lindsay yearned for a stronger conception of the 'common life' at the political level than he himself believed was possible. This difference reflected an ambiguity at the heart of the Idealist theory of the state which was discussed in earlier chapters.[14]

Barker also maintained that Lindsay had shown insufficient appreciation for the 'political machinery' of the state, so concerned was he with its role in enhancing the moral life of society. Here again, the two men were *prima facie*, at least, not so far apart since Lindsay had brought precisely the same charge against Bosanquet in 1928. It seemed to Lindsay that for Bosanquet, the 'general will' which underlay human society was somehow 'automatically' reflected in the state. It did not matter to Bosanquet whether the general will was consciously apprehended by citizens or not. Consequently, in Lindsay's view, Bosanquet had failed to appreciate the importance of the constitution in giving 'unity and regimentation to the common life of society'; he had 'too little interest in juristic questions to go into such matters'.[15] But this concern was not apparent to Barker in reviewing Lindsay's *The Essentials of Democracy*. Here, Barker's breach with Idealism became fairly wide. The Whig source of his dissatisfaction is evident in the following passage, which is worth quoting at length.

[13] M. Freedman, *Liberalism Divided: A Study in British Political Thought, 1914–1939* (Oxford, 1986), 128, although Freeden rather dramatises this retreat and is vague about its character. Thus, he argues, centrist-liberalism 'refused to subscribe any further to a faith in the state as the disinterested agent of the community, reverting instead to a more individualistic conception of human nature and social relations'. In addition, the 'old' liberal concern with constitutionalism as an ingredient of 'centrist-liberalism' is missing from Freeden's account.

[14] See chs. 3 and 4 below.

[15] A.D. Lindsay, 'Bosanquet's theory of the General Will', *Proceedings of the Aristotelian Society* (1928), supp. vol. 8, 41, 43.

One who has lectured for many years on English Constitutional History cannot but acquire a deep sense of the value of a 'law-state' which has guaranteed men's rights with singular success, and of a 'free State' which has developed, again with singular success, the working of a representative assembly and a system of responsible government. It is easy to smile at the paean on the English constitution with which Blackstone concludes his *Commentaries*; and yet, after all, what a scheme of ordered law and organised liberty it is, and how it lets each of us build up his own life in its shelter![16]

For Barker, the charm of this Whig vision of the English polity had grown over the years, and it continued to grow. In 1944 he openly acknowledged his allegiance to 'the constant stars of the ancient Whig tradition'.[17] Three years later, he described himself in similar terms as 'an old Liberal, [who] belongs to the tradition of 1688'.[18]

We should not, of course, make too much of Barker's differences with Lindsay in this 1930 review, nor his explicit identification with Whiggism in the following decade. Much of what he wrote in the 1930s was eminently continuous with ideas which he had expressed before. For example, he never abandoned the (mild) Idealist agenda for social change which he had adopted earlier in the century. In a speech to the Liberal Summer School in 1933, he emphasised the need to extend the central respect in Britain for 'the sanctity of human personality' into the economic realm, much of the force of this plea undoubtedly stemming from Green's remarks on the need for some limitations to be made on the right of 'freedom of contract'.[19] To this end, Barker signed the manifesto of resurgent progressivism in 1935 entitled *The Next Five Years: An Essay in Political Agreement.*[20] Furthermore, as has been stressed throughout this study, he had always insisted upon the primary political value of individual liberty; and he had always implicitly associated the 'external framework of rights' as the condition of moral goodness in Idealism with the English 'law-state' that was celebrated in Whiggism. Moreover, it would be plausible to explain Barker's reservations in 1930 about placing too high a premium on the moral aspect of the state against the backdrop of current events in Britain; most notably the campaign of the recent

16 E. Barker, 'Democracy and social justice', *Contemporary Review* (March 1930), 302.

17 E. Barker, 'Foreword' to Viscount Hinchingbrooke, *Full Speed Ahead! Essays in Tory Reform* (London, 1944).

18 E. Barker, 'Mr. Amery's thoughts on the Constitution', *The Fortnightly Review* (July 1947), 178.

19 Reported in *The Liberal Magazine*, 41 (September 1933), 434.

20 As Michael Freeden has argued, this document made rhetorical references to the ideal of 'economic justice' as the key to the future of the democratic state. However, its proposals fell markedly short of its radical vision. *Liberalism Divided*, 356–63.

Home Secretary, William Joynson Hicks, to purify public morals as a new mood of gaiety seized interwar Britain.[21] Certainly, this context illuminates his concern with highlighting the merely 'indirect' role of the state in improving the moral life of its citizens, expressed, as it was, 'in days when uninstructed goodwill is apt to cry to the State, "you must make men sober"'.[22]

However, Barker's review of Lindsay's *The Essentials of Democracy* suggests a much keener sense than at any time previously that the moral preoccupations of Idealism had impeded a fuller understanding of the legal fabric of the state. In addition, he repeated similar misgivings about Idealism four years after the review, indicating that they represented more than simply a passing response to developments on the home front in the latter half of the 1920s. In fact, they were closely bound up with a shift in his historical interests away from ancient Greek and recent political thought which had concerned him hitherto and towards the early-modern period, the heyday of natural law and social contract theory.[23] In this age he found ideas which were vital to combating the rising tide of Fascist and Communist dictatorship in Europe. In order to make room for them, though, the Idealist conception of the state as a moral community had to be diluted with older theories, theories which had assumed a new relevance to one whose Whig sensibilities had emerged to the forefront of his thought.

GIERKE AND THE INDEPENDENCE OF LAW

The place in which Barker's doubts about Idealism resurfaced in 1934 was the introduction to his translation of parts of the last volume of Otto Von Gierke's *Genossenschaftsrecht* published in 1913. In order to appreciate this dimension of the essay, however, it is first necessary to explore its wider themes.

The sections of Gierke's work with which Barker was concerned in this translation dealt with natural law theories of society and the state between 1500 and 1800. In undertaking the project, he consciously followed in the footsteps of Maitland who had translated sections of the third volume in 1900. However, less sympathetic than his mentor to the theory of human associations as 'real personalities' which

[21] R. Blythe, *The Age of Illusion: Glimpses of Britain between the Wars, 1919–1940* (Oxford, 1983), ch. 2.
[22] E. Barker, 'Democracy and social justice', 303.
[23] The special subject he offered in the History Tripos was 'English Political Thought during the American and French Revolutions'. *The Student's Handbook to Cambridge* (Cambridge, 1931).

Gierke had ardently espoused, Barker played up the merits of its rival which had emerged from the joint forces of Roman law and natural law.

The essence of this competing view was that groups – whether the state or 'voluntary' bodies more strictly conceived – were rooted in contract between individuals who were assumed to be free of all social ties. Contract being a universal act which transcended the customs and outlook of each society, it was depicted in the natural law tradition as subject to one overriding law. In his introduction, Barker traced this idea forward from Roman law to medieval jurisprudence. There the implications of a belief in the existence of a 'common law of humanity' – originally held by the Stoic thinkers of ancient Greece – were fully drawn out.[24]

That natural law might constitute a higher authority than positive law in some way was the main point of interest which he found in Gierke's analysis of the idea as it became secularised in the early-modern period. His attraction to natural law had much to do with his disdain for the intellectual force with which it came into sharp conflict in the eighteenth century: that is, historical law founded upon a 'folk-will'. He was considerably alarmed by the revival of the latter in his own time as he identified a new form of political activism on the Continent to which messianic nationalism had given rise. He had himself observed that phenomenon in Germany and Italy during visits to those two countries in 1934, fulfilling the hopes of the founders of his Chair that he would imbue his subject with first-hand experience of political systems abroad.[25] He included Soviet Communism in his understanding of the totalitarian outcome of the resurgence of Romanticism in modern politics; for all its rejection of mysticism and transcendentalism in favour of materialism, the ruling ideology in Russia transformed 'class' into 'folk' and mobilised an entire society in pursuit of its apocalyptic ideal.[26] He leant on the Nazi theorist Carl Schmitt here, emphasising the importance of Schmitt's conception of the distinctiveness of the twentieth-century state in

[24] His interest in the development of the idea of natural law was perhaps prompted by James Bryce's essay on 'The law of nature', in *Studies in History and Jurisprudence*, 2 vols., II (Oxford, 1901), 112–71. Certainly, Barker's account resembles Bryce's at several points, not least that natural law was by no means alien to English common law, 164–7.

[25] E. Barker, *Age and Youth*, 172–3.

[26] E. Barker, *Reflections on Government* (Oxford, 1942), 163. This book was based on lectures he had delivered in the 1930s. For other instances of his reaction to Soviet Communism, see 'Rival faiths?', in H. Wilson Harris (ed.), *Christianity and Communism* (Oxford, 1937), 1–9; and his response to George Bernard Shaw on 'Democracy and the Soviet' in *The Times*, 20 November 1933.

which the differences between Fascism and Communism dissolved. That distinctiveness lay in the supersession of the old Liberal-Democratic order – with its ineliminable 'dualism' between state and individual and state and society – by a new 'triune' system. By this, explained Barker, Schmitt meant the dominance of both state and society by a 'single movement or party', one which was bent on destroying all social and political opposition.[27]

The threat which Schmitt's 'friend and foe' – or 'comrade and stranger' – model of politics posed to the impersonality of the modern state greatly agitated Barker in the 1930s.[28] The 'militarization' of politics – the conception of the political as an arena of total war – offended all the virtues of decency, moderation, and the peaceful resolution of conflict which he found in historic parliamentary systems. He looked on developments in all three totalitarian countries as the apotheosis of the doctrine of the 'rights of groups' which had made such large strides in his own country at the turn of the century and which had been informed – through Gierke – by a Romantic theory of the group. 'Historical Law' – law that was grounded by its exponents in the national life of each community and believed to be infused with the 'soul' of its people – was not a concept to which Barker ever warmed. In his view it was a peculiarly German doctrine, the effect of which he described graphically as the transformation of whole societies into 'super-personal realities . . . great Brocken spectres, confronting us as we walk'. While it might ennoble the individual by lifting him out of his self-centred existence, the theory of groups as real persons also 'engulfs his life, and absorbs his individuality'.[29] Natural law provided an individualist and humanitarian antidote that was all the more welcome for its accessible philosophical foundations. On these scores it also embodied, in Barker's view, the ultimate tie between 'Christian principle and civil government', Christianity likewise being concerned with 'the common nature of man' and 'the rights of man as man'.[30]

[27] E. Barker, *The Citizen's Choice* (Cambridge, 1938), 12.

[28] E. Barker, *Reflections on Government*, 270.

[29] Otto Gierke, *Natural Law and the Theory of Society 1500–1800*, trans. with an introduction by E. Barker, 2 vols. (Cambridge, 1934), vol. 1, xvii.

[30] E. Barker, 'Christian principle and civil government', *The Guardian*, 10 November 1939. He rejected all attempts to formulate more specific conceptions of the relationship between Christianity and politics that could be applied to policy-making. Writing to M.B. Reckitt – a former pupil and Christian Socialist – in 1932, he argued that 'if we tie up our Faith with this or that solution of the detail, we box it in too small a receptacle'. Barker to Reckitt, 3 October 1932, Reckitt Papers, University of Sussex Library, 10/1.

Barker allowed his long-standing antipathy to German thought full expression in the Gierke Introduction.[31] Whereas he conceived German thought as a 'heaving and tumultuous thing', French thought seemed to possess a 'clearer air'; formal and even superficial though it might be, it had the merits of 'classicism' and 'simplicity'. It was with a mixture of pleasure, relief, and admiration that Barker read the lecture of the German historicist thinker, Ernst Troeltsch, in 1922 on 'The Ideas of Natural Law and Humanity'. This acknowledged the loss which Germany's departure from the natural law lines of Western European thought represented within the Romantic movement, and attempted to build bridges back to that mainstream. Barker included a translation of the lecture as an appendix to the Gierke volume.

In the same vein, he often extolled in the 1930s Gierke's similar appreciation for the natural law tradition. He never tired of quoting a passage from Gierke's book on Johannes Althusius published in 1880 which declared that 'the undying spirit of [natural] law can never be extinguished', the section from which it was taken forming another appendix to the Gierke volume. That assertion provided a constant source of strength as Nazism and Fascism gained ground in the 1930s, with their gospel of 'revolutionary legality'. As he argued in his Herbert Spencer Memorial Lecture delivered in 1938, natural law served as a reminder in these crisis-ridden times that: 'A people does not make its law for itself by an exclusive act of "autarky" in declaring what it will regard as law. It has and it needs a collaborator – the thought of its thinkers and thinkers of other countries, . . . pursued . . . through all the centuries, about what is just and right in the mutual relations of men.'[32]

This claim was fully in keeping with the twofold sanction which Gierke lent to natural law: one negative and the other positive. First, natural law for Gierke was not a set of laws deduced from the operation of reason by which the validity of positive laws could be

[31] Although at the time he wrote of this antipathy as a current mood only. In a letter to H.A.L. Fisher, he proclaimed that 'I have a general dislike for German *Lehre* at the moment. I am just finishing a biggish volume on Gierke's Political Theories of the Modern [*sic*] Age . . . and two years spent among German theorists have almost destroyed me.' The letter was a response to Fisher's suggestions that he write a book on Marx for the Home University Library, of which series Fisher was an editor. Barker declined in deference to other projects, and the contract went to Isaiah Berlin instead. Barker to Fisher, 30 July 1933, MS. Murray 408, fol. 165, Bodleian Library.

[32] E. Barker, 'Natural law in the political world', *The Hibbert Journal*, 36 (1938), 490.

tested.[33] Similarly, Barker insisted that the roots of natural law lay firmly in society and history, not in imaginings about a pre-political state of nature with which the natural law tradition had become temporarily associated in the early-modern period. It was important to Barker that natural law had a 2,000-year history, beginning with the Stoics in ancient Greece. It was thus no intellectual fantasy but a doctrine imbued with all 'the quality of historical fact'.[34] In this sense, it should be seen as having 'evolved' in the same way as national systems of law. The only difference with the latter was the aim of its votaries – mainly 'an elite of jurists and thinkers' – to devise a law for 'the community of mankind' based on common human needs and instincts. But Barker could find nothing discreditable in this endeavour. To denounce its universalist ambitions and to mistake its foundations as 'abstract' – as was the wont of nineteenth-century Burkean Whigs, for example – was to ignore a powerful spiritual force in human history. He seemed to revert here to one of his long-standing beliefs in the existence of a 'conviction' running through the centuries that:

> mankind has common rules of life with which the various positive laws, and the various communities or nations which have deposited those laws, must ultimately accord and ultimately be reconciled. No community, and no community-law is ultimate. Behind such things there stands what some might call . . . the sense of the civilised world, but what may better be called, in a simpler and more traditional term, the law of nature – the law of the nature of man, expressed in the conviction of human thought about the requirements and demands of that nature in the sphere of men's external relations with one another.[35]

The second – positive – basis of Gierke's appreciation of natural law and which, again, Barker echoed was its suggestion of 'the sovereign independence of the idea of Justice'. This was an insight, Gierke believed, which had also been embodied in historical law from its inception, although to a much lesser extent in recent times. Concerned about trends in Germany to reduce the substance of law to the idea of 'Utility' and its power to that of 'force', he praised the way in which the 'idea' of law was vindicated in natural law as bearing an 'original and independent' title to existence. Distancing himself from

[33] S. Mogi, *Otto Von Gierke: His Political Teaching and Jurisprudence* (London, 1932), 142. Gierke's sympathy with the natural law tradition, at any level, is overlooked by Roger Scruton in his recent recruitment of Gierke to the Conservative tradition. See 'Gierke and the corporate person', in *The Philosopher on Dover Beach* (Manchester, 1990).

[34] E. Barker, 'Natural law and the political world', 485.

[35] Ibid., 487–8.

the contemporary tendency to equate law with 'will' rather than conceiving it as a set of external standards for the actions of 'free wills', Gierke showed his full Idealist credentials.[36]

However, Gierke's Idealism was peculiar in this regard. As Sobrei Mogi perceptively noted in 1932, many Idealists attached only a secondary importance to law, as against the derivation of an ethical law from a general human idea. They either conceived law as an external aid to the fulfilment of an ethical purpose, or as an instrument in realising a social ideal which was also imposed upon it from outside. For Gierke, though, in Mogi's view, 'if any ideas at all can be seen operative in the history of mankind, the idea of law must be thought of as an original and unique spiritual emanation of human nature'.[37] Herein lay the main source of Gierke's attraction to natural law, and one which is equally visible in Barker's commendation of that tradition. When he praised natural law for showing 'how much a philosophy of law . . . can contribute to political theory', Barker revealed his thorough identification with Gierke's effort to elevate law in Idealist discourse.[38] The polemical edge of this claim in regard to British Idealism will become apparent presently.

Yet Barker felt that, important as Gierke's deference to natural law was, nevertheless he remained a 'Germanist of the Germanists, nurtured in the tradition of the Folk and instinct with the philosophy of *Volksgeist* and *Volksrecht*'.[39] Such avowals as the latter, he believed, were incompatible with the vision of individual liberty and human unity which had inspired natural law thinkers since the Stoics. For more forceful examples of the connections he perceived between positive law and natural law, he looked to English legal and political thought in the seventeenth and eighteenth centuries. This suggested that native respect for English law and institutions was not quite so divorced from the natural law project as the Burkean tradition presupposed. Again, we find Barker pressing natural law ideas into a Burkean mould, implying that the latter had not recognised a valuable ally when it saw one. He was particularly struck by the obeisance which Blackstone paid to the authority of natural law in the introduction to his *Commentaries*, despite his subsequent and incongruent eulogy to the unique liberties enjoyed by Englishmen in the rest of the book. Barker added to this example the *obiter dictum* of an English judge in 1641 to the effect that Acts of Parliament which transgressed the

36 Gierke, *Natural Law and the Theory of Society*, 224.
37 S. Mogi, *Otto Von Gierke*, 140–1.
38 Gierke, *Natural Law and the Theory of Society*, xxviii.
39 Ibid., lvi.

principles of 'natural equity' were null and void. Locke's political philosophy also counted for him as an important landmark in the English reception of natural law. As he wrote in *The Times* on the tercentenary of Locke's birth in 1932:

We are generally prone to think of Locke as the exponent of the Social Contract. It would be more just to think of him as the exponent of the sovereignty of Natural Law. He put into plain English, and he dressed in an English dress of sober grey cloth, doctrines which ultimately go back to the Porch and the Stoic teachers of antiquity.

It was primarily as a theorist of parliamentary government that Locke – and the Whig Party which adopted his principles – received Barker's acclaim; they stood behind an institution which, he maintained, 'may justly be called the great contribution of England to Europe, and, beyond Europe, to other continents'.[40] A cosmopolitan and imperialist Whig, Barker was inevitably attracted to the universal claims of natural law which underpinned Locke's theory of (English) government and made the latter ripe for export. He found a final illustration of the links between natural law and English law in the American Revolution. Whilst, on the one hand, American lawyers seized upon the right of revolution entailed by Blackstone's defence of the supremacy of natural law, yet they made their cause the 'ancient doctrine of the common law' which had allegedly been flouted in recent British policy towards the colony.[41]

Evidently, Barker loaded the concept of natural law with both Idealist and Whig meanings. But he did not do so in equal proportions, certainly if Idealism is taken in its British form. To the crucial value which, following Gierke, he perceived in natural law – that of expressing the *idea* of law as an independent and primordial force in human society and politics – he found English Idealism largely indifferent. The context in which his misgivings about the latter emerged on this score was a comparison between 'English political science' and its continental counterpart which went very much in the latter's favour. This important sub-text of Barker's Gierke essay will repay closer examination since it developed the themes which he had set out in his review of Lindsay's *The Essentials of Democracy* four years earlier.

[40] E. Barker, *The Times*, 29 August 1932.

[41] Gierke, *Natural Law and the Theory of Society*, xlvi–xlvii; E. Barker, 'Blackstone and the British Constitution', in *Essays on Government* (Oxford, 1945), 141. While this essay was written in 1943, its roots were in the previous decade when Barker lectured at Cambridge on the history of political ideas in England during the second half of the eighteenth century. Barker's cosmopolitanism and imperialism will be considered in more detail in ch. 8 below.

THE SHORTCOMINGS OF ENGLISH POLITICAL SCIENCE

Barker's focus on the centrality of law to politics was by now a familiar theme of his writings. However, it had acquired a special urgency of late with the erosion of constitutionalism in Europe; so much so, in fact, that he directly confronted the shortcomings of 'English political science' in this regard. At the outset of his introduction to Gierke, Barker ventured to argue that, as a result of an over-concentration on the moral dimensions of political life, '[o]ur English political science has had no great method'. By and large, the subject had been cultivated by 'politicians with a philosophic gift or philosophers with a practical interest'. In the former camp, he placed Sidney, Burke, Morley, and Bryce; in the latter, Adam Smith, Paley, Sidgwick, Green, and Bosanquet. Either way, the result had been that a concern for understanding the 'normative' character of the state had become the primary goal of political inquiry. The tradition of 'humanism' in the ancient universities was largely responsible for the heightened English interest in the moral foundations of politics. But while the importance of this focus could not be gainsaid, nevertheless without an equal regard for the legal side of the state, political science was simply 'a loose congeries of facile *aperçus*'. In this respect, English political thinkers could learn a few lessons from their continental colleagues, amongst whom the lawyers were represented in far higher numbers. Indeed:

> To study modern French political theory is to study the lawyers – Esmein, Hauriou, Barthélemy, Duguit: it is to study works which generally go by the style of *Traité du Droit constitutionnel.* To study modern German political theory is equally to study the lawyers – Jellinek, Kelson and Schmitt; and if treatises are written on the theory of the State (*allgemeine Staatslehre*), as well as *Staatsrecht* proper, we find they are written by professors of law.[42]

Of course, Barker had not forgotten a coterie that might count as an English equivalent, one which had aroused his keen sensitivity to the close relationship between law and politics in the first place. This comprised the Victorian jurists Maine, Dicey, and Maitland, and behind them in an earlier period, Blackstone, Bentham, and Austin. But against the towering influence of the lawyers on the discipline of political science in continental Europe, these names seemed merely 'scattered lights rather than a constellation'. It was not that their

[42] Gierke, *Natural Law and the Theory of Society*, xix–xxi.

impact on the subject had been negligible; on the contrary, as he argued in his inaugural lecture in 1928, they had made a substantial impact on English political thought. But their contribution was limited by the nature of the constitutional practices which they studied: because of the indeterminate nature of the English constitution, they had merely 'disengag[ed] . . . broad constitutional principles from the body of our law'. The upshot of the dominance of the common law in English constitutional development was that no 'separate' legal science of the state existed in England; no *Staatsrecht* on the model of Germany.[43] Consequently – he drove the message home in the Gierke Introduction – moral philosophy presided over the study of politics in England, with clear detrimental effects.

Barker's list of English thinkers who had – in effect – stifled political science in this way was sufficiently miscellaneous to avoid the suggestion that any one school of thought should shoulder the main responsibility. However, his projection of English political science as primarily concerned with ethics was undoubtedly inspired by the great sway which Idealism exercised over the discipline in his intellectually formative years; and his Gierke Introduction was undoubtedly something of a reaction against it. It came close to an admission that Idealism constituted, at best, simply a partial framework for the study of politics. His vision of political science was not one in which the pendulum had swung far in the opposite direction: to 'the arid regions of legal metaphysics'. If political inquiry considered the state as a legal association, it should never neglect the 'ends or purposes' which underpinned it. This would inevitably take the subject into the realm of morals to discover 'some ultimate ethical principle' that lay at the root of all human organisation. Yet whilst he attempted to salvage something from Idealist 'political science' here, his definition of 'ultimate ends' was more redolent of J.S. Mill than Green or any other Idealist thinker, especially when stated in the following, unqualified form. 'To many', maintained Barker, in his usual way demolishing the opposition by amassing unspecified support against it, 'that ultimate principle has always seemed the intrinsic value of the human personality.'

But nowadays, he believed, the primacy of individuality in political life was increasingly sacrificed before the needs of the group. This seemed clear in the ascendancy of conceptions of 'economic solidarity'

[43] E. Barker, 'The study of political science', in *Church, State, and Study* (London, 1930), 205–6.

or 'social utility' in recent social thought.[44] The immediate target of Barker's remarks here were the recent legal philosophies of Leon Duguit and Roscoe Pound; yet they were all of a piece with his wider strictures on the flames of nationalist feeling which were being strenuously fanned at the time. In these circumstances, he gave free reign to his individualist instincts. This is especially apparent in his endorsement of a qualified form of social contract theory. Barker was not so keen to dismiss the social contract phase in the development of natural law theory as other Idealists like Gierke, who, apart from this dimension was sympathetic to the wider tradition. He was unapologetic about the individualism of social contract thinkers given his view that 'individual personality is the one intrinsic value of human life'.[45] Furthermore, he sought to uphold the idea of contract as the root of political society, this being crucial to his idea that the state constituted a legal association above all else. Here again, his Whig view of English history seems to have got the better of his Idealism, even though, as ever, he aimed at a compromise. For his endorsement of a contract theory of government was much inspired by thoughts of the English Revolution of 1688, a landmark in the Whig interpretation of English history. Interpreting constitutionalism as fundamentally contractual in nature, he conceived that event as an act whereby a pre-existing national society made a legal covenant with itself; henceforth, it agreed that government should be conducted in accordance with certain 'articles of association'. In the lectures which Barker delivered at Cambridge and which he later published as *The Principles of Social and Political Theory* (1951), he projected this 'shift of ideas' in English national society as heralding similar movements worldwide; after the Hanoverian period when England finally acquired a 'settled state', constitutionalism spread to North America and France in the eighteenth century and then to the rest of Western Europe, South America and the countries of the British Commonwealth in the nineteenth century.

Of course, he maintained, the state in its constitutional guise existed in some form before these times, not least in England. Here, constitutionalism had gone hand in hand with the establishment and development of institutions of representative democracy since the thirteenth century. As Barker rather Whiggishly proposed in a German magazine in 1939, parliamentary democracy possessed a

[44] Gierke, *Natural Law and the Theory of Society*, xxvi–vii. [45] Ibid., xlix.

'long and continuous history' in Britain, older than 1832 when it was formally recognised as such. Addressing a nation which had now all but abandoned that path, he made what was perhaps a last-minute plea for a stay of its execution. Thus, he recommended the parliamentary system as one which in England had historically promoted national unity, 'whatever our differences and divisions'.[46]

But regardless of the form which the modern state may have taken and the liberties which may have existed before the seventeenth century, only afterwards did it become 'a specifically legal association'.[47] By implanting contract in historical time in this way, Barker attempted to extricate the notion from the hypothetical state of nature for which it had been much maligned. Yet, as he continually emphasised, such a usage would only support the idea of a political contract, not a wider social contract. He fully retained the Burkean/Idealist conception of society (and the state in its embryonic form) as an organic growth. Thus, he was at pains to point out that in establishing civil government the societies he mentioned had only turned part of themselves into a legal association.[48] Ever concerned to maintain a distinction between society and the state, he defined the former in terms of a 'common culture' and the latter in terms of law. He lent heavily here on Paul Vinogradoff, a legal theorist and historian of the generation of Maitland and Dicey, whom Barker had known during his Oxford years. A Russian emigré who greatly admired the English constitutional tradition, Vinogradoff defined the state in 1922 as a 'juridically organized nation, or a nation organized for action under legal rules'.[49] To Barker, this suggested the impersonal nature of the state which had historically prevailed in Western Europe at least, but which had been greatly undermined of late by what he termed the 'eruption of the personal' factor in politics. Nothing could be more remote from his ideal of the 'impersonal rule of law' and the impersonal institutions which gave effect to it than the ascendancy of the *Fuhrer-prinzip* in contemporary Germany.[50]

But again, in wanting the best of both worlds – a world of organic

[46] E. Barker, 'The rise of democracy in England', *Deutsche-Englesche Heft*, 3 (June 1939), 81.

[47] E. Barker, *Principles of Social and Political Theory* (Oxford, 1951; 1961), 205.

[48] Gierke, *Natural Law and the Theory of Society*, xxiii; E. Barker, *Principles of Social and Political Theory*, 190.

[49] P. Vinogradoff, *Historical Jurisprudence*, vol. I, 85, quoted in E. Barker, *Principles of Social and Political Theory*, 56. Vinogradoff also set out his theory of the state as a legal organisation in his essay 'The juridical nature of the state', *The Collected Papers of Paul Vinogradoff*, 2 vols. (Oxford, 1928), vol. II, 350–66.

[50] E. Barker, *Reflections on Government*, 136.

growth, on the one hand, and of contract, on the other – Barker reached an extremely delicate synthesis. This was apparent to contemporaries who, while praising his scholarship in bringing more of Gierke's work to the attention of English readers, nonetheless noted the inconsistencies into which he had been led in interpreting it. Michael Oakeshott, for example – who taught with Barker at Cambridge in the 1930s – detected all the pitfalls of seventeenth-century individualism in his senior colleague's theory. He considered Barker's conception of the 'partial' nature of the political contract as reminiscent of earlier, implicitly Lockean notions that some rights were reserved when individuals entered into civil society; and it was unsatisfactory as a result. Reviewing Barker's introduction to Gierke, Oakeshott remarked with evident disagreement that 'in dealing with society and the state we are presented with a relationship between two separate entities, the one lying "behind" or "stretching outside" the other'.[51] Despite their common sympathies in many areas of political philosophy, a substantial intellectual rift existed between the two men which is well reflected in their choice of early-modern heroes: while Barker followed Locke's route to the limited state, Oakeshott took the more unconventional path of Hobbes.[52]

Considerable attention has been given above to Barker's move away from Idealism in the 1930s. But how much distance had he actually moved from that philosophy? Whilst he certainly sought to modify its impact on the study of politics in order that law might exert a greater influence on the discipline, he found two other areas of concern in the 1930s to which it might be applied with fewer reservations. The first was sociology and social science; the second, the building of local communities.

SOCIAL SCIENCE AND COMMUNITY-BUILDING

Barker had always taken a keen interest in the social sciences. In writings such as his book on *Political Thought in England from Herbert Spencer to the Present Day* and his inaugural lecture on *The Study of*

[51] M. Oakeshott, 'The theory of society', *The Cambridge Review*, 56, 12 October 1934, 11.

[52] See Oakeshott's introduction to Hobbes' *Leviathan*, first published in 1937 and reprinted in M. Oakeshott, *Hobbes on Civil Association* (Oxford, 1946). Denying that Hobbes was an absolutist in government, Oakeshott wrote that '[t]he natural right surrendered is the unconditional right, on all occasions, to exercise one's individual will in the pursuit of felicity . . . But to surrender an absolute right to do something on all occasions, is not to give up the right of doing it on any occasion.' 62.

Political Science, he had sought to link all the various disciplines of social science to one common scholarly enterprise. However, this usually entailed their subordination to his own subject, political theory. From the outset of his career, he had been much attracted to Aristotle's notion of political science as 'the master science' on the grounds of its concern with the 'ultimate end' – that of man.[53] Moreover, he never ceased to affirm the Idealist understanding of human life as purposeful and rational. When adapted to this idiom, he lent his wholehearted support to disciplinary ventures such as sociology. For example, he attempted, in 1915, to narrow the divide between political philosophy and sociology which had been precipitated by the emphasis upon the primacy of instinct over reason in recent contributions to the latter subject. Addressing the sociological theory of Benjamin Kidd, Gabriel Tarde, and his friend Graham Wallas, he asserted:

> The sociologist will start from habits, instincts, emotions, but at any rate he will end in a conception of association as based on intelligent reason. The political theorist starts at the opposite end with rational association; but he admits that there exists, and must be taken into account, a sub-rational area of instinct. The difference between the two methods is not profound.[54]

Barker pursued his attempt to harness the study of politics and sociology – with the former as the superior partner – in the interwar period. For example, he became President of the Institute of Sociology in London in 1935, a post which he held for the next three years, and was a leading advocate of a new tripos in 'Social and Political Studies' at Cambridge six years earlier.[55] However, the grounds on which he urged such an alliance had changed slightly over the years. While earlier he had attempted to close the gap between the two subjects conceived as 'instinct' versus 'reason', in later years he associated sociology with the general study of groups, and political science proper with the legal side of the state. This is certainly the implication of his introduction to Gierke, despite some casual remarks there that 'political theory' was not only synonymous with political science but social science at large. What he wanted to emphasise by this comment was that the state could not be studied in

[53] E. Barker, *The Political Thought of Plato and Aristotle* (1906; New York, 1959), 239.

[54] E. Barker, *Political Thought in England from Herbert Spencer to the Present Day* (London, 1915), 160.

[55] He delivered three addresses as President of the Institute: 'The social background of recent political changes', *The Sociological Review*, 28 (1936), 117–32; 'Maitland as a sociologist', *The Sociological Review*, 29, no. 2, (1937), 121–35; and 'The contact of cultures in India', *The Sociological Review*, 30 (1938), 105–19.

isolation from other social forces.[56] However, the logic of his argument about the vital connection between legal and political science was to leave the study of the 'cohesions' and 'unities' in the wider society to the province of sociology. This was the consequence, as he understood it, of Gierke's conception of *Recht* as existing within a sphere of social organisms bound by 'living relations'.[57]

There was a good deal of Idealist aura surrounding this division of labour between legal-political science, on the one hand, and social-political science on the other. Significantly, though, Barker found it necessary to create these two distinct although related branches of the study of politics where one had proved adequate for an earlier generation of Idealists. His move in this direction is perhaps best interpreted as an effort to reconstitute Idealism as a theory of society rather than (principally) a theory of the state. This is suggested in his reservation of the term 'contract' for the establishment of political society, not society as such. Nor was he alone in this venture; A.D. Lindsay had carved out a similar future for Idealism in the 1920s, despite his inability to refrain from investing large communitarian hopes in the state. Lindsay clearly regarded this shift as not only the saving-grace of Idealism, much assailed recently for confusing the modern state with the Greek *polis*; it had also proved the redemption of modern disciplines like social psychology, economics, and sociology. For example, the latter, 'after many false starts, inspired by the mistaken belief that a scientific treatment of society should interpret higher forms in the light of lower, has now found it possible to study the manifold variety of institutional and social life on the basis provided by idealistic philosophy'.[58] It is likely that Lindsay's sense of triumph was occasioned by Hobhouse's sociological writings. Hobhouse had been a leading rebel against the Idealist theory of the state which he denounced during the First World War as a 'false and wicked' doctrine. With its alleged glorification of the state, Hobhouse held Idealism in large part accountable for that conflagration. He continued, however, to import many Idealist assumptions and values into his work as an evolutionary sociologist, conceiving the ideals of 'harmony' and 'rationality' as the underlying principles of social development.[59]

56 Gierke, *Natural Law and the Theory of Society*, xxv. 57 Ibid., xxxiii.

58 A.D. Lindsay, 'Political theory', in F.S. Marvin (ed.), *Developments in European Thought* (1920; 2nd edn, London, 1929), 169.

59 S. Collini, *Liberalism and Sociology: L.T. Hobhouse and Political Argument in England, 1880–1914* (Cambridge, 1979), 242.

Barker, at any rate, found much with which he could identify in Hobhouse's contribution to sociology. Called upon to write Hobhouse's obituary for the British Academy in 1930, he emphasised his colleague's reconciliation of the Comtean and Spencerian heritage of the subject with an Idealist philosophy of mind. The latter was all the more worthy because Hobhouse had shorn it of its 'mystical' elements and made it more 'realistic'. He stressed Hobhouse's individualist sensibilities in believing that 'ultimate good consisted in the liberation of human personality', a position with which he was in close sympathy. Perhaps most importantly, however, he was drawn to Hobhouse's idea of sociology as an inquiry into the evolution of moral life and the human quest for social justice conceived as an acceptance of mutual interdependence. In this respect, he saw Hobhouse as engaged in the same project as Plato, both being 'torn' between the two professions of philosophy and politics. If the questions which engaged Hobhouse could be termed 'Sociology', then that subject was 'old in human history'; and it had Plato as its father, rather than Comte.[60]

Again, we see Barker extending his goodwill to the discipline of sociology, once he had settled it in his own intellectual domain. Anxious to sustain a place in the human sciences for the Idealist concern with the ethical foundations of society, he saw this as a primary duty of 'social science'. Moreover, sociology not only accommodated the moral preoccupations of Idealism; it could also be made a locus for the issues raised by Pluralism earlier in the century. It will be recalled from an earlier chapter that Barker's tribute to 'Maitland as a Sociologist', which he made in his capacity as President of the Institute of Sociology in 1936, was based on Maitland's appreciation of the extent to which groups rather than individuals constituted the chief social nexus.[61] Well attuned to the image of the richness of group life in England which had forcefully emerged in Maitland's writings, Barker made the study of groups

[60] E. Barker, 'Leonard Trelawny Hobhouse, 1864–1929', *Proceedings of the British Academy*, 15 (1930), 554.

[61] E. Barker, 'Maitland as a sociologist', 121–35. Barker's claim to sociological authority for both Maitland and himself would not have seemed untoward to at least one member of the growing sociological profession after the Second World War. For example, T.H. Marshall – who became Professor of Sociology at the London School of Economics in 1946 – traced his route to the subject through the writings on medieval society of Seebohm, Vinogradoff, and Maitland while reading history at Cambridge; and subsequently his acquaintance with Wallas, Lowes Dickinson, and Barker. Marshall's 'A British sociological career', *International Social Science Journal*, 25 (1973), 88–99.

central to the field of sociology. Spelling out the content of sociology at a conference on the social sciences in London in 1936, he maintained that it was concerned with 'the action of the group on its individual members, and their reaction on the group: it deals with the relations and interactions of groups'.[62]

It is clear, however, that in Barker's mind, this specific study of groups would be underpinned by a general ethical-social theory of the kind which had been furnished by Hobhouse's writings. Certainly, he linked the study of groups and the study of morals in his attempt in 1930 to persuade Cambridge to provide for the study of sociology as well as political science. This would take the form of a Chair or Readership in Sociology together with a new Tripos in Social and Political Studies. Here he joined forces with W.R. Sorley – Professor of Moral Philosophy – Michael Oakeshott, and a few other sympathisers. They presented their case in terms of the fulfilment of 'the general plan for the development of the social sciences' intended by the Rockefeller Foundation when Barker's own Chair was established two years earlier.[63] The Senate of the university had then shown a distinct lack of enthusiasm for the foundation's proposal to reverse the poor fortunes of sociology in England by making Cambridge a centre for its study, alongside that of political science.[64] Barker's support for realising the full vision of the Rockefeller Memorial when he arrived at Cambridge was partly grounded in a desire to overcome his marginal intellectual position in the History Faculty; he anticipated that the establishment of a new tripos, even if restricted to Part II of another degree, would give him a more distinctive position at Cambridge.[65] But he had strong intellectual as well as personal reasons for pressing sociology's case. These are apparent in his response to a request for his definition of social science at a meeting of the General Board of Faculties at Cambridge in May 1930, at which a Majority Report of a committee in favour of developing the subject was discussed. According to a record of the proceedings, Barker maintained that 'social science' embraced:

the general study of all forms of groups, both considered historically and

[62] E. Barker, Foreword to J.E. Dugdale (ed.), *Further Papers on the Social Sciences: Their Relations in Theory and Teaching* (London, 1937), 10 (vol. III of The Institute of Sociology's *The Social Sciences: Their Relations in Theory and Teaching* (London, 1936–7)).

[63] W.R. Sorley and Ernest Barker, Memorandum accompanying letter to the Vice-Chancellor, 17 May 1930, General Board of Faculties: Notes on Agenda, 1929–30, 227.

[64] Bulmer, 'Sociology and political science at Cambridge', 158–9.

[65] E. Barker, *Age and Youth*, 157.

from the point of view of Anthropology and studied contemporaneously. Syndicates, Corporations, etc.; the study of social values, and social principles. He referred to Hobhouse's book on *The Elements of Social Justice* [1922] as an example of the lines along which he would expect a Reader in Sociology to lecture.[66]

Hobhouse's book made little reference to the sort of Pluralist concerns which Barker identified in the first part of his definition. It began with a classic Idealist statement about the subordination of politics to ethics, and proceeded to work out the practical implications of this perspective for an ideal of 'unity of aim' and 'co-operation' amongst men.[67] But Barker obviously believed that the two dimensions of 'social science', which roughly corresponded to the Pluralist and Idealist strands of his thought, formed a coherent sociological agenda. Moreover, by stressing the need for the separate endowment of sociology, Barker in all probability hoped to disencumber the field of political science proper for the study of the state from a legal point of view.

However, the fresh proposal for a tripos in 'Social and Political Studies' met with the same frosty reception as four years previously. A Minority Report signed by J.H. Clapham and J.M. Keynes found that the study of politics was already well covered at Cambridge in the History and Economics Triposes. Whilst the report recognised that this point failed to address all the subjects which touched on 'social science' as conceived by supporters of the proposed new tripos, its authors nonetheless believed that they had considered the scheme's 'main part'. The root of their objection seems to have been the inclusion of 'Social Psychology'; without being specific, they also doubted the value to undergraduate study of some of the suggested books for the degree.[68] Whether as a result of the Minority Report or otherwise, the proposal came to nothing.

However, Barker continued to organise his own work along the lines he had suggested to the General Board in conjunction with his essay on Gierke. As required by his complex intellectual heritage, he assumed the profession of both social and political scientist. His closest outlet for this dual role at Cambridge was the teaching of a compulsory course in the Economics Tripos after 1930 entitled 'The Principles of Politics', instigated by Keynes. The course embraced:

66 'Development of political and social science in the University', General Board of Faculties: Notes on Agenda, 1930–1, 189.

67 L.T. Hobhouse, *The Elements of Social Justice* (London, 1922), Preface.

68 Note from J.H. Clapham and J.M. Keynes, undated, General Board of Faculties: Notes on Agenda, 1930–1, 72. I have been unable to locate the Majority Report.

'(a) the distinction between society and the state (b) political values, such as justice and equality (c) the grounds and limits of political obligation and (d) the functions of government and the rights of individuals'.[69] He eventually published the lectures for the course as *The Principles of Social and Political Theory* in 1951, a book which gave greater attention to 'the social' than his services to the Economics Faculty would allow. This will be seen in the following chapter.

However, if Barker's scope for 'social science' was restricted at Cambridge, he found other opportunities outside of the university. As Chairman of the Community Centres and Associations Committee of the National Council of Social Service (NCSS) from 1930 to 1942, he became an enthusiastic practitioner as well as a theorist of social science.[70] And as with his approach to sociological theory, his work for the NCSS was greatly inspired by the Idealism whose hold on the study of politics he was simultaneously attempting to loosen. It is significant that the three other leading figures in this venture were also prominent teachers of politics at this time: A.D. Lindsay was Chairman of the Unemployment Committee, J.L. Stocks (Professor of Philosophy at the University of Manchester[71]) became an advisor on housing questions, and W.G.S. Adams (Gladstone Professor of Political Theory and Institutions at Oxford) had been Chairman of the NCSS since 1919. Both Lindsay and Stocks, as well as Barker, had strong Idealist leanings and perpetuated the Idealist tradition of giving philosophy a practical edge. In this light, and with sociology noticeable for its absence in English intellectual life during the interwar period, Barker and his colleagues were prime candidates for the role of community leaders.[72] But what precise intellectual relevance did Idealism hold for this activity?

69 *The Student's Handbook to Cambridge* (Cambridge, 1930).

70 The NCSS had been established after the First World War to co-ordinate the activities of the numerous voluntary bodies concerned with social work in Britain. See M. Brasnett, *Voluntary Social Action: A History of the National Council of Social Service, 1919–1969* (London, 1969). On the circumstances of Barker's recruitment to the organisation, see his contribution to E. Elath, N. Bentwich, and D. May (eds.), *Memories of Sir Wyndham Deedes* (London, 1958), 48–51.

71 On Stocks' responsibility for directing political studies at Manchester during the interwar period, see J. Stapleton, 'Academic political thought and the development of political studies in Britain, 1900–1950', unpublished Ph.D. thesis, University of Sussex, 1986, ch. 8.

72 There is now a large literature on the so-called failure of sociology to develop in Britain before the Second World War, most of it concentrating on the nineteenth century. The most comprehensive work relating to this period is still P. Abrams, *The Origins of British Sociology, 1834–1914* (Chicago, 1968). For an early to mid-twentieth century focus, see M. Bulmer, *Essays on the History of British Sociology* (Cambridge, 1985).

While Barker may have rejected the ideal of the *polis* – as interpreted by the English Idealists – for the modern state, he showed no hesitation in applying it to local communities. His main task as Chairman of the Community Centres Committee was to promote community life on the first municipal housing estates in Britain. He held high hopes for such surroundings, looking forward to an England which would be 'dotted' with reincarnations of the Athens of antiquity. Central to this vision was each community taking charge of its own cultural well-being, emulating the excellence that had been achieved in this sphere by the inhabitants of the *polis*.[73] As a further illustration of the model of the ancient city-state from which he worked, he adopted Aristotle as his guide in determining the size of local communities; he argued in 1943, '[w]hen I preach the town of limited size, fifty to seventy-five thousand, I remember Aristotle's love of limit, of measure, of mode'. Most importantly, he was strengthened in his work as a community-builder by the most valuable lesson he derived from Aristotle's *Politics*; that 'in a town or *polis*, a group of men different from one another and contributing different things, becomes a whole which is self-sufficient for the purposes of a good life'.[74] This was a vital tenet of his Idealist theory of society; and if he ever doubted its capacity to stand up in the rather spartan face of the early English council estate – deprived of any natural, 'organic' base – a few reflections upon the strength of English 'voluntarism' would have been sufficient to reassure him. Indeed, regarding his work for the NSCC as a signal success, this reinforced the Pluralist view of English society which he had found so attractive in Maitland's writings at the turn of the century. As he wrote of this experience in his autobiography:

I had always believed in voluntary effort and the value of voluntary societies, and I had always felt that much of what was great and fine in the history of my country . . . was ultimately based on my countrymen's habit of doing things together for themselves in voluntary co-operation. What I learned of community centres and associations, as I saw them with my own eyes, and

[73] E. Barker, 'Community centres', *The Archway* (organ of the Woolwich Council of Social Service), November 1937, 53.

[74] E. Barker, 'The civic and social background of industry', *Co-Partnership*, 49, 434 (May/August 1943). Other articles written by Barker in connection with his work for the NSCC are 'Community centres and circles', *The Fortnightly Review* (March 1939), 257–66; 'New housing estates: the problem', *The Social Service Review*, 12 (1931), 47–50; 'Community life', *Community* (January/February 1938), 85; and 'The community spirit: ten years of a movement', *The Times*, 31 March 1939.

saw them actually at work, confirmed, with a visible and tangible evidence, the thoughts that had simmered in my brain as a result of my reading of history.[75]

Here again, Barker hitched together the values and insights of Idealism, on the one hand, and Pluralism on the other. He fully retained his belief in their validity, but as theories of society rather than the state. Applied at the local level, they provided a means by which the harmony and warmth of the Greek city-state could be recovered. At the national level, however, he substituted a view of political institutions that was crucially derived from Whiggism – one which emphasised their impersonal, legal nature. He attempted to connect these two models of social organisation, not least in his Aristotelian account of 'friendship' and 'fellowship' as the indispensable bases of justice. He conceived himself as engaged in some such exercise in fostering the ties of community in his work for the NCSS. At another level, as we shall see in the next chapter, he traced the lines of voluntary association across the boundary of society into that of the state, certainly the English state. But if he identified border crossings between society and state, and thereby the different traditions of thought by which he construed those terms, he insisted upon the distinctiveness of the ideals which informed them. Such an outlook assumed the co-existence of two different spheres of social life, to mutual advantage; and by its means, Barker, at least, could hold on to both of the worlds he had inherited from late-nineteenth-century political thought.

[75] E. Barker, *Age and Youth*, 176.

CHAPTER 7

Traditions of civility: the construction of Englishness in the Second World War and beyond

PRIVATE AND PUBLIC ENGLISHNESS

While Barker had always construed his role as a teacher and writer in the broadest of terms, his retirement from the Cambridge Chair in 1939 opened up new and even richer possibilities for its enactment. This was largely on account of the fact that his retirement coincided with the outbreak of the Second World War. As he wrote to Jessica Brett Young, wife of the poet Francis Brett Young, in 1944, 'It is one result of this war that it galvanises the spirits of us older men into activity which the body can hardly rise to.'[1] He quickly became a leading authority on English cultural identity in Britain, developing many of themes which he had touched upon in earlier years. This focus of his work was instrumental in securing him a wide readership, a 'partial public' to which he could bid farewell in his penultimate book.[2]

A clear preoccupation with what one historian has termed 'the Englishness of England' had emerged in literary writing during the 1930s, not all of it elegiac. This gave all the appearance of 'a nation in love with itself', offsetting the harsh cultural dissent of the 'Auden generation' for which that decade is usually renowned.[3] After the experience of Dunkirk in 1940, the idea of Englishness acquired still

[1] Barker to Jessica Brett Young, 27 December 1944, University Library, Birmingham, MS. FBY 2545.

[2] See his preface to *From Alexander to Constantine: Passages Illustrating the History of Social and Political Ideas, 336 B.C.–A.D. 337*, translated with introductions, notes and essays (Oxford, 1956). In his final book he had to apologise for this premature farewell. See *Social and Political Thought of Byzantium, from Justinian I to the Last Palaeologus, Passages from Byzantine Writers and Documents*, translated with an introduction and notes (Oxford, 1957), ix.

[3] R. Samuel (ed.), *Patriotism: The Making and Unmaking of British National Identity*, 3 vols., vol. I: *History and Politics* (London, 1989), xxx, xxiv. On the need to 'demythologise' the 1930s, recognising 'the sheer size, range, diversity, even contradictory qualities of the literature of the period', see A. Croft, 'Forward to the 1930s: the literary politics of anamnesis', in C. Shaw and M. Chase (eds.), *The Imagined Past: History and Nostalgia* (Manchester, 1989).

further emotional charge, playing a crucial role in maintaining a high level of civilian morale and eliciting the patriotism of English intellectuals across a wide range of the political spectrum.[4] On the left, George Orwell provides the clearest illustration of this wave of intense patriotic identification, drawing a warm analogy in 1941 between England and a family, albeit with 'the wrong members in control'.[5]

For Barker, Englishness during the Second World War and beyond was fundamentally related to the attitudes, values, and behaviour which prevailed in his conception of the diurnal contexts of national life. Here, he echoed a broader movement in literature during the interwar years, one in which ideals of England had become firmly 'domesticated'.[6] As such, the English spirit was traced primarily to private and local space. This interpretation of Englishness reached perhaps its most extreme expression in the 'green' and 'mystical' but much threatened world of Mary Butts' novels. England was identified there – in Patrick Wright's world – with 'a *refusal* of publicity and a flight into *secrecy*'.[7] While other writers stopped short of associating Englishness with this degree of introversion – retaining at least a limited place for the public sphere in the literary imagination – nevertheless, the 'reclusive' tendencies of the English mind and character were strongly underlined in the late 1920s and 1930s. As the Dean of St Paul's wrote in 1926, 'what governs the Englishman is his inner atmosphere. It is never a precise reason or an outer fact that determines him to choose his work or his play or his religion but always the weather in his soul.'[8] This response harked back to the nineteenth century when, according to Peter Gay, outstanding virtues had been made of 'reserve, . . . modesty, reticence, propriety, to say nothing of prudishness and hypocrisy' amongst the middle classes throughout Europe and America. Such modes of conduct

[4] E. Homberger, 'Intellectuals, Englishness, and the "myths" of Dunkirk', *Revue Française de Civilization Britannique*, 4 (1986), 82–100. Cited in S. Collini, 'Intellectuals in Britain and France in the twentieth century: confusions, contrasts – and convergence?', in J. Jennings (ed.), *Intellectuals in Twentieth-Century France: Mandarins and Samurais* (Oxford, 1993).

[5] G. Orwell, 'The lion and the unicorn: socialism and the English genius' (1941), in *The Collected Essays, Journals, and Letters of George Orwell*, 2 vols. (London, 1968), vol. II, 68.

[6] On the 'privatization' of Englishness in this period, see A. Light, *Forever England: Femininity, Literature and Conservatism between the Wars* (London, 1991); P. Rich, 'Imperial decline and the resurgence of English national identity, 1918–1979', in T. Kushner and K. Lunn, *Traditions of Intolerance: Historical Perspectives on Fascism and Race Discourse in Britain* (Manchester, 1989), 33–52; and R. Samuel, introduction to *Patriotism*, vol. I, p. xxx.

[7] P. Wright, *On Living in an Old Country: The National Past in Contemporary Britain* (London, 1985), 127.

[8] W.R. Inge, *England* (London, 1926), 113.

created a 'privileged space' in which the challenges of 'a world in flux' might be negotiated with minimal psychological cost.[9] It was a legacy which assumed a distinctively English gloss between the wars, in the eyes of foreign and British observers alike. For example, J.B. Priestley then declared England 'a land of privacy', a quality about which there was much misunderstanding among foreigners:

> the stranger who comes here is at a disadvantage. He sees the high walls but not the gardens they enclose. He watches Englishmen hurrying silently through the streets to their homes and does not realize that they are hastening away out of his sight, only in order that they may unbend at last, turning themselves into persons he would not recognize.[10]

The high premium that was attached to the ordinary and unspectacular, and correspondingly the inward life in the interwar period represented a sharp reaction against the distinctively heroic, robust, and 'exterior' projections of Englishness in governing institutions and imperial expansion earlier in the century. This retreat from what were essentially militaristic ideals of England following the cataclysm of the First World War – and the relocation of the *patria* in home (mainly rural) places, and the private self – is well captured in the liberal-conservatism of Stanley Baldwin. Invoking the nation's rustic attachments and traditions, Baldwin celebrated the quiet and ancient pleasures of familiar landscapes and routines which historical change seemed to have passed by. A conception of the 'diversified individuality' of the English was central to his vision.[11]

However, never one to abandon old theoretical constructions when new ones emerged, Barker welded together the 'interior' and 'exterior' dimensions of English national consciousness during the early decades of twentieth century. The paradox of English reserve in his writings is that it had nonetheless generated the firmest of public

[9] P. Gay, *The Bourgeois Experience: Victoria to Freud*, vol. I, *Education of the Senses* (New York, 1984), 458. The importance which the Victorian middle classes attached to privacy was integrally linked to the significance they gave to home and family life. The way in which the latter became a primary locus of masculine identity in mid-Victorian Britain has been sensitively explored by John Tosh, 'Domesticity and manliness in the Victorian middle class: the family of Edward White Benson', in M. Roper and J. Tosh (eds.), *Manful Assertions: Masculinities in Britain since 1800* (London, 1991).

[10] J.B. Priestley, *English Humour* (London, 1929), quoted in A. Bryant, *The National Character* (London, 1934), 15.

[11] S. Baldwin, *On England* (London, 1926), p. 5. However, it has been pointed out by Philip Williamson that Baldwin's rural invocations of Englishness were by no means exercises in escapism from the pressures of industrial society; nor were they the *leit motif* of his writings. See his illuminating chapter, 'The doctrinal politics of Stanley Baldwin', in M. Bentley (ed.), *Public and Private Doctrine* (Cambridge, 1993).

ties relative to other European countries. This chapter considers the link he made between the private and public faces of Englishness at the level of national life in the 1940s, reserving for the next chapter the implications he drew for greater internationalism. The mediating concept here was that of 'civility', an ideal which was central to Barker's cultural and political reflections in later life.

GREEK ANTIQUITY AND ENGLISH MODERNITY

The idea of Englishness not only concentrated many British minds in the interwar years; in addition, it aroused considerable interest among foreigners. A spate of works appeared by admirers and critics alike from a range of European nationalities, all much exercised by the peculiarities of the English.[12] The experience of England as an enemy, ally, adopted homeland, and place of internment during the First World War seems to have been especially influential in stimulating the curiosity of outsiders.[13] Contributions to this genre also came from foreign academics who taught their native language and literature in English universities.[14] In other cases, a period of residence in England was sufficient to provoke extensive reflection upon the singular nature of the host society and culture.[15]

In exploring English national character in the 1940s and 1950s, Barker availed himself fully of these commentaries, particularly those written by Wilhelm Dibelius and George Santayana. This enabled him to enlist independent support for his warm appraisals of England, suggesting that they were not solely the product of a blind national pride. Indeed, he sometimes corrected flattering suggestions from abroad that the excellences of the English were exclusively English; such, for example, was the case with the English ideal of 'the gentleman' which he attempted to connect with wider European currents.[16] But the critical distance he took from the various qualities

[12] The examples that are given in the following three footnotes are included in the anthology edited by Francesca M. Wilson, *Strange Island: Britain through Foreign Eyes, 1395–1940* (London, 1950).

[13] Respective examples are W. Dibelius, *England*, transl. by Mary Agnes Hamilton, intro. by A. D. Lindsay (1923; London 1930); A. Maurois, *Three Letters on the English* (London, 1938); G. Santayana, *Soliloquies in England: And Later Soliloquies* (London, 1922); P. Cohen-Portheim, *England: The Unknown Isle*, transl. A. Harris (London, 1930).

[14] E. Cammaerts, *Discoveries in England* (London, 1930); S. de Madariaga, *Englishmen, Frenchmen, Spaniards: An Essay in Comparative Psychology* (London, 1928).

[15] O. Keun, *I Discover the English* (London, 1934); F. Renier, *The English: Are They Human?* (London, 1931).

[16] E. Barker, *Traditions of Civility: Eight Essays* (Cambridge, 1948), 124.

he perceived in the national culture was limited. He used a favourite strategy when discussing each national trait: first to address its defects but then moving on to its merits, thereby leaving a positive impression in the reader's mind. Similarly, if he was at pains to point out the wider context of European civilisation in which Englishness was immersed, he allowed little room for doubt that the virtues of the Western tradition were exemplified in England. Nor did he think that the various associations he made with English national character were anything less than applicable across the entire social spectrum: Englishness was an all-inclusive property, not confined to any one class or region. He delighted in poetry such as Francis Brett Young's *The Island* which captured this pervasive national glow.[17] In a letter to Brett Young praising the latter work he emphasised that 'it is not only the poet, but the interpreter of England – rivers and birds and flowers, and the people that have lived among them – who has moved my admiration and even gained my affection'.[18] As I shall emphasise later in this chapter, his conception of the English spirit was in fact markedly class specific, as well as highly personal.

These initial comments on Barker's treatment of Englishness towards the end of his life are best illustrated in the importance which the concept of 'civility' acquired for him at this time. He transformed this notion into a byword for Englishness in his *Traditions of Civility* published in 1948. The book will be interpreted here in conjunction with his concluding essay to *The Character of England* entitled 'An attempt at perspective'. This was a work which he edited for Oxford University Press and which was published in 1947.[19] As he explained in the preface, the project formed 'the culmination and fulfilment' of the Press' previous ventures in this area: *Shakespeare's England* (1916), *Johnson's England* (1933), and *Early Victorian England* (1934).[20] However, the latest work in this series was intended as a description of 'the spirit of England' not at any one point in time but in 'the whole course of its permanent and long-term operation'. The expansive inspiration behind this enterprise was evidently kindled by the aftermath of

[17] F. Brett Young, *The Island* (London, 1944).

[18] Barker to Francis Brett Young, 18 December 1944, University Library, Birmingham, MS. FBY 2544.

[19] E. Barker (ed.), *The Character of England* (Oxford, 1947).

[20] The editorship of *The Character of England* must have given him special pleasure, particularly as it was published by the Clarendon Press. In a letter to Elie Halévy in 1919 he referred to that publishing house as 'a great national Press'. This was mainly because it had acquired the title to the *Dictionary of National Biography*. Barker to Halévy, 31 July 1919, in the possession of H. Guy-Loë, Sucy En Brie, Paris.

triumph in the war when a degree of 'sympathy' with 'England's achievement' seemed permissible. The tone of both *Traditions of Civility* and *The Character of England* was overwhelmingly set by the aim of cultural inclusion rather than advanced scholarship; consequently, Englishness in the two works was often related to what the author of the first and editor of the second imagined to be common, everyday experiences. As Barker emphasised in the Preface of *The Character of England*, it was not only the doings of the 'great and famous' which had informed the book's picture of England, but – in addition – 'the general run of ordinary behaviour, and the simple tastes of the mass of the people'. This aligned with a wider elevation of the 'classless masses' as the heart and soul of the English nation by popular writers such as Arthur Bryant. However, in general, Barker managed to rise above their heavily patronising tone. Bryant, for example, writing in the previous decade, insisted that 'the rich varied meat of our native English character' lay below 'the upper crust', with its cosmopolitan ideals. He continued:

> When I travel in a first-class carriage, I sometimes find myself in a perhaps wider but alien world; when I go third, I feel that I have returned to England. There, spiritually starved as I hold them to be, yet rich in the accumulated traditions of their past, are my own people; that is my country and I love it.[21]

Traditions of Civility consisted of eight essays on various subjects in the history of European culture since antiquity. Yet continual references were made to English history, even in the chapters which took up non-English themes. Thus, in his chapter on 'Dante and the last voyage of Ulysses', Barker identified a resurgence of the image of the western quest of discovery signified in Ulysses' voyage in poems by Tennyson and Browning; the latter's *Paracelsus*, he believed, represented 'an imagination which comes nearest to that of Dante'.[22] Quite plausibly, this claim was underpinned by the centrality of the sea to English national identity, a theme which was frequently invoked in connection with Englishness during the first half of the twentieth century.[23]

[21] Bryant, *The National Character*, 154–5. [22] E. Barker, *Traditions in Civility*, 73.

[23] See Stanley Baldwin's remark at a dinner to celebrate 'our country and our patron saint', that '[t]he Patron Saint of sailors is surely the most suitable Patron Saint for men of the English stock'. *On England*, 2. Arthur Bryant also invoked the sea as an 'ancient and, I think, elemental influence in English history and character'. *The National Character*, 27. Also see the chapter by J.A. Williamson on 'England and the Sea', in *The Character of England*, ed. E. Barker.

The anchor of *Traditions of Civility* was undoubtedly the first chapter entitled 'Greek influence in English life and thought'. Barker never actually defined 'civility', other than referring – on the title page – to Dr Johnson's sense of the term as 'the state of being civilized: freedom from barbarity'. But he made clear his view that its origins lay deep in the political life and thought of ancient Greece. He began the essay with a quotation from Maine that '[e]xcept the blind forces of Nature, nothing moves in this world which is not Greek in its origin'. He was prepared to qualify this claim by the inclusion of certain Hebraic and Asiatic contributions to the modern European world. Yet the exclusion of Germanic culture as another primary force in shaping Western 'civility' is striking by comparison with the loud acclaim it had received in English scholarship in the previous century. Indeed, one reviewer was moved to exclaim, '[h]ow are the mighty fallen since the days of Bishop Stubbs!'[24]

Moreover, while Barker emphasised the Greek heritage as a common European inheritance, nevertheless it emerges quite forcefully in the first chapter that he regarded England as its most faithful heir. Modesty probably prevented him from being more explicit about this connection between ancient Greece and modern England, although here he could easily have leant on the work of contemporary Anglophiles from abroad who felt no such inhibitions.[25] Instead, he slid very casually from a discussion of Greek influences on European thought to Greek influences upon English education, poetry, and English political and economic thought, projecting an image of England as permeated with the Greek past. For example, he sought to convey the essence of Platonic thought by reference to Fabianism, with its 'belief in the scientific expert, its trend towards scientific experiment, and its movement towards a new social order imposed on the errors and confusion of the past'. By contrast, in his account, the spirit of Aristotle survived in English Whiggism; the former possessed a 'curious English quality', showing 'a Whig sense of the value of time and tradition, and of the wisdom of human co-operation with the working of time and tradition'.[26] Elsewhere at the same time he even went so far as to claim that Aristotle (not Aquinas, as Acton had

[24] *English Historical Review*, 64 (1949), 288.

[25] See for example, the Belgian writer E. Cammaert's *Discoveries in England*. 'As I became more familiar with my Classics, many similar images convinced me that England was indeed the spiritual heiress of Greece, and played, in modern days, on the Atlantic coast, the part which had been played by her ancestor in the eastern Mediterranean, twenty-five centuries ago.' 36.

[26] E. Barker, *Traditions of Civility*, 9–10.

maintained) was 'the first Whig'; it followed that 'if there is any modern climate of Aristotle's *Politics*, it is the climate of 1688'.[27] The suggestion here is that Plato and Fabianism were of a profoundly un-English temper, whereas Aristotle, Whiggism, and Englishness were all of the same, elevated disposition.

Barker confessed that his awareness of the 'congruity' between the Greek past and the English present was especially sharp as a scholar who had been trained in the foremost centre of Greek learning in Britain – the Oxford School of Literae Humaniores. This was also related to his view that the Greek classics had played a pivotal role in the education of English rulers, whether formally educated or – as in the case of the country gentleman – informally educated in their study.[28] But he was anxious to dispel any impression that the characteristics and outlook of ancient Greece had been appropriated in England by the governing class alone; on the contrary, he believed that they had made a far deeper, indeed a universal impact. Drawing upon Santayana's *Soliloquies in England* he underlined the shared landscape of the sea which had sensitised the English and Greek nations alike to 'the empire of personal liberty'.[29] In additional support of his claim that the spirit of Greece pervaded England in its entirety, he recalled a visit he had made to Preston during the First World War, and his delight upon finding a quotation from Thucydides running all the way around the building of the public library.[30] Further evidence also pointed to the affinity between the 'ordinary' Englishman and the thinkers and citizens of ancient Greece. He cited a comment which had been made to him by a German professor of Greek that a humanist quality ran deep in English veins, and that this was a function of Greek learning which had far outstretched the world of scholarship. To this Barker remarked: 'It is indeed a story which deserves to be told – Greek in the vicarage, the bank, the civil service, the Prime Minister's study, or the Viceroy's Lodge in India. A captain serving in Burmah will write to you to ask for a plain text of the *Republic*; and T.E. Lawrence could carry the *Odyssey* into strange places.'[31] This observation did not suggest quite the same extensive influence of Greek culture on English life as the example of Preston's

27 E. Barker (ed.), *The Politics of Aristotle* (Oxford, 1946), lxii, xxxi.
28 E. Barker, *Traditions of Civility*, 26; *British Statesmen* (London, 1941), 15–16.
29 E. Barker (ed.), *The Character of England*, 555; Santayana, *Soliloquies in England*, 34.
30 E. Barker, *Traditions of Civility*, 23.
31 Ibid., 32–3.

Hellenist Library Committee. Nonetheless, it serves to emphasise where Barker believed Englishness – as conduct and outlook in accordance with the norms of civility and humanism – was primarily situated and from where it radiated (we are not told precisely how) to the rest of society. This was the older, gentlemanly, and learned professions, the members of which Barker had educated throughout his university career and among whom he could count a number of distinguished pupils. Recalling in his autobiography a particularly gifted cohort of New College students after the First World War, he remarked that they had 'ripened into a rich harvest . . . [one which] is still there, and still a source of nutriment to the general life of the nation, at any rate in the realms of education and culture'.[32]

This association was crucial to his attempt to undermine the authority of the newer, welfare, and technocratic professions which had become the cornerstone of state planning in the 1940s. In counterposing the 'gentleman' to the 'expert' Barker sought substantial political mileage from a leading cultural idea, one which was perceived as a primary obstacle to reform by thinkers on the Left during the interwar period.[33] The concept of the 'gentleman' did not stand alone in his portrait of the national type during this period; rather, it was closely linked to other 'constants' in England which he identified, for example the cult of the 'amateur' and 'the voluntary habit'. These connections will become apparent if we first turn to Barker's construction of the gentlemanly ideal and the place he accorded to it in 'traditions of civility'.

THE CULTURAL CENTRALITY OF THE GENTLEMAN

As I have emphasised already, Barker was anxious to point out that the idea of the gentleman possessed strong European roots; it had been imported into England during the Renaissance, from Italy in the first instance, and Spain and France in the second. Nevertheless, he added, the idea had enjoyed a continuous life in England, in

[32] E. Barker, *Age and Youth: Memories of Three Universities and Father of the Man* (London, 1953), 83. Barker devoted a chapter to his Oxford pupils in his autobiography (he did not seem to forge the same number of close personal ties with his Cambridge students, for whom he functioned as a course, rather than a college, tutor). His British students included Father Bede Jarrett, Christopher Dawson, Sir Fred Clark, Ernest Jacob, Idris Deane Jones, Douglas Woodruff, Ada Levett, and T.S. Lawrence. Some of his other Oxford pupils are mentioned elsewhere in this study – C.E.G. Catlin, H.J. Laski, Clement Attlee, M.B. Reckitt, David Thomson, Dermot Morrah, and William Archer.

[33] See for example, Harold J. Laski, *The Danger of Being a Gentleman: And Other Essays* (London, 1939).

keeping with the great store that was set by continuity in all other aspects of national life. To this extent he identified the 'figure and the idea of the gentleman' as a mainstay of the English character. His understanding of the gentlemanly ideal, as in many other things English, owed much to Santayana's meditations on England during the First World War. For Barker, the gentleman 'is shy, yet also self-confident. He is the refinement of manliness; but the manliness is sometimes more obvious than the refinement. He is disquieted by men's eyes; but he is also a cynosure. He does gentlemanly things; but he seems to be even more marked by the things which he does not do.'[34]

This depiction accords well with the 'interiorisation' of Englishness which had developed in the interwar years – retreating to the private sphere of home and then further to the English psyche itself. It was clearly no objective description; rather, the passage suggests the author's approval of a certain degree of inwardness – of keeping oneself to oneself and eschewing bombast – as the chief emblem of cultural belonging in England.[35] Such shyness often being 'stiff' and 'awkward', it could also explain the 'patronising' attitudes which hostile critics abroad sometimes detected in the English.[36] It was certainly an ideal of character to which Barker had always warmed and, indeed, consciously cultivated himself. The above quotation, for example, has much to compare with his self-effacing response to the congratulations he received from H.J. Laski on receiving his knighthood in 1944. He wrote:

> I confess that I was pleased to be knighted; but I really think I was equally pleased by the letters I got from old pupils. And as for the knighting – it was really the Books Commission of the Allied Ministers of Education (for which I work, and which has done really good work) that deserved to be knighted. I think the honour has just ricocheted on me.[37]

The same modesty and reserve is evident in another letter he wrote to Laski during their often stormy relationship. Having sung Barker's

[34] E. Barker (ed.), *The Character of England*, 567; compare G. Santayana, *Soliloquies in England*, 4–5, 38.

[35] On a similar note, after a visit to Yorkshire in 1950 he had cause to take its inhabitants to task for their excessive county pride. 'The wise man refrains from blowing his own trumpet. He leaves it to others to recount his triumphs; and he amuses himself by playing a game which is peculiarly English; a game which he begins to learn in his later years at school, and at which he becomes proficient in his university years. This is the game of understatement.' E. Barker, 'Is Yorkshire Boastful?', *The Yorkshire Post*, 25 October 1950.

[36] E. Barker, 'The English character and attitude towards life', *England* (September 1950), 8.

[37] Barker to Laski, 15 January 1944; Laski Papers, Brynmor Jones Library, University of Hull. On Barker's work for the Book Commission, see ch. 8 below.

praises too highly for the latter's liking in 1920, when both men were in America, Laski received a note explaining his former teacher's subsequent annoyance. Barker wrote: 'What worried me . . . was that you made too much of me, and, as I thought, flattered me. I may be very foolish, but, quite honestly I didn't like it. I have a passion that way, which may be a sort of inverted vanity. But there it is – or was.'[38]

Barker explored the reception of the idea of the gentleman in England in his chapter in *Traditions of Civility* entitled 'The education of the English gentleman in the sixteenth century'. In his eyes, education provided the key to the character of the gentleman, particularly in England where that status had always been conferred by merit rather than birth. But the importance which education assumed for the cultivation of gentlemanly habits in the sixteenth century was firmly linked to the duties of scholarship and government, creating the role of 'scholar-governor-gentleman'. Barker was greatly responsive to what he perceived as the changing character of the gentlemanly ideal in Tudor England – from courtly love to 'public service'. This shift accorded with the central ethos of the Literae Humaniores School in the Oxford of his youth. Moreover, in analysing the content of the education of the Tudor gentleman, he especially highlighted the component of law, as well as moral and political philosophy which contemporary commentators such as Sir Thomas Elyot prescribed. Given that the gentleman was now expected to occupy high office, the study of law – or more precisely the laws of England – became an essential part of his training.

Here, Barker returned to a theme which has appeared throughout this account of his social and political thought: the notion that law constitutes the backbone of the English polity and should hence provide the basis of political education. Now he made the further connection between education, the law-state, and the ideal of 'civility'. He took his cue here from Thomas Starkey, whose *Dialogue between Cardinal Pole and Thomas Lipset* emphasised the vital importance of the education of the gentleman to 'good civility'. By the latter term,

[38] Barker to Laski, 8 November 1921; Laski Papers, Brynmor Jones Library, University of Hull. Temperamentally, Barker and Laski were poles apart. On Barker's attempt to distance himself from Laski at this time, see the letters from Laski to Graham Wallas, 21 March 1920 and 2 May 1920; and also S.K. Ratcliffe to Wallas, 15 October 1920. Wallas Papers, 1/64, British Library of Political and Economic Science. Writing to Wallas from Harvard, Laski expressed concern that Barker might jettison his chances of a post at the London School of Economics. However, when Laski applied for Wallas' Chair in 1925, Barker wrote in warm support of his former student. This, and other letters of support for Laski's promotion, are in the Laski Papers, International Institute of Social History, Amsterdam.

Barker pointed out, this Tudor writer primarily meant 'the constitution and government of "the very and true commonwealth"'.[39] The foundation of this sense of civility in the education of the gentleman – along the twin lines of morals and law – was something which in Barker's view marked England off from its European neighbours. The English mode of conducting 'civil' life was conspicuously that of 'intelligent amateurism'. On the continent, however, service to the state had been transformed into a 'science'.[40] It is evident where exactly Barker thought the balance of good fortune lay, as between the enjoyment of these two types of government. For example he remarked elsewhere that England, being 'a compact country of small extent and easy communications . . . has not needed administrative pressure to give it internal unity'.[41]

It will be seen presently that the ideal of limited government crucially informed Barker's concern to uphold the gentlemanly character of English polity. Before turning to this dimension of his concept of civility, however, it is important to emphasise the emollient effect which his work in this area – as in all others – was conceivably designed to achieve. A key part of his argument concerning the gentlemanly core of the civil ideal was that in England, class boundaries had always been markedly fluid. Thus in *The Character of England* he listed among the abiding elements of England that of social homogeneity. 'The habitat', he declared, 'has somehow produced understanding and even fusion.' Proof of this claim, he believed, could be found as far back as the twelfth century when, according to 'a sober treasury official', Saxons and Normans mixed freely. Further evidence, he thought, of the absence of rigid class boundaries in England was furnished by the two-way flow between 'sons' of the land and those of business.[42] Focusing upon social mobility further down the social scale the message which Barker gratefully received from Tudor commentators was that 'the common man' was by no means debarred from the gentlemanly estate. For all the Tudor concern to maintain a hierarchy of social

[39] E. Barker, *Traditions of Civility*, 137. [40] Ibid., 149.

[41] E. Barker, *The Development of Public Services in Western Europe, 1660–1930* (Oxford, 1944), 29; originally published as 'The development of administration, conscription, taxation, social services and education', in E. Eyre (ed.), *European Civilisation: Its Origins and Development*, vol. v (Oxford, 1937), part IV.

[42] E. Barker (ed.), *The Character of England*, 563. This powerful myth of an 'open elite' in England based on the assumed reciprocity of land and business has been challenged by L. Stone and J.C. Fawtier Stone in *An Open Elite? England, 1540–1880* (London, 1984).

orders, it gave Barker evident pleasure to record the opinion of authorities such as Cranmer that God had 'not fixed men irrevocably to the rung of their father's birth': movement was a real possibility, sanctioned by the belief that God may call individuals to a higher state than that to which they had been born. Gentlemen, then, 'be made good and cheap in England'.[43] It was an assertion to which Barker was understandably drawn, given his own rise from humble origins to positions of national importance. Far from seeing his success as an exception to the rule of the impenetrability of the British cultural and political elite, he wore it lightly. For example, of his Balliol days in 1893, he recalled:

> The senior Scholar of the year before me was the son of an engine driver who rose high in the Civil Service; the second Scholar was the son of a coachman who went on first to administrative work in South-East Asia and in later years to work on the *Dictionary of National Biography* and the *Oxford English Dictionary*. In my own year, I was the son of a miner; a contemporary, also a Scholar, had been a clerk in an engineering works; one of my seniors, the son of a domestic servant, was first an Oxford tutor and then a London professor. After all, we were not *so* benighted fifty years ago.[44]

This sense that his early life was nothing out of the ordinary helps to explain his confident belief in the flexible nature of social boundaries in England. It also placed him in a favourable position to sustain and exploit the spirit of national unity which had emerged in Britain during the 1930s and the Second World War.

AMATEUR AND LIMITED GOVERNMENT

Thus Barker securely linked civility to the concept of the gentleman, especially the gentleman-governor, and emphasised the 'democratic' possibilities of that status in England. Another characteristic which he associated with gentlemanly and hence civil rule was that of 'amateurism'. He attached a high premium to this quality, presenting it as a typically English virtue in his contribution to *The Character of England*. The cult of the amateur reigned in English sport, letters, scholarship, agriculture, and industry, as well as politics. It had its

[43] E. Barker, *Traditions of Civility*, 154–8.

[44] E. Barker, *Some Comparisons between Universities* (Blackwell, *c.* 1944). The quotation from this pamphlet – which I have been unable to trace – is cited in F. Brittain, 'On Certain Popular Errors', *The Cambridge Review*, 18 November 1944, 90. Barker made similar remarks about his contemporaries at Oxford in *British Universities* (London, 1946), 20.

defects, of course, as Barker was always ready to admit with every dimension of Englishness; for example, the amateur style was not always adequate to the problems of a complex and 'aggregated' world. As ever, though, for him, the merits of English characteristics far outweighed their deficiencies, and he sprang to the defence of amateurism for 'prevent[ing] life from being too hugely serious, [and] leaving a space for fun'. He also extolled its propensity to 'take away strain' and foster 'disinterestedness'. He was clearly making a direct political point here for, in his account, amateurs had particularly proved their worth in English government. In focusing on amateurism as a general feature of English life, Barker intended to give broad cultural sanction to a political ideal which was antithetical to large-scale planning through the application of professional expertise. For instance, he referred in his essay to 'the nervous tension in planning . . . which hardly accords with our instincts or the general tradition of our life'.[45] That tradition was essentially one of 'experimentalism', an echo of that which had most attracted Barker to Pluralism. It had generated socially beneficial results which would have completely eluded the planner. Running this claim into a central Burkean principle, he insisted that English government had traditionally met this experimental temper with 'a mass of skills and understandings'. Consequently, English political life was wholly at one, not only with the experimental grain of English society generally, but also with the English weather: the climate changed regularly, of course, but only with 'minor variations'.

It can be seen that Barker was here engaged in shrouding Englishness with a mystique which would make all attempts to govern in accordance with rational design seem culturally alien. Firm rejection of this political approach seemed especially urgent given the inroads which planning had made in the British state during the Second World War. Addressing suggestions that a 'planned society' was now an inevitable feature of English life, Barker played one of his favourite roles: that of offering calm and sober reflection, dampening down undue excitement at new developments in society and thought.

[45] E. Barker, *The Character of England*, 554–5. Barker's commendation of 'amateurism' is analogous to Johan Huizinga's account of 'play' in the development of civilization. For Huizinga, civilisation loses touch with its formative element of 'play' when it becomes more complex, 'more variegated, and more overladen'. J. Huizinga, *Homo Ludens: A Study of the Play Element in Culture* (1938), Eng. transl., (1949; London, 1970), 96. It is certainly significant that Huizinga was an Anglophile, and included a chapter 'In praise of government by gentlemen' in his *Confessions of a European in England* (London, 1958).

It was a tendency of the modern mind, he maintained, 'to magnify change, and to think with too ready a facility of "a changing world"'.[46] But to do so was to neglect the fact that constancy was always more apparent than change, and of no nation was this truer than the English.

However, these outwardly calm reflections upon English polity failed to conceal Barker's considerable unease with the agenda of British politics after 1945. In his eyes it was increasingly at odds with the liberal tradition, which he clearly identified with the English tradition. He voiced his anxiety about the economic and social policies of the Labour government in his 1949 Ramsay Muir Memorial Lecture. Addressing the subject of *Change and Continuity* he denounced what he saw as the Labour Party's 'sweeping policy of nationalization; its consequent methods of bureaucratic control . . .; and its resultant challenge to what many of us regard as the old and established liberties of the realm'. The changes introduced by Labour were not ones with which liberals should come to terms. Their response should be one of reasserting the claims of 'continuity' with the English past, an essentially liberal past. Liberals had never renounced the 'supervisory state', the state in the (Idealist) guise of 'the hinderer of hindrances'; but they had set themselves firmly against 'the managing and manipulating State which sets its fingers on every lever and prefers automatism to the surge and throb of individual human initiative'. Liberalism now stood in closest proximity to conservatism. While the latter had sometimes lacked flexibility – for example, in its opposition to Irish Home Rule and the abolition of the privileges enjoyed by the House of Lords – it generally shared liberalism's concern with change that was consistent with previous practice. Identifying with the conservative rather than the radical wing of liberalism, Barker concluded his lecture by insisting that '[o]ne can be a Liberal, and yet believe in tradition. Indeed, I do not see how one can be a Liberal *without* believing in tradition.'[47] His remark echoed his recommendation of Viscount Hinchingbrooke's book several years earlier when he made light of his Whig differences with his Tory friend: if there were differences, there was also agreement, not least that of both being 'good Englishmen under the skin'.[48] He had likewise set party differences aside in assisting Lord

[46] E. Barker, *The Character of England*, 554.

[47] E. Barker, *Change and Continuity*, the Ramsay Muir Memorial Lecture delivered at Oxford, 31 July 1949 (London, 1949), 13–16.

[48] E. Barker, Foreword to Viscount Hinchingbrooke, *Full Speed Ahead: Essays in Tory Reform* (London, 1944).

Henry Bentinck to write his *Tory Democracy* in 1918, leaving him with a similar respect for British conservatism. The aristocratic tradition of government represented by the Bentinck family constituted 'a source of our national strength for many centuries'.[49]

The amateur-gentleman governor, then, was the supreme guardian of the English tradition of 'experimentalism', and there was no reason to suppose that peacetime needed to be organised by the same structures of central planning which had been instituted to prosecute the war. Professions there had always been in England; but the traditional professions such as law, medicine, teaching, and the civil service were built very solidly along the 'anti-professional' lines which ran throughout English society. Flexibility and a willingness to compromise, together with trial and error were their keynotes; and in this they were at one with English national character generally.

VOLUNTARY AND POLITICAL ASSOCIATION

For Barker, the propriety of amateurism in government based on the rule of gentlemen was reinforced by a third characteristic of Englishness which he emphasised in the 1940s: that of 'the voluntary habit'. This was also reminiscent of the Pluralist themes of his early career, from which he now sought to reap the full benefits for a rejuvenated national culture. It consorted well with anti-professional modes of government on a number of scores.

First, the gentleman-ruler shared the same spirit of spontaneity and experimentation which Barker – following Maitland – found so congenial a feature of English club life. The approach of the gentleman-governor was typically that of playing by ear, responding to problems as the need arose rather than imposing grand schemes upon society informed by 'scientific' knowledge. This preference clearly underlay Barker's characterisation of planning in terms of 'strain' and 'tension', evils which were thankfully absent from the life of the voluntary association.

Second, given that Barker had identified 'amateur' government very closely with limited government, this too seemed well suited to the English capacity for free association. Preferring mutual self-help to organisation by the state, Englishmen had formed associations for

[49] E. Barker, *Age and Youth: Memories of Three Universities and Father of the Man* (London, 1953), 105–6.

all manner of social and political purposes. As Barker expressed this, one of his favourite themes, in his *Principles of Social and Political Theory* published in 1951: 'The club and the committee are part of the general grain [of English life]. They proliferate equally on allotments and in Pall Mall: in the "combination" rooms of colleges and in "combinations" of employers or workers.'[50] The quotation furnishes another instance of his attempt to assimilate English intellectual life into the national culture at large, providing a focus for the latter and hence an integrating force. But beyond this, the centrality which he gave to voluntary association in English development underlined a seminal cultural belief: that society in England had not been absorbed by the state, performing much of the business which had elsewhere – as J.S. Mill observed – devolved upon government.[51]

Yet while, in this sense, a clear division existed between state and society in England, in another sense the frontier had become almost imperceptible. This highlights a third association which Barker made between amateur government and 'the voluntary habit' in his account of Englishness after the Second World War: the idea that large tracts of the English state (and English law) had themselves originated in voluntary organisation. It was this, he believed, which gave English legal and political institutions their unique liberal character. The informal, almost casual, and certainly amateur guise in which the English state appeared in Barker's later work is best illustrated in another passage from his *Principles of Social and Political Theory*, one which is worth quoting at length:

> The English State itself has had some of the qualities of a club, and it has thus had a fellow feeling for clubs which has made it generally kind. Not only is the House of Commons something in the nature of a club: political parties . . . have long combined the character of social formations with the activity of political forces; and in the area of local self-government, during the two centuries which followed the Revolution of 1688, the Quarter Sessions of the Justices of the Peace were a sort of county club, which might meet in a county hotel (as the Berkshire justices did when they passed 'the Speenhamland Act' of 1795) to settle issues of county policy. Similarly, English law may be regarded as largely the product of a club, or rather of a group of clubs, the Inns of Court with their barrister members from whom the judges are drawn; and it is certain that in one of its elements, its peculiar law of trusts, English law has provided a shelter and shield for voluntary society.[52]

[50] E. Barker, *Principles of Social and Political Theory* (Oxford, 1951; 1961), 51.
[51] E. Barker (ed.), *The Character of England*, 567.
[52] E. Barker, *Principles of Social and Political Theory*, 52.

There was hence a continuum between state and society in England which Barker took great delight in emphasising, whether in his academic text-books or more 'middlebrow' writings of the 1940s. As an example of the latter, we may consider a short book entitled *Britain and the British People* published in 1942, which Barker fondly regarded as 'the best little book I have written in my life'.[53] In this work he made the same point as the above quotation by explaining the significance of the number 11 bus route in London, from Liverpool Street station to Westminster. This would carry the passenger through all three major institutional areas of 'England': the area of society, symbolised in the Stock Exchange and representing the device of the trust which had generated all manner of other voluntary societies in England; the 'borderland' area between society and state signified in the Inns of Courts which, like political parties, were 'half social formation and half political machine'; and finally the state itself through Whitehall and the Houses of Parliament.[54] It was significant that he boarded his readers on the number 11 bus in the City rather than Westminster, indicating his belief that the English state had been decisively shaped by English 'society' and not the other way round. It was a lesson which he had learned from George Unwin much earlier in the century as he attempted to take the anti-statist sting out of Pluralism; and it struck the same note as the view of Englishness which emerged more broadly between the wars: that 'private', local life constituted its essential repository, whilst being replete with major 'public' implications.

There was no question, however, of inferring from this apparent intimacy between society and state that the boundaries between the two – in so far as they existed – could be broken down entirely. While the state could not be confined to any one sphere of human life, its sole concern was with 'external acts', those which could be 'brought under a rule of law and thus made a matter of compulsory uniformity'.[55] In holding this view of the state, Barker may be compared with his contemporary, R.G. Collingwood. In 1928, Collingwood had defined political action as undertaken by the state in terms of 'orderliness, regularity, submission to a rule which applies equally to all'.[56] Indeed, there are further parallels in their political thought which are

[53] Barker to C.T. Onions, 3 July 1942, University Library, Birmingham, MS. Onions 9.
[54] E. Barker, *Britain and the British People* (Oxford, 1942), 82–3.
[55] E. Barker, *Principles of Social and Political Theory*, 45.
[56] R.G. Collingwood, 'Political action', *Proceedings of the Aristotelian Society*, 29 (1928), 162.

rooted in a common embrace of the ideal of 'civility'. Collingwood devoted considerable attention to the latter in his last work, *The New Leviathan*, published in 1942.[57] Like Barker, he tied the concept to a set of attitudes and practices in 'civilization' which included the conservation and wide accessibility of knowledge, a disdain for experts in public life, the settlement of disputes by peaceful – that is, legal – means, and a measure of openness between the ruling and ruled classes. Reviewing the book for *The Oxford Magazine*, Barker felt that the last two sections in which Collingwood developed his ideas about 'civilization' and 'barbarism' were too much soiled by the emotions of war (and Collingwood's failing health) to merit serious attention; Collingwood had launched a bitter attack upon the ingrained 'herd-worship' of the German people, and the latest outbreak of 'barbarism' to which it had led.[58] Yet despite the aggressive style in which it was sometimes expressed and which contrasted markedly with his constant desire to avoid giving offence, Barker acknowledged the value of Collingwood's philosophy. In an essay of 1945, he applauded Collingwood's distinction between 'society' and the 'non-social' community that lay at the heart of the latter's understanding of 'civility'.[59] For Collingwood, relations between human beings in 'society' are characterised by respect for others as free agents capable of exercising autonomous will, and where – contrary to the 'non-social community' – the use of force is ruled out in most cases of conflict. To this extent, therefore, 'society' was integrally 'well-mannered', 'converting occasions of non-agreement into occasions of agreement and thus averting quarrels before they happen'.[60]

Barker's definition of the state in terms of legal action was grounded in his Idealist emphasis on the state's capacity to create the conditions of the good life only, not the good life itself. It was a political ideal which now acquired a keen topical edge as conservative political theorists, especially, assailed the post-war expansion of the state.[61] The image of the state as a 'lifeboat' repelled such disparate thinkers as F.A. Hayek, Edward Shils, and Michael Oakeshott, this

[57] R.G. Collingwood, *The New Leviathan: Or Man, Society, Civilization, and Barbarism* (Oxford, 1942), 385. On Collingwood's political philosophy see the recent illuminating study by D. Boucher, *The Social and Political Thought of R.G. Collingwood* (Cambridge, 1989).

[58] E. Barker, 'Man and society', *The Oxford Magazine*, 4 February 1943, 160–3.

[59] E. Barker, *Essays on Government* (Oxford, 1945), 238, n.2.

[60] Collingwood, *The New Leviathan*, 338.

[61] On this reaction, from both conservative and other quarters, see R. Barker, *Political Ideas in Modern Britain* (London, 1978), 190–205.

being the root cause of despotism and totalitarianism in their view. Barker added his voice to this chorus of conservative scepticism in his assertion that:

There is no salvation in the State: there is only a sovereign safeguard. Salvation lies in ourselves, and we have to win it ourselves – in the shelter of the sovereign safeguard. We may dream of a State which itself is an institute of salvation. We only dream; and our dream is one which denatures the State and unspheres law.[62]

The gentleman-governor was the safeguard of this safeguard of law, and hence a central pillar of 'civility' which Barker had linked firmly to rule in accordance with law.

THE MISSING ENGLAND

Evidently, Barker's view of Englishness was much influenced by the political conclusions he fervently wished to uphold. As such, it excluded lifestyles and institutions which fell outside of what he deemed the cultural mainstream in England. It is apparent in the above account that Barker presented a scholar's picture of England above all else, its inhabitants engaging in learned pursuits after the fashion of the members of an Oxbridge college. In this respect, it was far from the diverse experiences of the timeless 'ordinary [English]man' whose spirit he was most concerned to capture in *The Character of England* and similar works. His identification of Englishness with the values and interests of the educated middle class did not escape criticism. Several reviewers of his books in the 1940s drew attention to the England which was strikingly absent from his peaceful and erudite images of the national culture. One such reviewer was David Thomson, who had been one of Barker's students at Cambridge. While he praised Barker's social and political theory in reviews of his tutor's books on that theme,[63] he was plainly exasperated with the general tone of *The Character of England*. He argued:

Much of it reads as if the writers wrote full-time for the British Council, and thought only of the politer, more elegant and least controversial aspects of English social life. Surely the suburbanite who digs his allotment on

62 E. Barker, *Principles of Social and Political Theory*, 47.

63 D. Thomson, review of *Reflections on Government*, *The Cambridge Review*, 10 October 1942, 8; and *Principles of Social and Political Theory*, *The Spectator*, 187, 21 December 1951, 859.

Saturday afternoons, takes the dog and children for a walk on Sunday mornings, reads Picture Post and Penguin Books, enjoys 'British films', and spends his weekdays in the office is as much a manifestation of the English character today as the villager digging his garden and the country gentleman riding after the fox.[64]

Other reviewers expressed similar dissatisfaction with Barker's England, finding further parts of the English social and cultural map missing from it. For example, A.J.P. Taylor thought it difficult to discover from *Britain and the British People* 'the most important fact about contemporary England: that it is the most industrialized community in the world'.[65] Jacques Barzun discerned the same silence in the book on matters relating to 'the way England earns its living'. He continued by noting one particular glaring void in Barker's account: 'There are chapters on Government, Law, Church, and Social Services, but none on Trade Unionism.'[66] It must be said in his defence that Barker made some effort to ensure that due weight was given to 'Labour' in *The Character of England*, a point on which he commended the book to Clement Attlee when he sent a copy to his former Oxford student, now Prime Minister.[67] However, the chapter he commissioned on 'The human side of industry' by Sir George T. Reid made little reference to working-class associations, concentrating instead on the individual English worker. Reid reached a conclusion which could hardly have pleased even moderate supporters of the Labour movement, that the English worker possessed the normal English characteristics of 'keeping his thoughts to himself'. To a high degree, therefore, 'he' was unfathomable. Nor could his 'view of life and affairs' be gathered from 'those who speak publicly on his behalf' – an obvious broadside against organised Labour.[68] To the extent that there was an 'anti-industrial spirit' in England in the twentieth century – indifferent to the culture of both capital and labour – then Barker could well illustrate that mood.[69]

64 D. Thomson, *The Cambridge Review*, 69, 21 February 1948, 372.

65 A.J.P. Taylor, *Manchester Guardian*, 13 January 1943.

66 J. Barzun, *The Nation*, 157, 14 August 1943, 188.

67 Barker to Attlee, 15 October 1947, MS. Attlee dep. 61, fol. 232, Bodleian Library. He continued, 'I hope that, in a spare hour at Chequers, you will glance at the last chapter. You will not agree with me, and you may think me an old Romantic . . .; but I know that you will forgive me.' Attlee was to have been a contributor himself but was apparently prevented from doing so by the General Election. See Barker's Preface.

68 E. Barker (ed.), *The Character of England*, 175.

69 See Martin Wiener, *English Culture and the Decline of the Industrial Spirit, 1850–1980* (Cambridge, 1981).

The fact was that Barker's meditations upon England were suspended between an idealised view of the past and a selective view of the present. His cultivated, consensual, and rural images of England were clearly intended as balm in crisis-ridden and rapidly changing times, designed to exert a steadying influence as much as anything else. The effect would have been spoiled by the intrusion of discordant and disaffected voices and experiences. In this respect, his work is comparable to the anodyne English history written by his Cambridge colleague and fellow late-Whig, G.M. Trevelyan, who predictably wrote an enthusiastic review of *Britain and the British People*.[70] Many facets of contemporary life were hostile to the kind of inward restraint and quiet contemplation – both solitary and in the company of others – where Barker located the benison of Englishness.[71] In particular, he saw the decreasing amount of time occupied by 'work' in the lives of modern individuals relative to their Victorian ancestors as leaving a worrying lacuna, something over which he had brooded since his involvement in the Hadow Committee in the 1920s. He shared this concern with other prominent contemporary liberals, most notably, J.M. Keynes.[72] It was a void which, in Barker's view, was in danger of being filled with mere 'recreation' rather than 'leisure' in the high Greek meaning of *schole*, or the enhancement of the mind and thereby the soul for its own intrinsic worth.[73] The worst aspect of 'recreation' was that it invariably involved some temporary communal excitement which left individuals out of touch with their inner selves. Writing in 1936, he maintained that:

The sad thing about modern English society is that there is so little leisure in

[70] G.M. Trevelyan, *The Cambridge Review*, 64, 6 February 1943, 64. On Trevelyan, see David Cannadine, *G.M. Trevelyan: A Life in History* (London, 1992); and J.M. Hernon, Jr., 'The last Whig historian and consensus history: George Macaulay Trevelyan, 1876–1962', *American Historical Review*, 81 (1976), 66–97.

[71] The adverse climate of late-modernity to 'civility' has been emphasised by the American sociologist, Richard Sennett. He has linked a healthy public life to one in which the ethic of 'intimacy' is kept well in check, something which failed to occur in Western societies in the post-war period. He defines the ideal of civility in terms which were close to Barker's: 'It is the activity which protects people from each other and yet allows them to enjoy each other's company. Wearing a mask is the essence of civility. Masks permit pure sociability, detached from the circumstances of power, malaise, and private feeling of those who wear them.' *The Fall of Public Man* (Cambridge, 1974), 264.

[72] J.M. Keynes, 'Economic possibilities for our grandchildren' (1930), *The Collected Writings of John Maynard Keynes*, vol. IX, *Essays in Persuasion* (London, 1972). Speaking of a hundred years hence, Keynes maintained that, 'for the first time since his creation man will be faced with his real, his permanent problem – how to use the freedom from pressing economic cares, how to occupy the leisure, which science and compound interest will have won for him, to live wisely and agreeably and well.' 328.

[73] E. Barker, *Traditions of Civility*, 17–20.

this higher sense . . . Perhaps the monotony and uniformity of work sends us in reaction to the hazards of games, or the excitement of watching them, or the still greater excitement of betting upon them: perhaps the urban aggregations in which men now live make them unhappy unless they are crowding together to some common game or spectacle.[74]

Yet despite such worries, his English world was still one in which good manners – founded upon a degree of introversion – remained the hallmark of the national identity. The well-hidden depths of the English psyche explained the seemingly impregnable structures of the English state too, together with the large area of voluntary social life in which the essentially 'private' nature of English sociability found free expression.

The reassuring nature of Barker's English vision was crucial to the success he achieved as a public figure during the 1940s, however politically and culturally skewed his outline of England may have been. His firm belief in the strength of the Western ideal of civility provided an important source of his optimism about the future of both his own country and Europe at large. In contrast, G.M. Trevelyan, many of whose values he shared, was overcome by a powerful sense of disillusion and alienation as the pre-1914 English world which provided all his moral and political markers became rapidly eclipsed. The ideal of civility offered Barker a welcome refuge from the chill winds of intensified group loyalties which greatly agitated him during the interwar period and beyond, a theme which will be resumed in the conclusion of this book. It also sanctioned the global dissemination of European values and institutions, particularly in their English form, as we shall see in chapter 8.

[74] E. Barker, *The Uses of Leisure* (London, 1936), 7, 11.

CHAPTER 8

The expansion of Englishness: the Books Commission, Europe, and the Commonwealth

ENGLISH INTERNATIONALISM

Reviewing works by A.J. Toynbee and E.H. Carr immediately after the Second World War, Barker was made painfully aware of the ever-widening generation gap between himself and younger scholars. He could not share their dark, melancholy view of the world, rooted as it was in an analysis of 'the disease of nationalism' which appeared to have left Western civilisation in a state of terminal decline. All too conscious of his advancing years and no doubt the remoteness of the Mazzinian influences of his youth, he inquired '[d]oes a disease of nationalism [i.e. German nationalism] prove that nationalism is itself a disease?' The unspoken answer was evidently no, and the silent example which supported it was the English nation; at any rate, he had always maintained that the latter was generally free of nationalism's vices. Gone too, or so it seemed, was the hope which an older generation had derived from contemplating the 'spiritual' forces at work in history; they now appeared as 'quenched stars, or even as baleful lights', yielding to the realities of 'power and economics' in international affairs.[1]

Yet despite the loss of face which both nationalism and internationalism suffered after the war in some quarters, Barker continued to sanction both ideals and to assert – in true Mazzinian style – the inextricable link between them.[2] Predictably, he regarded England as particularly well placed to strengthen this tie in world affairs. What precise contribution did the war make to affirming his view of the English nation's continuing international significance? What prospects did he think Englishness held for a lessening of international tension

[1] E. Barker, review of E.H. Carr, *Nationalism and After*, *Britain Today*, August 1945, 41–2; and review of A.J. Toynbee, *Civilisation on Trial*, *The Spectator*, 17 December 1948, 810.

[2] For example, see footnote 34 on p. 210.

in the future? And what wider forces in the history of Western civilisation did he invoke in support of England's world role after the war? In addressing these questions it will become clear how his unassuming account of English national character in terms of modesty, simplicity, and inwardness helped to restore confidence, albeit fleetingly, in the much-beleaguered idea of Britain as a major world power in the 1940s and 1950s.

CULTURAL DIPLOMACY

An analysis of Barker's internationalist commitment and its relationship to his understanding of Englishness in this period must begin in the context of Europe. Here, his concern that England should transcend its parochial borders is signalled by his involvement during the Second World War with the Books and Periodicals Commission. This body was established by the Conference of Allied Ministers of Education which represented eight allied governments then resident in London. The conference was initially envisaged as the basis of an international educational organisation, UNESCO being the eventual outcome. Strongly aware of the wider hopes behind the conference, Barker strove to make the work of the Books Commission an enduring testimony to the special role which Britain had played in nurturing them.[3]

The Books Commission began work in February 1943 with Barker as its chairman, a post which he held until the commission was disbanded in November 1945. His work for the commission well illustrates the considerable stature he had achieved as a national figure by the time of the war, the extent of his connections in governing circles, and his ease of communication with the wartime political elite as a warm supporter of Establishment Englishness. The various projects which the commission initiated under his aegis also underline the public importance which he attached to scholarship and education in the democratic era. Most importantly, however, for the purposes of this chapter, Barker found extensive affirmation of England's high cultural standing in Europe in the course of his commission activities. Fortified by this acclaim, he did his utmost to ensure that the bonds between England and the rest of Europe would be well sealed in the future, to mutual advantage. This will emerge if

[3] E. Barker, 'Books for the Allies', *The Spectator*, 29 September 1944, 284–5.

we consider the various responsibilities which were entrusted to the commission, and, in addition, one which Barker pursued on his own initiative.

The most important function of the commission was to ensure the replenishment of libraries in occupied allied countries after the war from the proceeds of a book salvage drive in Britain. A fund for the purchase of recent British books and periodicals was made available by the British government together with Allied governments, these being supplied from a list drawn up by Barker and his colleagues.[4] Both new and old books were distributed from the Inter-Allied Book Centre for which the commission also pressed and managed to secure in government premises in London in 1944. The commission's control of the supply of British books to Allied countries represented a discreet coup on Barker's part against the ambitions of the British Council. Joining forces with W.R. Richardson at the Board of Education, he wrested the operation from a body which he regarded as too much imbued with 'Machiavellianism . . . a looking to *raison d'état*'. For the British Council's 'cloven hoof', he was anxious to substitute what he believed to be the more respectable educational channels of the board, acting through the Books Commission.[5] In his view, the effectiveness of the spread of English influence and goodwill in the form of 'books to the allies' was vitally dependent upon this outcome.

Indeed, Barker's enthusiasm for the work of the commission was kindled by the opportunity he perceived it offered for strengthening Britain's international authority after the Second World War through the broad dissemination of English learning and literature. He derived much pleasure from the expressions of gratitude he encountered from members of foreign academic communities who worked closely with his committee for the refuge they had found in Britain. Their lavish praise of England as a result of this hospitality gave additional fuel to his national pride and his eagerness to make the rich sources of English culture widely available. Throughout 1944 he exerted considerable pressure upon the Board of Education, not least its president, R.A. Butler, to secure an increase in the quota of paper for the publication of educational books which might make their way to the Continent.[6] For example, writing to an official at the board in

[4] E. Barker, 'Books for the Allies'; and W.R. Richardson to the Accountant-General, 11 November 1943, ED42/5, Public Record Office (PRO).

[5] Barker to Richardson, 13 December 1943, ED42/6, PRO.

[6] Barker to Butler, 20 November 1944, ED42/5, PRO.

September of that year he invoked – on the evidence of his commission colleagues – 'a genuine hunger for English books' in Europe. This had resulted from a desire for the products of 'free thought and a free press'; from England being the 'friend' of many European countries during the war; and from a desire to 'escape the German intellectual monopoly'.[7] Seeking to capitalise on this goodwill towards Britain, he urged the board not to allow the springs of English scholarship to run dry, as seemed likely at the beginning of the year. It was of sufficient concern that Britain, together with the British Empire, might be faced with an acute shortage of books for use in schools and universities, thus threatening the 'disappearance of the English spirit'; but when the possibility that Britain might become a key supplier to the European continent was also considered, the case for immediate action seemed overwhelming. Holding out the prospect that these parts of the world would despair of Britain and turn instead to the United States for the books of which they were in desperate need, Barker pleaded for the board's intervention.[8] This was not the only instance of his resistance to the increasing competition for cultural and political influence which the United States posed to Britain in the 1940s, as will be seen presently.

It is worth pursuing further Barker's persistence with the question of paper supplies for educational purposes since it well reflects the high priority he attached to education in matters of politics and culture, in keeping with his understanding of the ideal of 'civility'. This concern now acquired the added dimension of extending British culture abroad, providing a new context in which to assert the primary claims of education upon national resources. Faced with a Board of Education that was reluctant to engage in special pleading on its own behalf lest the state be accused of 'discrimination', Barker insisted on its duty to ensure that educational needs were met before all others in the publishing trade. The present supply of paper, he emphasised, was being rapidly used up by publishers of 'novels and ephemerals' to the detriment of educational books because of the greater income generated by the former. But the criterion of which type of book 'paid best' was inappropriate in considering the distribution of scarce resources of paper. Sharing none of the department's anxiety about courting the state's favour as between one type of publication and another, he admonished: '[m]ust we let

[7] Barker to R. Pares, 30 September 1944, ED42/5, PRO.
[8] Barker to Richardson, 30 January 1944, ED42/5, PRO.

civilization go down the drain in the name of *laissez-faire*?'[9] Venturing a still further suggestion in another exchange on the same subject, he expressed his view that:

> even if a Board of Education quota meant that other departments had a less quota, the Board should still have its own quota. You may say I am prejudiced. I am in favour of sound learning and genuine education. I think that the needs of some of the other departments are, in comparison, ephemeral, and that, on a long view, they do not count equally in the balance.[10]

Ever concerned to elevate the academic profession to positions of major public importance he suggested that, in the event of the board securing its own paper supply, its use should be controlled by a committee of scholars as well as publishers.[11]

However, Barker's efforts to encourage the Board of Education to advance its own claims on the limited supply of paper at the end of the war met with little success. Despite the evidence he submitted from publishers like the Cambridge University Press that the recent increase in the supply of paper for the book trade 'would not go any appreciable way in meeting the European demand', he encountered polite rebuffs from the board.[12] Whilst assuring him that the board would take 'energetic steps' to further the reprinting of books for British students and scholars, and Allied purchasers alike, the President could offer him little hope of any further increase.[13]

If Barker's ambitions for a much increased output of current British educational books were thwarted, he could at least take comfort in the fact that some 600,000 books had been collected for distribution in Allied countries by the time the project closed in 1946. Heartened by this achievement, he invited the Prime Minister to preside over the closing down of the Inter-Allied Book Centre. 'I am genuinely proud of what my country has done', he informed Attlee.[14]

It was the same enhanced sense of national pride which underpinned a further scheme which he attempted to launch in the course of his work for the Books Commission: an Inter-Allied War Museum. Like his pleas for the increased production of educational books through an additional allocation of paper to the Board of Education, the

[9] Barker to Richardson, 3 February 1944, ED/42/5, PRO.
[10] Barker to Richardson, 2 May 1944, ED42/5, PRO.
[11] Barker to Richardson, 5 May 1944, ED42/5, PRO.
[12] Barker to Pares, 30 September 1944, ED42/5, PRO.
[13] Butler to Barker, 21 December 1944, ED42/5, PRO.
[14] Barker to Attlee, 13 October 1946, ED42/6, PRO.

museum project fell on stony ground, a fate which he greatly regretted. But like that campaign also, his museum initiative fully reflected the broad intermixture of patriotism, internationalism, and the primacy of public education which especially preoccupied him during the Second World War and beyond.

The idea of a War Museum was not originally Barker's but that of another member of the Books Commission: Jan Opočenský, a Yugoslav scholar and colleague from Barker's days at King's College. But Barker quickly became the moving force behind it, together with Jacquetta Hawkes at the Board of Education. What particularly seems to have stirred his imagination was the idea of 'Europe in London' to which the museum was intended as a lasting testament. As he expressed his hopes in a memorandum on the project in June 1944, a separate War Museum – with a Library and Research Centre as well – would provide the British public with 'a reminder of a great phase in British history; to the peoples of the Allied countries it would be a permanent memorial and a regular place of pilgrimage'.[15] Realising, however, that this proposal would be costly, he offered an alternative: that of incorporating such a memorial in the existing Imperial War Museum which had been established after the First World War.

Negotiation between these two schemes continued throughout 1945. But the project came to grief on the different dimensions and clientele which its promoters attempted to accommodate; the lack of extensive support among Allied governments; and the reluctance of the Imperial War Museum Trustees to dilute its exclusively English focus, for the purpose of exhibits at least. The expansion of the latter to include European items was central to Barker's vision of the Inter-Allied Museum, providing a memorial to the experiences of civilian populations throughout Europe and a source of enduring public as well as scholarly interest in the war.[16]

The failure of the museum cast a dark shadow over Barker's work for the Books Commission as a whole. As he confided to Richardson with uncharacteristic gloom in 1948, after going over old papers connected with the Commission he was left with a sense that 'much of the work I did came to nothing'. He accepted Richardson's

[15] Memorandum by the Chairman, War Museum, Library and Research Centre, 12 June 1944, ED/42/6, PRO.

[16] Conference of Allied Ministers of Education, History Committee, Memorandum by the Chairman (undated), ED42/6, PRO.

reassurance that considerable good had come out of the commission under his leadership; but he was inconsolable about the eclipse of the museum project. Whilst he could explain his disappointment as the result of a deep dissatisfaction with all unfinished business, the distinct popular, patriotic, and internationalist appeal of the museum meant that he felt its lack of success even more acutely.[17] In his brief account of the Books Commission in his autobiography he made no mention of his keen aspirations for a War Museum, although his remarks there about the Commission being 'a little sanguine' and 'planning for a new world, which we expected with too ready a confidence' evidently referred to that thwarted scheme.[18]

The project for a War Museum in London was an offshoot of the main business of the Books Commission's History Committee, also chaired by Barker: the writing of 'objective' history books. Specifically, the committee pursued the possibility of three publications in the wake of the war: first, a 'handbook' for teachers of history; second, a history of the war; and third, a 'History of European Civilisation'. All three proposals bore Barker's distinct pedagogical imprint. For example, in his initial statement he insisted that the proposed books be free of government control, resulting instead from independent scholarly collaboration. This was the essence of his understanding of 'objective' inquiry, a signal example of 'non-objective' history being provided by 'enemy versions and distortions' of 'the actual course of [recent] events' in occupied countries. In the creation of national myths, the pride engendered by those which were antique and therefore relatively innocuous was one thing; the prejudice and animosity towards other nations bred by the 'new and burning and contemporary' legend which characterised Germany recently was quite another.[19] Barker certainly assumed that there was a single truth to be found in historical study, given sincere and disinterested scholarship. In his mind, the dispassionate effort to understand was inextricably tied to the duties of citizenship. Thus he expressed his concern that 'a general educational purpose should pervade all three works' proposed.[20]

This certainly characterised the style of the one work which came

[17] Barker to Richardson, 2 April, 1948; 24 April 1948, ED42/6, PRO.

[18] E. Barker, *Age and Youth: Memories of Three Universities and Father of the Man* (London, 1953), 213.

[19] E. Barker, Foreword to *A Nazi School History Text Book, 1914–1933*, Friends of Europe Publications, no. 11 (London, 1934).

[20] The History Committee: Memorandum by Ernest Barker on Objective History Books (AME/B/42), ED42/6, PRO.

to fruition, *The European Inheritance*. Published in 1954 in three volumes, it constituted another success for the Books Commission. It was jointly edited by Barker, George Clark, and Paul Vaucher. However, as the other editors acknowledged at the outset, the book had originally been conceived by Barker and he undertook most of the editorial work connected with it. It is not difficult to understand the importance of this enterprise to him; like the museum project, *The European Inheritance* aimed at emphasising the idea of European unity and strengthening public attachment to Europe as a result of Allied co-operation and victory during the war. This was hardly likely to result in 'objective' history. Indeed, as A.J.P. Taylor pointed out in his review of the three volumes, the contributors clearly regarded the notion of 'inheritance' as an unmitigated good, never involving 'burdens and handicaps' but only gains. He added, sardonically, they 'still believe that history is always up and up and up and on and on and on'.[21] Certainly, accustomed to a celebratory and consensual treatment of his own national tradition, Barker was well equipped to write European history in the same bland style when the need arose. We have seen that his enthusiasm for all things English was intricately linked to his appreciation of European development more widely, with its roots in Greek antiquity. *The European Inheritance* paid full homage to this broader cultural and historical environment with which he had always identified, but never with so much zest as during the Second World War. Work for the Books Commission, he claimed in his autobiography, had given him 'a new European outlook'.[22] Indeed, in 1950 he even looked forward to an 'Association of Western Europe', overcoming his usual cautiousness about schemes for re-ordering the political world, particularly at an international level.[23] As well as commissioning many of the contributions to *The European Inheritance*, he wrote a typically expansive 'Review and Epilogue', drawing attention to the main spatial, temporal, and ethnic outlines of Europe.

However, perhaps the most striking feature of his treatment of the book's guiding theme was its consistently applied Whiggism. His observations were not only marked by a heavy dose of Whig optimism; for example, he claimed that Europe was destined to be neither 'Russianized' nor 'Americanized', but instead would remain

[21] A.J.P. Taylor, *New Statesman*, 15 May 1954, 637–8. [22] E. Barker, *Age and Youth*, 212.
[23] Barker to Lionel Curtis, 20 November 1950. MS. Curtis 63, fol. 88, Bodleian Library.

a 'laboratory for the world'.[24] In addition, he read the same Whig sense of temporal continuity, cultural uniqueness, ethnic hybridisation, and striving for free institutions in English history into European history more broadly. The following quotations (in which I have italicised the characteristic language of Whiggism) well capture this 'Whig interpretation of European history' which had been prompted by the war:

Europe has developed, in the course of *a long and continuous history, a unique and peculiar complex* of all the different elements [of religion, morals and manners, law, government, arts, sciences], which is at once peculiarly rich and peculiarly interconnected by the mutual sympathy of its ingredients. (p. 353)

The many marches of Europe – the Spanish; the English marches on the Welsh and Scottish borders; the march of the Rhineland, or middle Kingdom; the marches of east Germany, between the Teuton and the Slav; the marches of east Russia, between the Slav and the Tartar – all these have been areas of *contact* as well as areas of conflict. It is on the marches that we may trace *the cross-fertilization of cultures*. (p. 309)

Civilization began, indeed, outside the periphery of Europe . . . But these early civilizations, while they radiated their influence far afield, were by their very nature enclosed in their river-valleys; and though they attempted expansion and conquest, *their peoples were managed multitudes rather than free communities*, nor had they the salt of the open sea to invigorate their life and stimulate their motion. (p. 308)

This theme of overseas expansion as a distinctive and ennobling trait of European history will be resumed presently. What needs to be underlined first is the extent to which Barker was prepared to share with other European nations what, to a former generation of Whig historians, was a pre-eminently English inheritance. In making common cause between England and Europe, he undoubtedly attempted to give the liberal traditions of his own country – now threatened by encroaching technocracy – greater sanction and legitimacy. The striving for parliamentary freedom and democracy which he primarily discerned in English history could be made part of a general European quest which happened to have been most successfully and continuously worked out in Britain. This is clear from one of his *Essays on Government* published in 1945. There he expressed his belief that the British achievement in developing parliamentary government had been due more to the good fortune of being an island

24 E. Barker, G. Clark, and P. Vaucher (eds.), *The European Inheritance*, 3 vols. (Oxford, 1954), vol. III, 346.

race with a relatively smooth path of social, economic, and religious development than through 'native genius'; althugh the latter had undoubtedly helped in the guise of a strong capacity for tolerance and an empirical and illogical temper. Certainly, the 'spirit' of parliament had seized France as well as England, the setbacks which it had suffered in the former country since 1789 never having succeeded in crushing it entirely. The stormier terrain which the parliamentary movement had encountered in France was purely a function of the 'hard conditions' imposed by geographical frontiers, the sharper social cleavages bequeathed by the *ancien régime*, and the less favourable climate of religion in France.[25]

The concerns of English Whiggism seemed further vindicated after the war in the liberation of the formerly democratic republics in Eastern Europe from Nazi control. Having cultivated a strong and sympathetic interest in this region since his years at King's College London, Barker discerned the ethos of parliamentary liberty in Czechoslovakia, in particular, as well as Britain and France. This is apparent in the course of several close comparisons he made in the 1940s between the polity and general cultural and religious concerns of Czechoslovakia with those of the English.[26]

However, this welcoming of other nations into the Whig fold was by no means confined to European nations. If the experience of the Second World War focused Barker's attention on the European scale of the Whig project, it also seemed to strengthen his belief in the latter's universality. He clearly regarded the British Commonwealth as the main instrument in the universalisation of Whiggism in the twentieth century, despite recognising France as jointly appointed by history to roll forward the parliamentary tide.[27]

A PLURALIST VIEW OF THE BRITISH COMMONWEALTH

Historians have noted that the empire lost much of its former appeal in Britain during the interwar years. Following the Balfour declaration

[25] E. Barker, 'The Parliamentary system of government', in *Essays on Government* (Oxford, 1945), 61–3.

[26] E. Barker, 'British and Czech democracy', in J. Opočenský (ed.), *Edward Beneš: Essays and Reflections on the Occasion of his Sixtieth Birthday* (London, 1945), 41–53; 'The debt of Europe to Czechoslovakia and to Comenius', in J. Needham (ed.), *The Teacher of Nations: Addresses and Essays in Commemoration of the Visit to England of the Great Czech Educationalist Jan Amos Komenský Comenius* (Cambridge, 1942), 78–85; and preface to E. Táborský, *Czechoslovak Democracy at Work* (London, 1945).

[27] E. Barker, *Essays on Government*, 81.

of dominion autonomy at the Imperial Conference of 1926, the enthusiasm of an earlier generation for the idea of Britain as an imperial power began to wane. The decline of Tariff Reform as a burning political issue in the 1920s proved another symptom of the decline of the imperialist cause. The latter also fell victim to the deep suspicion of 'atavistic' territorial ambitions which overcame British society in the wake of the First World War.[28] However, with the outbreak of the Second World War, the empire regained some of its old, turn-of-the-century strength in the public imagination. As A.P. Thornton has remarked, 'the Empire was on the march again', lending renewed credence to the notion that 'Britain's old and much abused role of guardian was in fact essential to the preservation of peace and civilisation'.[29] In this return of interest and confidence in the imperial project, Barker's suggestion that the English nation had inherited the old, classical mantle of empire (that of fulfilling a 'mission of culture – and of something higher than culture') was likely to secure widespread agreement. Empires had always been more than 'mere power', he declared in *The Ideas and Ideals of the British Empire* of 1941; whether in their Hellenistic, Roman, or medieval guise they had always 'carried' some higher aim – that which was expressed in Stoicism, the concept of *jus*, or Christianity respectively.[30] As one might expect in the light of his synthesising instincts, the 'mission' with which Barker envisaged the British Empire as being charged was a combination of all three 'transcendent' ends in previous empires. It was, however, *sui generis*, both in relation to the 'classical' empires and the 'modern maritime' empires; 'not only in the extent and dimensions, and the peculiar liberty, of its colonies of agricultural settlement, but also in the composite character which unites these colonies, in one mixed structure, with colonies largely inhabited by native populations, and involving problems of biological, economic and cultural contact'.[31]

Barker ardently promoted this elevated view of the British Empire during the Second World War, emphasising the important implications for world harmony which had grown out of its pious beginnings in seventeenth-century Puritanism. It was vital to his attempt to reassert the dignity and authority of the empire that its origins be located here

[28] J.H. Grainger, *Patriotisms: Britain, 1900–1939* (London, 1986), 323–6, 329.
[29] A.P. Thornton, *The Imperial Idea and its Enemies* (1959; London, 1985), 317, 319.
[30] E. Barker, *The Ideas and Ideals of the British Empire* (Cambridge, 1941), 19–20.
[31] Ibid., 36–7.

rather than in the colonial military adventure with which it had been associated earlier in the century. He made much of George Unwin's refutation of Sir John Seeley's claim in *The Expansion of England* (1883) that the roots of empire lay in statesmanship, diplomacy, and war during the reign of Elizabeth I and beyond. Echoing Unwin, Barker insisted that British imperial ties had been forged out of the 'peaceful' expansion of English *society*.[32] It was certainly an idiosyncratic view of the British Empire, but it came into its own in the 1940s when the 'ordinary man' became a pivotal symbol of national strength and virtue. Barker cast the pioneer imperialists in analogous terms. He attributed 'the expansion of England' to the Protestant search for an 'escape' from religious uniformity, a movement which began around 1620. In other words, the British Empire in its initial phase was not so much the outcome of the English state's territorial ambitions abroad as a concerted attempt by 'the Englishman in the congregation' to evade its imperiousness at home. The active force in this movement, he believed, was the 'voluntary principle', the spontaneous association of individuals to achieve common ends which was soon to become the hallmark of English life generally.[33]

The roots of this argument in early-twentieth-century Pluralism are not difficult to discern, providing a theoretical foundation which yielded several advantages to the case for the empire. First, in claiming that the British Empire had developed from the English impulse to form groups, Barker could imply that it was as praiseworthy an enterprise as many others with the same origins; for example, the voluntary schools which had pioneered universal education in England. Moreover, extensively ruled through the device of 'the trust' of government on behalf of native populations, the empire could be portrayed as possessing the same high legal standing as the English voluntary association.[34] Finally, 'free association' could be seen as the pervading principle of the Commonwealth – as it was that of English society generally – when newly independent dominions remained within the organisation of their own accord.[35]

[32] G. Unwin, Introduction to C. Gill, *National Power and Prosperity* (1916), in R.H. Tawney (ed.), *Studies in Economic History: The Collected Papers of George Unwin* (London, 1927), 341. Unwin was a vigorous opponent of imperialism, as R.H. Tawney pointed out in his memoir. He would not have sanctioned the existence of a dependent empire. This is clear from the rest of the passage which Barker quoted, in which Unwin delights in emphasising that the British Empire exists 'for the purposes of rhetoric only'. He presumably meant the 'White' empire.

[33] E. Barker, *Ideas and Ideals*, 55–8. [34] Ibid., 65.

[35] E. Barker, Clark, and Vaucher, *The European Inheritance*, 351.

The earliest English settlements overseas had thus been inbued with a religious purpose which had left its distinct mark upon the empire subsequently. Springing to Cromwell's defence, Barker could argue that even when – in the middle of the seventeenth century – the state began to take an interest in the colonies, it was moved primarily by considerations of religious faith.[36] He by no means ignored the operation of other, less noble impulses in the expansion of England; in particular, 'jingoism' and the pursuit of riches had scarred the higher vision which had initially underlain British expansion overseas.[37] But with his usual propensity to see the dark side of English institutions vastly overshadowed by the bright, he expressed his firm faith in the future vitality and role of the empire, especially following its transition to a commonwealth of 'equal' nations with the Statute of Westminster in 1931. Writing in 1950, he emphasised the 'growing force' of the Commonwealth's ideals.[38] Earlier, in 1941, he was similarly confident that the idea of political liberty which was so centrally enshrined in the Commonwealth had not only taken root in the colonies by settlement, but in those which had been acquired by 'conquest and cession' as well.[39] While always maintaining his distance from exponents of imperial federation – such as Lionel Curtis – Barker nevertheless shared their highly idealistic and spiritual conception of empire as a great force for improvement in the world.[40] In this he was also at one with the 'evangelistic' strain of Imperial historiography developed by contemporary Oxford scholars such as Margery Perham and Reginald Coupland.[41] Originally a cross between a *Völkerwanderung* and a 'business proposition', the British Empire in his view had gradually evolved into 'a subtle and intricate structure for the development of human freedom'.[42] Decking out the imperial idea with the full regalia of Dicey's *The Law of the Constitution*, Barker made the empire a vehicle for exporting the twin pillars of British political success: the rule of law – 'ensuring the liberty of every "subject" under the common law' – on the one hand, and representative government, on the other.[43]

It was a vision of empire in which power and force were markedly

36 E. Barker, *Traditions of Civility: Eight Essays* (Cambridge, 1948), 163.

37 E. Barker, *Ideas and Ideals*, 163.

38 E. Barker, 'The ideals of the Commonwealth', *Parliamentary Affairs*, 4, 1 (1950), 18.

39 E. Barker, *Ideas and Ideals*, 49.

40 See his critical review of Curtis' *The Problem of the Commonwealth* (London, 1916), in *Times Literary Supplement*, 749, 26 May 1916, 241–2.

41 Grainger, *Patriotisms*, 325.

42 E. Barker, *Ideas and Ideals*, 8.

43 Ibid., 52 and 162.

absent, as critics such as Leonard Woolf were quick to point out. Reviewing the book for *The Political Quarterly*, Woolf found great merit in it as: 'an elegant portrait of the British Empire – an Academy portrait – seen through the eyes of a Liberal imperialist; idealism has guided the brush to smooth out any wrinkles or creases, blemishes or irregularities'.[44] Woolf certainly underlined here a tendency which pervaded all of Barker's work; an habitual readiness to play up the successes while playing down the failures of British policy, the extent to which British (and European) 'ideas and ideals' had been realised against the extent to which they had not. Woolf conceded that there was undoubtedly some truth in Barker's claim that one half of the purpose of the Dual Trust had been faithfully fulfilled: that which was concerned with 'the advancement of the well-being and the liberty of native populations'. But what of the colour bar in South Africa, Rhodesia, and Kenya which now threatened to spread to the whole of British Africa?[45]

As we have seen, Barker did acknowledge the more questionable sides of British imperial expansion so that it was not quite accurate of Woolf to say that he had presented a 'map and picture' of 'unmitigated rosiness'. But never one to dwell on these things, he left himself open to the charge that he did not take the misdeeds and shortcomings of governing institutions seriously enough. It was not that he harboured dark ideological motives which induced a 'silence' whenever he encountered awkward facts. Rather, his passing over such difficulties derived from an ingrained late-Victorian optimism which had survived out of its due season. He certainly did not belong to the Liberal imperialist camp of Grey, Haldane, and Asquith, where Woolf had placed him and from which he explicitly distanced himself in a reply to Woolf.[46] Whilst he shared the idealism of these earlier imperialists, he was quite indifferent to their equally significant vision of the empire as a major power bloc in world affairs.

The absence of a significant power dimension to Barker's conception of the British Empire/Commonwealth is most apparent in his view that the diffusion of the 'Westminster plus the Strand' model of

[44] L. Woolf, review of E. Barker, *Ideas and Ideals of the British Empire*, *The Political Quarterly*, 12 (1941), 351–2.

[45] Two books which were published in the same year as Barker's *Ideas and Ideals of the British Empire* gave the empire a far less rosy glow. N. Leys, *The Colour Bar in East Africa* (London, 1941); and W.M. MacMillan, *Democratise the Empire* (London, 1941).

[46] He wrote, 'By the way, I was never a Liberal Imperialist, and so far as I know myself I am not one now.' Barker to Woolf, 9 August 1941, Woolf Papers, University of Sussex Library, IM.5.47.

government was not its ultimate end. Rather, he was more inclined to conceive the latter as the promotion of international harmony. This is clearly illustrated in his support for the independence of India, a country which he visited in 1937 as part of a British Association delegation to the Indian Science Congress. Privately, in the same year, he expressed some doubts to a former Cambridge student and now Indian civil servant – W.G. Archer – about the Indians' capacity to overcome their inveterate habit of 'criticism'. As he continued:

> I see, of course, the national spirit which leads to the assertion that no constitution can be a constitution, or can function, unless it is nationally made. But I rather think that that is a bit of westernism, inappropriate to India. The real thing that I want to know is whether [they] can work things, and make them go . . . I feel that they ape opposition too much, and don't face the duty that at last confronts an opposition – the duty of taking on, and of showing what you can do.[47]

However, publicly, he withheld his reservations, especially after Independence and the Indians' adoption of a constitution whose principles were decidedly Western in spirit.[48] Significantly, in his *Ideas and Ideals* of 1941 he maintained that the attainment of dominion status by India would not only strengthen the Commonwealth; it would also 'determine for the better . . . the relations between Occident and Orient, the two main halves of mankind'.[49] There was no question that the Occident was the dynamic force in this process of change; and that it was through absorbing Western ideas of nationalism (in the limited sense of a common national identity which transcended all other social and ethnic divisions) and constitutionalism that India would contribute to the heart of the imperial agenda: the 'general progress of man'.[50] Still, if Barker's ethnocentricity and selective use of the criterion of 'westernism' are evident in such beliefs, he was generally free of European condescension towards colonised

[47] Barker to W.G. Archer, 2 April 1937, Archer Papers, India Office Library and Records, EUR F236/239.

[48] Barker included the Preamble to the Indian Constitution of 1949 after the contents page of his *Principles of Social and Political Theory* (Oxford, 1951). As he remarked in the Preface, 'I am the more moved to quote it because I am proud that the people of India should begin their independent life by subscribing to the principles of a political tradition which we in the West call Western, but which is now something more than Western.' On the deliberations of the Constituent Assembly, and the opposition of those in India who wanted a constitution more in keeping with Indian traditions, see G. Austin, *The Indian Constitution: Cornerstone of a Nation* (Oxford, 1966). [49] E. Barker, *Ideas and Ideals*, 137.

[50] Ibid., 114. Elsewhere he wrote that 'nationality is our gift to India'. E. Barker, 'The contact of colours and civilisations', *The Contemporary Review*, 779 (November 1930), 585.

peoples. Picking up on Archer's concern that Europeans should try to understand and mix with Indians, Barker wrote a sympathetic response which is worth quoting at length:

> My College has now a master who was Commander-in-Chief in India . . ., and a bursar who was director of posts and telegraphs . . . They are very nice people but they are both spoiled by India. They have become conventionalized specimens of good Englishmen, very nice to 'natives' (in a patronizing way) but so 'ruling-classy' that they move my bile. I suppose, as you say, it is the fault of the system, and not of the men themselves – though a good man can rise superior to the temptations of the system. There is a man who lives near us (. . . once a governor of the Punjab), who has a brain and insight. If there were more like him![51]

I have found no record of Barker's attitude to the Suez crisis four years before his death in 1956. But it is doubtful whether even that major post-war blow to imperial pride would have dented his unwavering conviction in the necessity for the Commonwealth and its potential for welding together disparate parts of the globe. Nor could he think that the role of the Commonwealth in diffusing liberal values and acting as a 'bridge' between East and West had been overtaken by the rise of the United States as a world power after the Second World War. Responding to a letter in 1949 from his old Oxford colleague and fellow classicist, Alfred Zimmern – now attached to a UNESCO research centre in Connecticut – he contended that Zimmern had erred in underestimating the sustained international significance of Britain:

> My one reaction is a feeling that you left my country and the British Commonwealth a little out of the picture. I cannot do that. To me – and to some friends whom I have in the USA – the hope of the world is the continuance of our Commonwealth as the great sane *via media* power of the world. I am more passionate about that than about anything else. I would beg you, now that you are settled on the other side of the Atlantic, to remember this side of the Atlantic, and I beg you to remember England. A good quiet country, which does its work (or used to do) without too much talking, but does work.[52]

Again, English national grandeur is here dressed down to the humblest of levels, this undoubtedly being suggested by the reticence and modesty which Barker celebrated in the English character more widely. In tying Englishness to unpretentiousness and general

[51] Barker to Archer, 7 July 1936, Archer Papers, EUR F236/239.
[52] Barker to Zimmern, 10 April 1949, MS. Zimmern 56, fols 110–11, Bodleian Library.

'civility', he could channel the quintessential English virtues of privacy, domesticity, and 'free fellowship' deep into the cause of international co-operation. To some extent this mirrored the Baldwinite attempt in the 1920s and 1930s to ground empire in the simple values of family, home, and countryside, the dominions in this version of the imperial story having developed from the archetypal yearning for the domestic space that was increasingly at a discount in 'England'.[53] Barker also shared Baldwin's constitutionalist vision of the empire, both in the sense of the central values it was seen to have imparted to each member country and the legal rules by which it was governed. (For Barker, the Statute of Westminster of 1931 'involved, in a sense, the making of a new constitution for the British Commonwealth of Nations'.[54] Such an emphasis represented a notable departure from previous accounts of the British Empire, for example those of the historians J.A. Froude and Seeley at the end of the nineteenth century, in which a concern with the constitutional development of 'Greater Britain' was markedly absent.[55] At this time, Whiggism – as the main intellectual protagonist of constitutionalism – and Imperialist thought maintained separate spheres. As will become apparent in the following section, Barker brought this political estrangement to an end. However, the parallel between Barker and Baldwin on matters of empire breaks down at the cosmopolitan vision to which Barker hitched them, in contrast with the more parochial contours of Baldwin's imperialism and his general insularity.[56] In considering the intellectual underpinnings of this cosmopolitanism, it is necessary to return to his conception of 'civility'.

THE GLOBALISATION OF CIVILITY

An intellectual movement which had always preoccupied Barker but which his retirement gave him the leisure to pursue in greater depth than before was that of Stoicism. At the age of eighty-two, in 1956, he published *From Alexander to Constantine*, a collection of documents illustrating 'the history of social and political ideas' from the fourth century B.C. to the fourth century A.D. Nine years earlier, in *Traditions of Civility*, he made clear the impetus behind this project: in his view,

[53] See Bill Schwarz, 'Conservatism, nationalism, and imperialism', in J. Donald and S. Hall (eds.), *Politics and Ideology* (Milton Keynes, 1986), 168–72.

[54] E. Barker, *Ideas and Ideals*, 97.

[55] J.W. Burrow, *A Liberal Descent: Victorian Historians and the English Past* (Cambridge, 1981), 233.

[56] Grainger, *Patriotisms*, 361.

Greek political thought was too much associated with the writings of Plato and Aristotle, the 'post-classical' ideas of the Cynics and Stoics being insufficiently known. But the impact of these later movements was equally significant, carrying the Greek philosophical world deep into that of the Roman. Barker's concern to bring Stoicism – especially – to light lay in that doctrine's conception of a universal natural law transcending the laws of particular communities. To the earlier notion of the *polis* as the locus of citizenship the Stoics, under their founder Zeno, added the notion of the *cosmopolis*. Yet had not the Stoics left a legacy of unresolved conflict here? Barker felt that they certainly had, though this did not diminish but rather enhanced their achievement in his eyes. With his usual aversion to absolutes, he admired the way in which the Stoics could appreciate the imperatives of both the city-state and the world-state, holding together 'different, and yet somehow allied, ideas in an undifferentiated unity'.[57] It was a prescription which he thought had retained its full validity, and never more so than in the twentieth century. One of the great tasks of the time, he thought, was to bring Germany back to this specifically universalist spirit of the 'ancient classical heritage', after its eclipse in the nineteenth century by the 'rolling clouds of a folk-philosophy'.[58]

This argument rehearsed similar ones he had made in the 1930s in contemplating 'the eruption of the group' on the European continent. However, it took on a new, decidedly Whig gloss when grafted upon his articulation of Western *Traditions of civility*. It would be unwise to impose too much coherence on the consciously eclectic character of that work; as Barker acknowledged at the outset, while all but one of the chapters had not been published before, they had originated at different times and for different occasions over a number of years. But given his regular references to the 'continuous' nature of the traditions identified in the book, an attempt to see the work as a whole is not entirely misplaced.

The enigmatic character of the book begins to recede in the light of the common themes between its first and final chapters; between 'Greek influences in English life and thought' and 'Natural law and the American Revolution'. In the early chapters, he asserted that a 'continuous' road existed between Zeno and the French Revolution, between a philosophy which immersed human affairs in the world of

[57] E. Barker, *From Alexander to Constantine: Passages and Documents Illustrating the History of Social and Political Ideas, 336 B.C.–A.D. 337* (Oxford, 1956), 40.

[58] E. Barker, *Traditions of Civility*, 12.

nature and the jettisoning of traditional laws and institutions in the name of 'the natural rights of man'.[59] However, it was more the American Revolution thirteen years previously which interested Barker as the incarnation of Stoic ideals in the modern world. The concluding essay of *Traditions in Civility* on this subject arose out of the Lowell Lectures he gave at Harvard in 1929. In a long and detailed account of the colonists' grievances with English rule, he described how the basis of their case for secession oscillated between an appeal to the 'laws of nature', on the one hand, and 'the rights of Englishmen', on the other. When the revolutionaries drew up their Bill of Rights in 1791, their formulations were thus 'mainly recitals of old English common-law rights'.[60] Furthermore, he maintained, the attractions of natural law to influential American lawyers of the time stemmed in large part from their confusion of it with 'fundamental' or constitutional law; and their keen embrace of the latter was attributable to their high regard for the British constitution.[61]

Therefore, in Barker's account, American resistance to British rule was thoroughly in tune with the deeply ingrained Englishness of the American people. In affirming that Englishness, Barker to some extent echoed the thoughts of his mentor, Lord Bryce. But Bryce's handling of this theme had been more scolding. In *Modern Democracies* (1921), he berated the Americans for 'fancying' themselves a 'new nation' after the Revolution; they had forgotten, 'in the pride of their new nationalism, that both their character and their institutions were due to causes that had been at work centuries before, as far back as Magna Carta and even as the Folk Mots of their primitive ancestors in the days of Ecghbert and Alfred'.[62] Predictably, there was no such hint of recrimination in Barker's analysis. His sympathy with the colonists most closely resembled that of Sir George Trevelyan who, in his *The American Revolution* (1899–1916), had emphasised the decisive English character of that event.[63] In Barker's eyes, not the least important evidence testifying to the English heritage of the Americans and the English basis of their bid for independence – whether they were conscious of it or not – was their legal-mindedness. This was especially reflected in their interest in natural law.[64] The latter was

[59] Ibid., 12. [60] Ibid., 344. [61] Ibid., 330.

[62] J. Bryce, *Modern Democracies*, 2 vols. (London, 1921), vol. II, 8. On Barker's admiration for Bryce, see ch. 2 above, footnote 69.

[63] H.A.L. Fisher, 'The Whig historians', Raleigh lecture on history, *Proceedings of the British Academy* (1928), 335–6. [64] E. Barker, *Traditions of Civility*, 321.

not some 'abstract' conception to which they resorted as the exigencies of the time required; rather, for the revolutionaries it was fully embodied in English legal and political theory from which English practice had wrongfully departed. Accordingly, in this interpretation of the American Revolution, natural law underpinned English law and became the vehicle through which the latter was disseminated beyond English shores. With the support of Lord Acton, Barker characterised the Declaration of American Independence as the universalisation of 'the old and parochial philosophy of Whiggism, making it an "international extra-territorial power"'. In this way, natural law was transformed from a negative, destructive force into one which was 'entirely positive and wholly constructive'.[65]

It is perhaps understandable that, like Burke and the Whig historians who followed him, Barker should have wanted to put as patriotic a face as possible upon the first disruption in the British Empire. But to what further destination was he taking this unmasking of American appeals to natural law, with its revelation of an inner Whig core? He certainly did not believe that the cause which the Americans had espoused was unique to their revolutionary epoch. Rather, the central message he found there was that the 'uprooted and generalised Whig was necessarily also a world-Whig'.[66] Natural law, empire, and Whiggism had thus become inextricably fused, and it is clear that for Barker the process which the Americans had set in motion had continued to be played out in the twentieth century, and on a far wider geographical stage. The universalisation of the Whig concern for 'the common rights of men under the law' had been sanctioned by natural law's cosmopolitan premises, beginning in the American Revolution.

This conception of the British Empire as cemented by the export of Whig ideals can be seen as an attempt to reassert its unity as the fragmentary movement towards independence gathered pace after the middle of the twentieth century; the empire was grounded, he insisted, in 'the liberty of *every* subject of the Crown'.[67] There is of course a danger of reading too much into Barker's reference to natural law as the 'common law of all men'. But it is at least plausible that his strong sympathies with the idea of natural law derived primarily from his identification with another conception of 'the common law', the common law which was native to England. At any rate, he argued

[65] Ibid., 326–7. [66] Ibid., 323. [67] E. Barker, *Ideas and Ideals*, 62.

that the extension of the Whig revolution abroad in the eighteenth century had sealed 'a long line of connection in the tradition of civility which runs from the end of the fourth century B.C.'.[68] Is it not the case that he saw the further progress of the empire and its transformation into the Commonwealth as a continuation of the same project? Certainly, his use of Acton's ideas about the 'detachment' of Whiggism from 'parchments and precedents, . . . leading families and historic conditions', together with his Diceyan analysis of the key objectives of empire, suggest that he did. England/Britain had played a seminal role in transporting overseas all that was best in the European political heritage, all that was best having acquired a pronounced English flavour.

[68] E. Barker, *Traditions of Civility*, 355.

CONCLUSION

A late-Victorian liberal-conservative

THE HOSTILITY OF POSTERITY

On the twenty-fifth anniversary of the Political Studies Association (PSA) in 1975, Wilfred Harrison found it necessary to explain to younger members of the profession why articles by Ernest Barker and G.D.H. Cole had been included in the first edition of *Political Studies* (1953).[1] 'Odd' though those pieces now seemed, Harrison stressed that at the time Barker and Cole had been two 'leading scholars'. Moreover, for those who required further retrospective justification, he added that references had been made to the two authors in recent works of political theory, this being evidence of sustained interest in their writings.[2]

Nevertheless, that attention notwithstanding, Harrison's almost apologetic statement emphasises the semi-obscurity into which Barker quickly plunged not long after his death on 17 February 1960. Until a decade or so previously, he could still count on an audience who upheld the political importance of liberal internationalism, individual freedom, reason, and conciliating class differences. If only among the survivors of his own generation, he could also assume continuing support for the view that the political philosophy and practice of the ancient world contained many valuable lessons for contemporary society. But the liberal underpinnings of these beliefs gave way quite dramatically after the Second World War as Green, Mazzini, and other Victorian prophets of spiritual betterment lost much of their remaining authority.

[1] E. Barker, 'Reflections on English political theory'; G.D.H. Cole, 'What is socialism? I & II'. Both in *Political Studies*, 1 (1953), 6–12, 21–33, 175–83.

[2] W. Harrison, 'The early years of *Political Studies*', in F.F. Ridley (ed.), *Studies in Politics: Essays to Mark the 25th Anniversary of the Political Studies Association* (Oxford, 1975), 186. The books to which Harrison referred where Barker's work was discussed were D.F. Thompson, *The Democratic Citizen* (Cambridge, 1970) and Barry Holden, *The Nature of Democracy* (London, 1970).

Furthermore, Barker never attempted to found a 'school' in the manner of American political science this century, with an extensive research programme and a distinctive methodology by which his legacy might have been carried forward. Such exercises in professional 'cloning' were quite alien to his conception of political inquiry as the reflections of individual scholars working within broad and well-established cultural traditions. It was because the original vision of the PSA was so much in harmony with this ideal of learning that he could give the organisation his wholehearted support. The low-key tone of the circular inviting membership – which bore Barker's name amongst thirteen others – read as follows:

> [i]t is not suggested that the Association should immediately embark on any ambitious functions or projects. An annual meeting for the discussion of papers and the exchange of ideas ought to be possible. The arranging of other meetings, the publication of some kind of research and information bulletin, perhaps even of a journal, would also come up for consideration.[3]

Not surprisingly, Barker's aspirations for a political science that was partially rooted in law came to nothing in these circumstances: in the absence of collaborators and disciples, his project effectively retired with him in 1939. Moreover, his equation of political science with political and legal theory became increasingly unfashionable in the 1950s as the field expanded and took a positivist turn under the influence of Amcrican bchaviouralism. Indeed, political theorists themselves – for example, Michael Oakeshott – were anxious to decouple the two terms, given the 'rationalist' hopes that were now pinned to the term 'political science'. Law – with its liberal doctrine of free agency and concern with 'restraints' upon political rule – would have been considered inappropriate as the handmaiden of political science by most practitioners of the latter after the Second World War. The more politically expansive and deterministic domain of sociology assumed that role instead.[4] Without wishing to jettison the term 'political science' entirely, Barker had always been wary of claims that the subject could yield exact and serviceable truths about political life. Consequently, his authority in the discipline increasingly

[3] Quoted in Norman Chester, 'Political studies in Britain: recollections and comments', in Ridley (ed.), *Studies in Politics*, 30.

[4] A recent account of this conflict on the wider front of the history of the human sciences – one which is framed in terms of 'Nomos' versus 'Physis' and clearly champions the former – is Donald R. Kelley, *The Human Measure: Social Thought in the Western Legal Tradition* (Cambridge, Mass., 1990).

became confined to the sphere of political theory. Indeed, in the years immediately before his death his books enjoyed the status of being 'probably the most widely read' by students of that subject, along with those of H.J. Laski and A.D. Lindsay.[5]

Not that there was much else in this line of work around at the time. One sympathetic reviewer of Barker's *Principles of Social and Political Theory* (1951) had to admit that, despite the book's 'highly conservative flavour', it nonetheless represented 'an immensely valuable addition to the all-too-empty shelf of modern contributions to political philosophy in the round'.[6] The problem was that by the 1950s political theory and philosophy had received the full wrath of the logical positivists. When T.D. Weldon published *The Vocabulary of Politics* in 1953, the kind of normative reflection upon political life in which Barker engaged was sentenced to death. It is true that the subject in this guise failed to expire, major contributions being made in subsequent years by Isaiah Berlin, H.L.A. Hart, F.A. Hayek, and Michael Oakeshott, for example.[7] However, it did suffer stiff competition from the appoach of linguistic analysis, which was confined to examining the uses of political terms in 'ordinary language'.

Weldon's dismissal of 'classical political philosophy' was reinforced by the work of empiricists like W.J.M. Mackenzie. While critical of the positivist excesses of American political science and while also appreciative of the 'Greats tradition' of the study of politics in Britain earlier in the century, nevertheless Mackenzie attempted to reshape the latter through focusing primarily upon policy, administration, and political actors.[8] There is perhaps no more telling indication of the distance between prewar and post-war political science in Britain than Mackenzie's review of Barker's *Principles of Social and Political Theory*. He began by quoting a passage from the book in which Barker asserted the 'drabness' of a world organised around the satisfaction of 'social wants' by 'social engineers'. For Barker, this ideal was antithetical to the notion of 'a world of persons' and hence 'a world of values' which constituted 'a fact of all time'. To this extent,

[5] W.A. Robson, *The University Teaching of the Social Sciences: Political Science* (Paris, 1954), 216.

[6] D. Thomson, *The Spectator*, 187, 21 December 1951, 860.

[7] J. Gray, 'Against the new liberalism: Rawls, Dworkin and the emptying of political life', *Times Literary Supplement*, 3 July 1992, 13.

[8] Mackenzie had been inspired by Weldon's interest in science at Oxford in the 1930s, and he defended the integrity of Weldon's linguistic approach to political theory in a short autobiographical essay. W.J.M. Mackenzie, *Explorations in Government: Collected Papers: 1951–1968* (London, 1975), xxi.

Mackenzie remarked, the book belonged to 'a great tradition'. But he could scarcely conceal his disdain ('[t]his is grand', he commented, with more than a hint of facetiousness), suggesting that Barker's vision was inadequate to the reforming tasks ahead of British politics and political science. He concluded the review on an ominous note:

> Anyone (and there are very many) who has worked for the State since 1939 will be startled to hear that 'the movement of the State is the regular revolution of steady and unfailing machinery' . . . In fact, Sir Ernest's reformulation of an unending tradition is related to a point in time, and that point is 1938 rather than 1951. His book will probably be the classic of a period . . ., it will be a powerful instrument of education for a very long time. But it may soon need its own gloss.[9]

Barker's work evidently ceased to command a high level of respect as the climate of political studies changed in Britain after 1945. However, one can argue that it has become less marginal to current political concerns, for all its roseate view of the workings of (British) government at which Mackenzie correctly looked askance. The empirical model of political science which displaced Barker's was itself short-lived; rooted in the technocratic optimism of the post-war world, particularly the view that society could be permanently reshaped for the better by the piecemeal reforms of an enlightened state, it lost much ground when the approach of the engineers became discredited in the 1970s. There was by no means an intellectual void in the discipline when sociology fell from grace as the cornerstone of political understanding; economics – in the form of rational choice theory – quickly stepped into the breach. Nonetheless, dissatisfaction has grown with the sustained instrumental and reductionist conception of politics, despite this recent change of paradigm. In both the political science of the 1960s, on the one hand, and the 1980s, on the other, the idea of the political was obscured by external projects for which it became the agent: the 'planned society', economic growth, social welfare, and so forth. By contrast, classical notions of political life have acquired a new purchase of late through a heightened interest in constitutional issues. For example, the organisation 'Charter 88' in Britain has helped to switch the focus of political debate away from issues of material well-being to an older location in the formal and procedural basis of government. As I emphasise later in this conclusion, Barker by no means neglected questions concerning

[9] *The Guardian*, 23 November 1951, 4.

social justice and 'the good life'. But these were ancillary to what he regarded as of primary importance in 'the great sphere of politics'. There, as he wrote in 1937, 'the process of life is greater than its objectives, and the method of governing superior to the aim of government'.[10]

The present affirmation of the distinctiveness of politics in some circles can gain much from thinkers of an earlier generation, particularly Barker, R.G. Collingwood, and Michael Oakeshott. While the common ground between the last two figures is frequently underlined, Barker's similarities with (as well as differences from) his near-contemporaries have been overlooked.[11] The superiority of the work of all three writers over much post-war political thought lies in their shared emphasis upon the centrality of political order to civilisation more generally. This enabled them to catch the wider historical dynamic of the political world, something that was lost in the static, empiricist outlook which prevailed in political studies during later decades. The framework of 'civilisation' also influenced their association of politics with modes of specifically public conduct and relations, in some sense separated from ordinary, private existence, which they regarded as integral to the ideal of 'civility'.[12] While this sense of the autonomy of things political was confused with the search for social and moral cohesion in the British Idealist tradition, nevertheless the latter underpinned its clearest articulations in British political thought in the twentieth century. Barker, Collingwood, and Oakeshott all developed the potential in Idealism for a legal and hence limited conception of politics, this being embodied in the idea that the state's overriding concern is with 'external' acts.[13] It may seem that their ideas were too much steeped

[10] E. Barker, 'The conflict of ideologies', *The Citizen's Choice* (Cambridge, 1937), 14.

[11] I briefly touched upon the parallels in the political thought of Barker and Collingwood in ch. 7 above. It is also significant that both Barker and Collingwood were much influenced by the Italian Idealist, Benedetto Croce. The latter provided them with an antidote to the historical deficiencies in British Idealism. I mentioned Barker's admiration for Croce in the Introduction. See also the Conclusion below, p. 216. On Collingwood's debt to Croce, see D. Boucher, *The Social and Political Thought of R.G. Collingwood* (Cambridge, 1989), 10–21. On the affinities between the political thought of Collingwood and Oakeshott, see P. Franco, *The Political Philosophy of Michael Oakeshott* (New Haven, 1990), *passim*.

[12] I by no means wish to endorse the prevailing distinction between the public and private spheres of life in Western society, one which is detrimental to women who are confined to the latter sphere and which has been much contested by feminist thinkers. I simply assert the importance of maintaining a distinction, albeit in non-gendered terms.

[13] See above, ch. 6, for Barker's debt to Gierke's Idealism in fashioning a legal conception of politics. On Collingwood, see above, ch. 7. Oakeshott also separated the potential for a 'negative politics' in Idealism from its rationalist tendencies. See R. Grant, *Oakeshott*

in an elite celebration of English political culture and institutions to be of much interest now. Yet as I argue below in relation to Barker, his complacency and sanguinity often represented a triumph of faith over considerable anxiety about modern social and political life. That anxiety is not so easily dismissed as his now rare optimism.

INDIVIDUALITY AND THE PROBLEM OF GROUPS

Before further evaluation of Barker's political thought, it is first necessary to summarise his outlook and situate it within a broader intellectual spectrum. While recognising that such endeavours are always rough and arbitrary, I suggest that Barker's ideas about society and politics are best located in the large although sparsely populated terrain of liberal-conservatism. It was one which other prominent liberals of his generation came to inhabit as the twentieth century unfolded, for example G.M. Trevelyan and Gilbert Murray. Writing to Barker in 1939, Murray asserted his continued loyalty to Gladstonian liberalism but, at the same time, the increasing attraction which conservative principles held for him. He continued:

> I do not in the least mean the principles of the Primrose League or the Central Conservative Association; I mean the truth that the anthropologists teach us so emphatically, that every savage tribe, or indeed every human community, is held together and supported by an immense network of customs, traditions and beliefs, and is apt to fall to bits if you remove them too rapidly or violently. It is the network of normal expectations that holds society together, and once you begin not to know what to expect, things are dangerous.[14]

Barker heartily concurred, replying that 'some security of expectation is the basis of manners, morals, politics'.[15] Yet despite his long-standing sympathies with British conservatism and his association with prominent Tory figures,[16] his identification with the conservative tradition was qualified. In much of the analysis which follows, his *Reflections upon Government* of 1942 will be used to assess the balance and

(London, 1990), 30–2. The prominence of the concept of 'civility' in his thought, as in that of Collingwood and Barker, is apparent in Oakeshott's later work, *On Human Conduct* (Oxford, 1975).

14 Murray to Barker, 18 March 1939, MS. Murray 86, fol. 142, Bodleian Library. On Trevelyan's shift from liberalism to conservatism in the interwar period, specifically through his friendship with Stanley Baldwin, see D. Cannadine, *G.M. Trevelyan: A Life in History* (London, 1992), 158–60.

15 Barker to Murray, 20 March 1939, MS. Murray 86, fol. 144.

16 See ch. 7 above, pp. 168–9.

coherence of his political convictions, that work representing perhaps the most comprehensive statement of his ideas.

Initially, the general tenor of his liberal-conservatism is well captured in a passing remark which he made towards the end of his autobiography while ruminating upon the changing character of English roads between his youth and his old age. Previously associated with peacefulness and solitude, if coarse surfaces, they had now become 'macadamized' and regulated. These developments were the inevitable consequence of 'speed and congestion', and in Barker's mind they provided an allegory of a wider transformation in twentieth-century society. Not all social changes in the last few years of his life displeased him. For example, he welcomed the new domestic circumstances of his family in the post-war world, one in which 'daily keeps' (a cook and a house maid) had taken the place of 'live-in' servants. The latter, he wrote to Violet Markham, felt themselves to be 'slaves', whereas the former ensured 'a more human and pleasant way of life' rooted in a spirit of 'unenvious and friendly' equality.[17] That remark was perhaps negatively inspired by the policies of 'compulsory' and 'organised' equality which he associated with the Labour Party. Yet, in general, he was unenthusiastic about the pace and direction of change in Britain in the 1950s. His reflection upon the roads prompted this reaction: 'I suppose there is a mulish Victorian in me which wants to go slow, and, even more, wants to be let alone.'[18] At what levels are these two personal, and yet at the same time fundamentally political impulses – embodying this conservatism and liberalism respectively – interwoven in his writings?

We may begin a response to this question by considering Barker's perpetual tendency to make virtues of retreat, solitude, and the keeping of one's distance from society, a feature of his thought which has been accentuated throughout this study. It is a point which he made with almost obsessive regularity, never losing an opportunity to assert the 'personal and the private' as necessities of the human spirit.[19] This insistence was rooted in his Nonconformist background, attracting him to 'classical' liberal thinkers such as J.S. Mill even while he rejected what he perceived as their too rigid divorce between the individual and society, on the one hand, and their political

[17] Barker to Violet Markham, 18 January 1955, Markham Papers, British Library of Political and Economic Science, 25/1.

[18] E. Barker, *Age and Youth: Memories of Three Universities and Father of the Man* (London, 1953), 230.

[19] For example, see E. Barker, *Age and Youth*, 235.

intransigence, on the other.[20] He took from these writers a defence of what he termed 'the integrity of individual personality', and an urgent sense of the need to protect it against excessive intrusions from both society and the state. It is in this context that the remark cited earlier about his 'Victorian' impulse to be 'left alone' is best placed. Naturally, this concern would have heightened his high Burkean regard for English liberties. But in registering this esteem, one should not underestimate the quest of the Puritan soul for occasional refuge from society – the sense of feeling overwhelmed even by the society of the Congregation – which constituted its essential source. As such, his individualism must be distinguished from that popular mid-Victorian sense of freedom as 'doing what one likes', against which Matthew Arnold attempted to set the higher aspirations of 'our best self'.[21] It must also be detached from the individualism of the circle of writers which developed around Herbert Spencer's political thought in the late-nineteenth century: Wordsworth Donisthorpe, Auberon Herbert, and others. Their stalwart defence of liberty as – above all else – an absolute right to property was no part of Barker's intellectual brief. He always regretted that the nobility of Puritanism had become tarnished by its adoption of 'Midas' as an ally, just as much as it had degenerated into a Bible-despotism in New England.[22] While never an all-round enthusiast of state intervention, he rejected the principle of *laissez-faire* to which the concern for property rights and free competition gave rise. His conception of the state as a culture-state as well as a law-state firmly ruled out the Spencerian brand of individualism, and the peculiar type of 'liberal conservatism' which accompanied it.[23]

These dual Nonconformist/Burkean sympathies lie at the root of Barker's distinctiveness as a political theorist in the first half of the

[20] In a BBC talk in 1946, Barker agreed with critics of Mill who denied 'the validity of [his] distinction between the other-regarding part of a man's life and the self-regarding part . . . All we are and all we do touches others as well as ourselves.' Yet he added, revealingly, '[b]ut all the same I have always been moved by Mill's argument. His plea for the rights of individuality may be defective, but it is precious.' Swedish News Talk entitled 'John Stuart Mill and his essay *On Liberty*', 8 January 1946, typescript in the Barker Papers, Peterhouse, Box VIII.

[21] M. Arnold, *Culture and Anarchy: An Essay in Political and Social Criticism* (London, 1869), ch. 2.

[22] E. Barker, 'The discredited state: thoughts on politics before the war', *Political Quarterly*, 2 (February 1915), 104; also see his essay on 'Puritanism' (1929), reprinted in *Church, State, and Study* (London, 1930).

[23] On these writers, see M.W. Taylor, *Men Versus the State: Herbert Spencer and Late Victorian Individualism* (Oxford, 1992).

twentieth century. But they opened up a large gulf in his thought, even while they reinforced each other at the limited level of endorsing the importance of human liberty. The division is reproduced and perhaps best explored in other allegiances which he formed around these two influences; for example, between Idealism, on the one hand, and liberal individualism, on the other. While he readily endorsed Idealist accounts of the self as inseparable from institutions and communities, nevertheless he was always quick to defend the greater claim of individual liberty against the requirements and pressures of group solidarity. Indeed it is noticeable that he used Idealist assertions of the *social* framework of moral freedom to qualify the stronger emphasis he continually placed upon *individual* liberty. He never reversed this sequence, that is, by qualifying Idealist theories of the 'social' self by a residual individualism. Thus, after some forceful statements on the 'ultimate liberty of individual personality' in his *Reflections Upon Government* he asserted that, of course, the moral action of individuals entailed by human freedom vitally required the context of society: 'If we abolish the notion of this interplay of like agents, we abolish the very idea of moral action, and we thus extinguish moral personality, which exists in and by such action.' But he ensured that the discourse of individualism regained the upper hand in his argument. The 'common thought and will' which was both the condition and consequence of this moral interaction must not be construed as separate from individuals, standing over and against them; rather, it existed 'within' them, and might be rejected as well as accepted by them. The Nonconformist in Barker spoke loud and clear here, committing – from a conservative perspective – the ultimate heresy of believing that: 'There are times and seasons when we may feel it our duty, and our true liberty, to guide ourselves by a conception of good which is beyond social thought and social will, and proceeds immediately from our own deepest self.'[24]

Barker's concerted defence of the liberty and dignity of individuals against groups, crowds, multitudes, races, 'confessions', and so forth formed the *leit motif* of all his writings. It is perhaps no exaggeration to say that, throughout his life, he was greatly unnerved by the spectre of heightened group consciousness. This is clear from his habit of conveying the daunting nature of communal politics by the use of vivid spatial imagery; for example, 'surging', 'heaving', 'rolling',

[24] E. Barker, *Reflections upon Government* (Oxford, 1942), 16–18.

'Titanic', 'eruption', and 'colliding wills'. The small-scale, informal, convivial atmosphere of the English club or voluntary association was one thing; the mobilisation of whole sectors of society quite another. In shrinking from the latter, a number of comparisons may be drawn between Barker and other nineteenth- and twentieth-century writers for whom group life proved similarly disconcerting. However, the singularity of Barker's attitudes will become readily apparent.

First, a parallel may be drawn with Sir Henry Maine's analysis of the movement of 'progressive' societies in his *Ancient Law* of 1861. Maine, too, was much exercised by the tendency of groups, particularly the family, to 'swallow up' the individuality of persons. But in his confident, mid-Victorian view, such a phenomenon was most typical of primitive societies organised around the principle of 'status'; by and large, it had been eclipsed in the modern world by the individualist bonds of 'contract'. For all Maine's awareness of the rarity and fragility of 'progress', nevertheless he could assert that once achieved the change in question – to date at any rate – 'has not been subject to reaction or recoil'.[25]

Barker's contrasting sense that human 'gregariousness' had acquired a new and unsettling prominence in modern society was shared with contemporary European thinkers, particularly the Spanish philosopher José Ortega y Gassett. In *The Revolt of the Masses* (1930), the latter wrote of the menacing threat to civilisation posed by the upheaval of human 'agglomerations' which had been 'let loose' upon history by the nineteenth century; they now bestrode the modern world 'like giants'.[26] Unlike Ortega, though, Barker did not depict this development in terms of an atavistic tribalism. Instead, he emphasised the *sui generis* character of group life in the modern world. Whatever its affinities with the early condition of mankind, the reascendance of groups sprang from developments that were unique to modernity.

Venturing an analogy with a third modern thinker, we might compare this insistence with the views of the early-twentieth-century social psychologist William MacDougall. MacDougall had devoted a short chapter of his *Social Psychology* (1908) to 'the gregarious instinct', emphasising that in modern times it no longer served its positive function in early social evolution of providing 'the conditions of aggregation in which alone the higher evolution of the social

[25] H. Maine, *Ancient Law: Its Connection with the Early History of Society* (1861; London, 1905), 169, 183.

[26] J. Ortega y Gassett, *The Revolt of the Masses* (1930; English transl. London, 1932), 23.

attributes was possible'. For MacDougall, gregariousness among humans had now become counterproductive, constituting 'one of the greatest demoralising factors of the present time in this country'.[27] Yet MacDougall's tendency to explain all social life in terms of the different conditions which affected the play of 'instinct' always remained alien to Barker's explanation of society in terms of 'Mind'.[28] Essentially, for Barker, the developments in question boiled down to 'numbers', particularly: 'the new physical contacts of numbers produced by a new material civilization, from the new *mental* filaments of connection between numbers spun by all the new agencies of education'.[29] Modern group identities, that is, were marked by a high degree of reflectiveness of the kind he had outlined in his initial response to Pluralist ideas: that which centred upon the 'organising ideas' at the heart of collective life. Given his Idealist understanding of the basis of group cohesion in contemporary society, his response to the latter was not entirely negative. In particular he recognised that groups inspired nobility, heroism, and devotion, properties which undoubtedly appealed to the surviving Hellenist in him. However, any good which might come from the revival of these qualities in the modern world was in his view considerably outweighed by the intensity and exclusiveness to which group life tended. Groups easily dominated their members, becoming 'something above them and apart from them, for which they must live and to which they are means'.[30]

When groups laid claim to sovereignty, Barker's disquiet at 'the cult of the group' in modern political life and thought was associated with the distinction which he constantly drew between state and society. He defined the former in the impersonal terms of law and the latter as a more intimate realm of free association and the pursuit of common purposes. Indeed, so insistent was he about the sharpness of this distinction that he even detected its absence in the conservatism of Burke. He classed Burke with Plato (and Aristotle) as offering a vision of the 'total' state because of his conception of the latter as 'a partnership in all science; a partnership in all art; a partnership in every virtue; and in all perfection'. A state which subsumed society

27 W. MacDougall, *An Introduction to Social Psychology* (London, 1908; eighteenth edn, 1923), 296–301.

28 This difference emerged clearly in Barker's *Political Thought in England from Herbert Spencer to the Present Day* (London, 1915), 157.

29 E. Barker, *Reflections upon Government*, 266. (My italics.)

30 Ibid., 151.

was unsustainable, inviting challenge from individuals who rejected its excessive demands and from subordinate bodies which would seek their own 'enthronement' instead. The essential generality of the state would be supplanted by the particular goals of groups, be they classes, nations, occupations, or whatever. I emphasised in an earlier chapter that Barker's anxiety about the threat which organised groups posed to the 'universal' nature of the state originated in the political turmoil before and after the First World War. In his view, the outbreak of Syndicalism, Bolshevism, and Nationalism in Europe represented an evasion of the complex problem of conflicting loyalties in society by demanding that loyalty to the groups which these movements represented should override every other. In doing so, the latter sought to abrogate the role of the state as the 'ultimate' centre of adjustment and reconciliation in society by elevating their own specific and limited ends.[31]

Barker attributed the eclipse of the distinction between society and state when the latter fell prey to particular group purposes to the upsurge of 'the personal' in modern politics. He not only linked this to the increasing significance of individual political leaders; he also invoked the same term to characterise the reification of groups in the twentieth century. He was exceptionally wary of exaggerated notions of group solidarity reflected, in particular, in misguided attempts to convert their legal personality into a 'real' personality. He most feared the adverse consequences here for the essentially 'juridical' nature of the state. The state being no more (but no less) than a framework of rights and duties in a certain territory, it was necessarily impartial, impersonal, and limited. But once dominant groups laid claim to 'transcendent' personalities – thereby 'negating' the personalities of their individual members – and once they sought to lodge that personality in the state, all other purposes in society would dissolve. The triumphant group would seek to universalise its cause, thereby inaugurating a totalitarian state. An inherited system of law – enforcing 'external' standards of conduct only – would be superseded by the will of the group's leaders masquerading as 'the general will' and discarding all previous constraints upon political rule.

Hence for Barker, 'organic' theories of both the state and lesser groups erred in endowing it with a transcendent personality and will, and were thus replete with totalitarian implications. Again, traditional

[31] Ibid., 23.

conservatism was as much the target of his attack as the more strident exponents of 'group personality'. This clearly emerged in his earliest work, *The Political Thought of Plato and Aristotle*, where he castigated the 'over-conservatism' of Burke arising out of his organicist leanings.[32] Perceiving totalitarianism as the apotheosis of the group in modern society, Barker sought to separate loyalty to the state from specific communal attachments. To Barker, intense forms of nationalism especially represented the antithesis of the liberal state, obscuring perhaps the *only* political principle which he failed to water down with any other: that is, that in democratic societies at least, 'the idea of personality has a statuesque precision, . . . each person stand[ing] out firm and clear in his own existence'.[33] Highly receptive though he was to the importance of national character and tradition in human life, he regarded the political application of nationalism with acute misgivings. In this he was close to the conservatism of Michael Oakeshott who also stripped the state of 'substantive' collective goals.[34]

DEMOCRACY AND THE PRIORITY OF IDEALS

A further illustration of Barker's distance from mainstream British conservatism is his wholehearted commitment to democracy – democracy by discussion, that is. This also set him apart from critics of mass society like Ortega y Gassett whose political concerns he otherwise shared. He denied the contradiction between democracy and liberty which had troubled many nineteenth-century thinkers in Britain, such as Maine and W.E.H. Lecky. This followed Tocqueville's insights into the uniformity of ideas and aspirations in American democracy arising out of its egalitarian pressures, an outcome which Barker was more inclined to attribute to an 'original Puritan temper' rather than defects in the democratic ideal itself.[35] Democracy, he believed, had suffered much discredit from the view that it was

[32] See ch. 2 below, pp. 48–9. [33] E. Barker, *Reflections upon Government*, 194.

[34] Oakeshott, *On Human Conduct*. However, Barker departed from Oakeshott in upholding the liberal causes of 'humanity' and international unity at the same time as he rejected state-centred nationalism. He regarded the discredit which the ideal of internationalism suffered when groups such as nations closed in upon themselves as not the least regrettable aspect of the latter phenomenon. He wrote: 'If the self-conscious nation persists in its own self-consciousness, and sets its attention wholly towards the unique and incommunicable character of its own ideals and its place in the world, it will deny the very idea of any international system in which it can be included and by which it can be limited.' E. Barker, *Reflections upon Government*, 277.

[35] E. Barker, *National Character and the Factors in its Formation* (London, 1927; 1928), 170.

'quantitative' rather than 'qualitative' in nature, pitting 'numbers' against intelligent political leadership. In reality, however, democracy was logically entailed by the central assumption in liberalism of the 'intrinsic individuality' of the human spirit. Liberalism should not be construed as 'mere negativism', constantly imposing vetoes on the claims of the organised state. Nor was the 'mass-vote' the essence of democracy as Joseph Schumpeter argued in his *Capitalism, Socialism, and Democracy* which was published in the same year as Barker's *Reflections upon Government.* Rather, both liberalism and democracy entailed: 'the thinking and discoursing mind which can dare to raise and to face conflicting views of the Good, and to seek by the way of discussion some agreed and accepted compromise whereby a true (because) national will is attained, as it cannot otherwise be, and a national Good is secured which is really good because it is freely willed'.[36] Placing himself squarely in the tradition of Milton and Mill, Barker maintained that liberty and democracy constituted one inseparable cause rather than two which existed in a state of tension. More central than the prevalence of the 'will of the people' to democracy was 'the grand dialectic of public debate' underlying popular sovereignty. The only alternative to democracy in the modern world was 'dictatorship', the substitution of the 'simplistic' and 'immediate' representation of the people in the will of a single person or party for an 'impersonal system of representative institutions'.[37]

The importance which Barker attached to democracy as integral to a liberal society contrasts with the far more muted response which the democratic ideal has received in the conservative tradition. Certainly conservative thinkers have endorsed democracy, but with no great degree of enthusiasm and with none of the high hopes of enhancing the moral and intellectual level of human life which liberals have characteristically nurtured in connection with that system of government. According to Oakeshott, for example, 'the major part of mankind has nothing to say';[38] hence the right of free speech which liberals have regarded as part and parcel of democracy is less significant – although by no means insignificant – than other liberties such as freedom of association and freedom to own property.

[36] E. Barker, *Reflections upon Government*, 4.

[37] E. Barker, 'Democracy since the war and its prospects for the future', *International Affairs*, 13, 6 (1934), 756.

[38] Quoted in R. Eccleshall, 'Michael Oakeshott and sceptical conservatism', in L. Tivey and A. Wright (eds.), *Political Thought since 1945: Philosophy, Science, Ideology* (Aldershot, 1992), 179.

Democracy is not to be looked upon as an 'ideal', offering limitless scope for human improvement; for improvement, in the conservative's world, is a mirage, certainly as pursued through public institutions. Democracy, for Oakeshott at least, is essentially an inherited 'practice' which is distorted if abridged by theory. If it is to be exported, for example, far better that 'the workmen travel with the tools', as occurred in British overseas expansion, than that it be 'packed up and shipped abroad' in the form of a compact set of abstract ideas.[39] Democracy is thus to be revered simply as a constitutional device of representation which provides a check upon arbitrary power and one which, moreover, preceded all modern theories of the popular will.

The qualified support which conservatives have given to democracy is closely linked to a pessimistic view of human nature and a corresponding emphasis upon human imperfection. Conservatives characteristically scorn utopian styles of politics which seek to eradicate the ills of humankind and to secure a lasting reign of virtue in human society. Much the same antipathy can be seen in Barker's thought; in, for example, his hostility towards planning and technocracy and the widespread modern preference for state action at the expense of voluntary agencies. His attachment to the 'amateur' nature of English government against the 'science of the state' which had been perfected on the Continent well illustrates the cautious, moderate conservative within him, one who always recoiled from ambitious schemes for reconstructing society where existing practices seemed solid. The significance of this qualification will become apparent presently.

Yet it was not on account of any inordinate pessimism about the human condition that he adopted this stance; rather his scepticism of the reforming impulse in politics lay in his habitual concern for 'individuality'. In harbouring few doubts about the moral and political capacities of the bulk of humankind, given sufficient educational provision, his distance from conservatism is particularly marked. He would not have endorsed Burke's doubts about the capacities of the 'swinish multitude' for self-government which have continued to inform the conservative tradition subsequently. As long as the *esprit de corps* of both groups and society as a whole was kept within bounds, all would be well. While never underestimating the difficulty of this task, nevertheless he was at least hopeful that it could be achieved.

[39] M. Oakeshott, 'Political education', *Rationalism in Politics: and other Essays* (London, 1962), 122.

Barker's greater confidence in the political aptitudes of 'ordinary' humanity than is usual among conservative thinkers is well captured in the letter he wrote to Graham Wallas in 1914 praising the latter's recent book, *The Great Society*. He expressed his pleasure in sharing the thoughts on modern political life of one who could 'see the worst and yet believe in the best'.[40] He was obviously referring to Wallas' emphasis upon the continuing role of rational thought in politics, despite the weight of evidence against it in the political behaviour and attitudes of mass electorates. But the remark possesses a wider resonance too in that it reflects the invincible optimism which informed all of Barker's work. This also led him to focus upon 'ideals' at the expense of the failure of human institutions to live up to their ideals, a shortcoming of Idealist political thought generally in the eyes of its critics. In a correspondence with Leonard Woolf following the latter's critical review of his *Ideas and Ideals of the British Empire* in 1941,[41] Barker accepted Woolf's dissatisfaction with the book. He admitted that his 'disposition' to 'look at the ideal sought' could lead to a 'facile optimism and to a condoning of wrong'. Replying to Woolf's point that the colour bar in South Africa represented a shameful face of the empire, he confessed that he had always been 'hurt' by this development. But as was his wont, after acknowledging the defects of a particular approach he wanted to defend, he emphasised – without being specific in this case – that it had its 'advantages' too. He also made it clear that he was unlikely to abandon his course of concentrating upon 'ideals' above all else in political analysis. As he continued: 'It is probably grounded in a sort of "softness" in my own character; but I think the study of Aristotle (and of his general theory that the end sought is the reality and the true "nature") has helped to confirm it.'[42]

The disclosure of this Aristotelian source of his equanimity highlights the enduring legacy of his early contact with Idealist political philosophy. The latter – as interpreted through the texts of Aristotle, especially – imbued him with a sense of the primacy of 'spirit' in human affairs and its capacity to overcome all adversity. He also derived from Idealism a conception of the importance of external – political – organisation for the fulfilment of the individual's potential

[40] Barker to Wallas, 15 July 1914, Wallas Papers, British Library of Political and Economic Science, 1/57, 2 (111). [41] See above, ch. 8, p. 190.

[42] Barker to Woolf, 19 August 1941, Woolf Papers, University of Sussex Library. IM5, 47. I am indebted to Jan Aart Scholte for this reference.

for 'spiritual growth'. The balance between the 'inward' and 'outward' parts of human life was a very difficult one to strike, as Barker no doubt learned from Green and Bosanquet. But clear evidence that such a medium was possible could be found in the development of English polity, grounded as it was in the dual principles of 'the rule of law' and representative government. Inoculated against gloom by Idealism and Whiggism jointly, he maintained an unswerving faith in the ultimate triumph of social and political ideals which gave a high priority to personal freedom.

POLITICS, ECONOMICS, HISTORY

Obviously, Barker's liberalism is of a peculiarly late-nineteenth-century English variety. Just as his conservatism is well removed from some aspects of traditional and contemporary conservatism, so his liberalism withstands little comparison with current versions of the latter, even those which border closely on conservatism. If we consider the liberalism of F.A. Hayek, for example, there might, on the surface, appear to be a good deal in common with Barker's political thought. Focusing, in particular, upon Hayek's constitutionalism and his conception of the 'rule of law' as the cornerstone of political life, a common liberal vision is readily apparent. This affinity is especially evident when Hayek's Burkean defence of customary law and traditional institutions as the mainstays of a secure social order are also taken into account. The analogy breaks down, however, in view of the instrumental value which Hayek primarily attaches to liberty. As commentators on Hayek have pointed out, he accorded a high premium to liberty not so much because it enhances individual self-development but as a necessary precondition of progress defined as economic prosperity. The importance to his vision of human life of a fixed set of laws revolves crucially around their role in providing the best climate for wealth-creation.[43] To appreciate the distance of this central concern of neo-liberalism from the liberalism which Barker upheld, we need only note the latter's acerbic remarks in *Reflections upon Government* about the pursuit of what he termed 'unitarianism' in politics. This was the passion for fusing essentially different modes of human activity, in politics the most typical form being the subsuming of politics in economics; it presumed individuals to be merely

[43] N. Barry, 'F.A. Hayek and market liberalism', in Tivey and Wright (eds.), *Political Thought since 1945*, 137–8, 148.

'economic agents' rather than 'civilized beings with a tradition of humane culture'. However, invoking the collective and conditional 'we may doubt' when what he really meant was that *he* certainly doubted the merits of this conflation, he attributed 'full dignity' only to man as a 'political being and a citizen'. The mere existence of doubt, at any rate, made it essential to 'cling to the essence of the political mode within its own field and for its own purpose': that is, the adjustment of claims and counterclaims of right 'in the spiritual field of personal relations'.[44]

There is also only a surface comparison between Barker's liberal-conservatism and the contemporary vogue of 'anti-foundationalism' within liberalism. This has developed from the challenge of 'post-modernism' to the 'false universalism' of mainstream ideologies like liberalism. Certainly his work is well in tune with this tide of liberal-conservative opinion in so far as the latter seeks to understand cardinal liberal values by situating them within the evolving traditions and institutions of 'civil association'. Liberal society, in this perspective, becomes an achievement which the political theorist explores so that its members may attain a greater degree of collective self-knowledge. Liberalism should hence surrender its universalist pretensions, extending its claims only to the actual societies in which it has developed. As John Gray has defended this view in relation to the focus in liberalism upon the individual: 'we seek to understand, not personhood, but ourselves, just as we are'. Liberalism, he insists, must give up the ghost of 'abstract' theories of human rights, those 'hallucinatory perspectives' which have only encouraged 'a legalistic politics of adversarial confrontation and weakened the understanding of political life as a sphere in which interests are moderated and subject to reasonable compromise'.[45]

But as we saw in the previous chapter, Barker could not rest content with a liberalism which held only limited prescriptive power. Instead, he attempted to secure global significance for the Burkean idea of an English 'liberal descent' through the historical basis he believed it provided for a wider doctrine of the 'Rights of Man', possessing independent value. In this way his thought epitomises the 'incoherence' into which 'Pyrrhonic' liberalism inevitably falls – according to Gray – once it attempts to privilege one set of liberties over another, and over other political values too.

[44] E. Barker, *Reflections upon Government*, 242–3.

[45] John Gray, *Liberalisms: Essays in Political Philosophy* (1989; London, 1990), 263, 215.

Yet however discordant these two facets of his political thought may have been, Barker made a persuasive case for appealing to liberal principles in relieving the tendency towards self-validation and hence immobility in historical traditions of liberal practice. The return to a pure form of Burkeanism in recent Liberal thought is based upon an overly confident view of the capacity of 'liberal' societies to engage in the 'repair and renewal' of their political inheritance without critical debate.[46] Barker recognised that tradition may reach a point at which it ceases to be creative, when it then becomes a burden on the present. Thus he suggested that Burke's attitude towards the French Revolution had been blinkered. Burke was 'far too tender to the *ancien regime*', he noted in an essay of 1939, echoing the sentiment of his earlier criticism of Burke's defence of rotten boroughs.[47] Burke had signally failed to see his own values at work across the Channel, most notably the spirit of 'experimentalism' which he found so salutary a feature of his own country's history. He was so preoccupied with attacking 'the dead hand of metaphysics' that he fell instead into 'a worship of the dead hand of history'. Fixed and abstract political principles can indeed be tyrannical. But broad guiding 'ideals' were of a different order (although Barker was perhaps too ready to associate these ideals with Western ideals); and the liberal triumphed over the conservative in him when he emphasised their positive role in political life. In Burke's harsh contempt for the 'ideals of the Revolution – its passion for liberty, and its still deeper passion for equality', he failed to discern 'some of the profoundest and the most permanent of its actual tendencies and achievements'.[48]

This criticism of Burke is consistent with Barker's lifelong predilection for striking a balance between history and philosophy, historical law and natural law, nationalism and internationalism. As ever, the evils of inflated national pride were foremost in his mind in his insistence upon the need for all these middle ways. As he argued in the address he delivered to the Historical Association in 1922 which was inspired by Croce's thought:

> We are always cheating ourselves into the conviction that continuity of duration or antiquity of origin is itself a value; but we must always criticize continuities and antiquities by a criterion which is beyond time. In a word, the historian, with all his historical values, must come before the bar of

[46] This criticism is made of Oakeshott's thought by R. Eccleshall, 'Michael Oakeshott and sceptical conservatism', 189–90. [47] See above, ch. 2, p. 47.

[48] E. Barker, 'Burke on the French Revolution', in *Essays on Government* (Oxford, 1945), 217, 234.

philosophy. And there – to take one instance – all the many nationalisms which feed on the historic method, with their memories of Cuchulain and Stephen Dushan and other heroes and glories, will be asked to change their language; and the question will be, not 'What have you been?', but 'What can you do for the moral betterment of humanity.'[49]

While Croce believed that philosophical knowledge is based on history, nevertheless – emphasised Barker in a review of Croce's *History* in 1941 – his perspective was not one of 'escapist' contemplation. Instead, it imposed 'stern duties' upon individuals to apply their minds to contemporary problems and circumstances in the overriding interest of the free human spirit. The lesson to be drawn from Croce's philosophy was that 'thought must think the past in the service of the future and for the sake of action; must always think it afresh by perpetual effort, never burying its head in the sands of a fixed *dottrina* or an eschatological Utopia'.[50]

ASSESSMENT

How might this injunction be applied now to the national traditions, images, purposes, and practices which are loudly fêted in Barker's intellectual legacy? At a time when much public discussion is preoccupied with the twin problems of long-term British decline and the attenuated sense of national identity, such a question provides a fitting point on which to conclude this book. Certainly, in some quarters, the political and cultural values with which Barker and his like-minded contemporaries associated Englishness require little if any scrutiny, merely re-assertion when contrasted with the degenerate standards of contemporary British society. Here, the broad middle-class character of England expressed in the prevalence of decency, restraint, tolerance, duty, and law-abidingness – qualities which emerged in the late eighteenth century and which Barker did so much to amplify in the second quarter of the twentieth century – is rapidly acquiring the lustre of nostalgia.[51] But to vindicate this avowedly healthier time for English national culture begs the question as to why its vitality was

[49] E. Barker, 'History and philosophy', in *Church, State, and Study* (London, 1930), 219.

[50] E. Barker, review of Croce's *History as the Story of Liberty*, translated by Sylvia Sprigge, *The Observer*, 23 March 1941.

[51] For example, J. Richards, 'How today's heroes are destroying our national character', *Daily Mail*, 20 March 1993, 6–7. The article begins with a quotation from Barker on the mutability of national character.

eroded once the homogenising pressures of war and its immediate aftermath had been removed.

One reason for the diminishing influence of the view of England which Barker elaborated was the growing exclusiveness of its root idea at a political level. For all the sincerity of his belief in the ecumenical possibilities of English civility – the extension of the principle of democracy by discussion throughout British society and the world at large – developments since the 1960s have taken an opposite turn. In the United Kingdom itself the continuing tensions of race, nation, religion, gender, and class have led to a denial of full British status to a wide range of those who are *de facto* citizens, not least those of Commonwealth origin. Furthermore, the globalisation of English culture in the guise of civility and therewith the close and permanent association of nations which Barker believed was the central task of the Commonwealth has been unceremoniously abandoned. As Britain forged closer ties with Europe, the antipodal Commonwealth ceased to feature prominently, if at all, in the collective sense of Britishness, confounding an essential part of the identities of its member nations at the same time.[52] Consequently, the Englishness which captured Barker's imagination and for which he had high, inclusive hopes became monopolised by a privileged section of primarily southern England. This has been exacerbated by the reluctance of cultural and political elites to redefine British national identity in relation to Europe – a cause which Barker keenly embraced – particularly in view of the threatening spectre of uniformity posed by European bureaucracy.

Understandably, responses to the increasing insularity of England in the period following Barker's death have taken the form of vigorous, often militant assertions of group identity, which in his mind constituted the nemesis of civility. A similar process may be under way now as 'Europe' selects which nations on the Eurasian continent can safely be judged 'European'.[53] Does it follow, therefore, that his wider social and political thought has lost credibility – that the legitimate demands of excluded groups for equity within British and other national and supra-national cultures in the West means that his anxiety about groups has been overtaken by events? That anxiety – as I have stressed in this conclusion – forms something like

[52] On this consequence of the abandonment of the British imperial project, see J.G.A. Pocock, 'Deconstructing Europe', *London Review of Books*, 19 December 1991, 6–10.

[53] Pocock, 'Deconstructing Europe', 8.

the defining feature of his work overall, and is all the more poignant in the light of the group closure which has been practised by the English nation itself.

We may perhaps salvage two interrelated themes from the vision of an expansive, civil England and Europe which Barker successfully expressed in his lifetime. This is despite the subsequent upsurge of sectarianism – bordering upon a new tribalism – which he believed that wider vision would forestall. First, his alertness to the dangers of the organisation and repesentation of corporate interests in politics – however much prompted by the state's shortcomings as the universal ideal of society – may still carry conviction. He never lost an opportunity to denounce the acute social and political fragmentation, authoritarianism, and deep-seated animosity which frequently accompanied such endeavours. To Barker, they were firmly rooted in the translation of the ideal of citizenship into comradeship which Carl Schmitt had hauntingly encapsulated in his friend/foe depiction of modern political life. Barker's account of the fissures opened up by the politicisation of groups provides a salutary rejoinder to the enhanced groupism of the late twentieth century, whether at the level of identity politics generally (as in Western Europe and North America) or the claim of hitherto oppressed nationalities to sovereignty in large parts of Eastern Europe and the former Soviet Union. In this respect, his writings accord well with that current of contemporary liberalism which rejects the communitarian idea that selves are in some sense 'constituted' by primary group attachments such as nation, region, tribe, and family. As Stephen Macedo has argued, this view places loyalties 'beyond critical reflection and choice'. He continues, 'Humanity is ill-served by tribalism in any of its forms. The fact that a liberal public morality, when institutionalized and practised, helps people to gain a critical distance on their local attachments is one of its greatest achievements.'[54] It may well be, as Will Kymlicka asserts, that contemporary liberalism will have to rise to the political challenge of extending rights from individuals to minority groups in order to prevent the kind of marginalisation which non-Anglo-Saxon communities have experienced in Britain. Nonetheless, Barker's reservations about according political status to groups may at least require its advocates to defend their confidence in a just outcome, one in which 'all members of society, individually and in community with

[54] S. Macedo, *Liberal Virtues: Citizenship, Virtue, and Community in Liberal Constitutionalism* (Oxford, 1990), 246–7.

others, can intelligently form and successfully pursue their understandings of the good'.[55] Indeed, his cautiousness here could serve to strengthen debate as to how citizenship may be made more effective through the reform of conventional constitutional mechanisms which focus upon the relationship between individuals and the state, unmediated by group loyalties.

The second theme of continuing value is Barker's insistence upon the need – within the parameters of a democratic state – for a 'general personal liberty' that is irreducible to any communal purpose beyond itself. Culturally bound though these two dimensions of his political tbought may be, they signal a profound respect for human personality and its need – in substantial parts of western society, at least – for moral and political space.[56] These concerns by no means implied the anti-social individual who is often assumed to be central to the liberal tradition, particularly in the wake of the recent communitarian attack upon it; as can be seen from his many tributes to the history of free association in England, Barker exalted the values of civility, sociability, and conviviality, as well as the importance of cultural membership more generally. Neither did his liberal political vision point to a minimal state, although he did stress the need for a limited one. He maintained that the state was responsible for ensuring adequate public provision of 'mental' and 'material' goods, as well as upholding a framework of civil and political rights. He perceived this provision as especially vital to the preservation of the state's impartial and impersonal nature, and with that, the individual liberty he so highly prized. As he wrote in his *Reflections upon Government*; 'the liberty of all, shared equally by all, is so far from being a natural condition that it may be described, without any paradox, as the most artificial of all conditions'. In the absence among citizens of a common level of 'equipment' (a term he borrowed from Aristotle) for participating in society, the democratic state would be unable 'to meet and direct the movements impinging on its life'.[57]

In both of these respects, at least, Barker's writings deserve greater attention. Together, they offer a resonant analysis of the complex conditions of, and threats to, individuality, an ideal which historically

[55] W. Kymlicka, *Liberalism, Community, and Culture* (Oxford, 1989), 254.

[56] An interesting analysis of the limited cultural relevance of liberal values and anxieties is given by B. Parekh, 'The cultural particularity of liberal democracy', *Political Studies*, 40 (1992), special issue on 'Prospects for Democracy', 160–75.

[57] E. Barker, *Reflections upon Government*, 189–91, 420.

has been central to the self-understanding and self-esteem of the English nation and which informed all of his work. It is certainly difficult to dissociate Barker's general political theory from the keen sense of national consciousness and what George Orwell aptly termed the 'emotional unity' of the English with which it was imbued. It is unlikely that the high level of instinctual patriotism which inspired the political thought of so many of his generation will be recovered in the very different circumstances of the late twentieth century. Nevertheless, in the contemporary reconstruction of both liberalism and Englishness or Britishness, there are luminous dimensions of his work which a later generation might fruitfully adapt and make its own.

Select Bibliography

THE BARKER PAPERS

Most of Barker's published work is held at Peterhouse, Cambridge. This includes his books, books to which he contributed, and journal and newspaper articles. The collection also contains a small amount of correspondence and unpublished material.

MANUSCRIPT COLLECTIONS

The following collections contain letters to and from Barker which I have cited.

William Archer Papers (The British Library, Oriental and India Office Collections)
Clement Attlee Papers (University College, Oxford)
Francis and Jessica Brett Young Papers (University Library, Birmingham)
James Bryce Papers (Bodleian Library, Oxford)
Lionel Curtis Papers (Bodleian Library, Oxford)
H.A.L. Fisher Papers (Bodleian Library, Oxford)
J.L. and B. Hammond Papers (Bodleian Library, Oxford)
E. Halévy Papers (in the possession of H. Guy-Loë, Sucy en Brie, Paris)
H.J. Laski Papers (The Brynmor Jones Library, University of Hull)

A.D. Lindsay Papers (University Library, Keele)
Violet Markham Papers (The British Library of Political and Economic Science)
F.S. Marvin Papers (Bodleian Library, Oxford)
Gilbert Murray Papers (Bodleian Library, Oxford)
C.T. Onions Papers (University Library, Birmingham)
Maurice Reckitt Papers (University Library, Sussex)
Round Table Papers (Bodleian Library, Oxford)
A.L. Smith Papers (Balliol College, Oxford)
T.F. Tout Papers (John Rylands University Library of Manchester)
Graham Wallas Papers (British Library of Political and Economic Science)
Leonard Woolf Papers (University of Sussex Library)
Alfred Zimmern Papers (Bodleian Library, Oxford)

OTHER ARCHIVAL MATERIAL

Hebdomadal Council Papers (1915–20), University of Oxford (Bodleian Library)
Minutes of Council, King's College London (1920–7)
Minutes of the Delegacy, King's College London (1920–7)
Minutes of the Board of the Faculty of History (1927–32), University of Cambridge. Faculty of History
General Board of Faculties: Notes on Agenda (1929–32), University of Cambridge. Cambridge University Library
Treasury Files (1948–51), Public Record Office, T199/352 and 353
Board of Education Files (1943–8), Public Record Office, ED42/5 and 6

BARKER'S WRITINGS

I have not attempted to give a complete bibliography of Barker's work; however, I have listed a substantial part of it. I have included most of his scholarly output, together with a broad selection of his work addressed to popular audiences. My primary aim in compiling this bibliography has been to convey the range of Barker's contributions to British scholarship and cultural life. I have also sought to capture the high esteem in which he was held. This is reflected in the volume of his writings, many of which were undoubtedly commissioned; and the requests he received to give lectures and addresses, and to write prefaces in the books of others. I have omitted the articles he wrote for newspapers, except for book reviews. Many of his contributions to newspapers are among the Barker Papers at Peterhouse.

BOOKS

The Political Thought of Plato and Aristotle (London, 1906)
The Dominican Order and Convocation: A Study of the Growth of Representation in the Church during the Thirteenth Century (Oxford, 1913)

Political Thought in England from Herbert Spencer to the Present Day (London, 1915)
Mothers and Sons in War Time: And Other Pieces Reprinted from The Times (London, 1915)
Ireland in the Last Fifty Years, 1866–1916 (Oxford, 1917)
Ireland in the Last Fifty Years, 1866–1918 (2nd edn, Oxford, 1919)
Greek Political Theory: Plato and his Predecessors (London, 1918)
The Crusades (London, 1925)
National Character and the Factors in its Formation (London, 1927)
Church, State, and Study: Essays (London, 1930)
Universities in Great Britain: Their Position and Their Problems (London, 1931)
Natural Law and the Theory of Society, 1500 to 1800, by Otto Gierke, translated with an introduction by Ernest Barker (Cambridge, 1934)
Oliver Cromwell and the English People (Cambridge, 1937)
The Citizen's Choice (Cambridge, 1937)
The Values of Life: Essays on the Circles and Centres of Duty (London, 1939)
British Statesmen (London, 1941)
The Ideas and Ideals of the British Empire (Cambridge, 1941)
Britain and the British People (Oxford, 1942)
Reflections on Government (Oxford, 1942)
The Development of Public Services in Western Europe, 1660–1930 (Oxford, 1944)
British Constitutional Monarchy (Oxford, 1945)
Essays on Government (Oxford, 1945)
British Universities (London, 1946)
The Politics of Aristotle, translated with an introduction, notes, and appendices by Ernest Barker (Oxford, 1946)
Social Contract: Essays by Locke, Hume, and Rousseau (London, 1947)
The Character of England, edited by Ernest Barker (Oxford, 1947)
Traditions of Civility: Eight Essays (Cambridge, 1948)
The Principles of Social and Political Theory (Oxford, 1951)
Age and Youth: Memories of Three Universities and Father of the Man (London, 1953)
The European Inheritance, edited by Ernest Barker, George Clark, and Paul Vaucher, 3 vols. (Oxford, 1954)
From Alexander to Constantine: Passages and Documents Illustrating the History of Social and Political Ideas, 336 B.C.–A.D. 337, translated with introductions, notes, and essays by Ernest Barker (Oxford, 1956)
Social and Political Thought in Byzantium from Justinian I to the Last Palaeologus: Passages from Byzantine Writers and Documents, translated with an introduction and notes by Ernest Barker (Oxford, 1957)

PAMPHLETS AND LECTURES

Nietzsche and Treitschke: The Worship of Power in Modern Germany, Oxford Pamphlets no. 20 (London, 1914)
The Submerged Nationalities of the German Empire (Oxford, 1915)
Nationalism and Internationalism, Christian Social Union Pamphlet no. 45

(London, 1915)
Great Britain's Reasons for Going to War (London, 1915)
The Relations of England to Holland (London, 1915)
A Confederation of the Nations: Its Power and Constitution (Oxford, 1918)
Linguistic Oppression in the German Empire (London, 1918)
Social Ideas and Educational Systems, an address to the Co-operative Union Ltd. at Southport (Manchester, 1925)
Christianity and Nationality, Burge Memorial Lecture (Oxford, 1927)
The Study of Political Science and its Relation to Cognate Studies (Cambridge, 1928)
Burke and Bristol: A Study of the Relations between Burke and his Constituency during the Years 1774–1780, Lewis Fry Memorial Lecture (Bristol, 1931)
The Highway and the Ladder, The 7th George Cadbury Memorial Lecture (Birmingham, 1933)
Philosophy and Politics, The 6th Annual Haldane Memorial Lecture (London, 1934)
The Uses of Leisure, an address to the World Association for Adult Education (London, 1936)
Education for Citizenship, a lecture for the University of London Institute of Education. Studies and Reports no. 10 (Oxford, 1936)
'Natural law in the political world', Herbert Spencer Memorial Lecture, *The Hibbert Journal*, 36 (1938), 481–91
British Constitutional Monarchy, Central Office of Information (London, 1944)
Winston Churchill, Central Office of Information (London, 1945)
Reflections on Family Life, an address delivered to the Parents' Association (London, 1947)
Cultural Influences in Britain, Central Office of Information (London, 1948)
Change and Continuity, Ramsay Muir Memorial Lecture (London, 1949)
'Happiness and success', The Fripp Memorial Lecture, *Theology* (March, 1950), 83–90
The Development of Education in England during the last Fifty Years, The Arthur Mellows Memorial Lecture (Peterborough, 1951)
British Constitutional Monarchy, Central Office of Information (London, 1952)

CHAPTERS IN BOOKS

'Italy and the West, 410–476', *Cambridge Medieval History*, vol. I (Cambridge, 1911)
E. Barker, C.R.L. Fletcher, L.G. Wickham Legg, H.W.C. Davis, Arthur Hassall, and F. Morgan, *Why We Are At War: Great Britain's Case* (Oxford, 1914)
'History and the position of women', in Z. Fairfield (ed.), *Some Aspects of the Women's Movement* (London, 1915)
'Social relations of men after the war', in L. Gardner (ed.), *The Hope for Society: Essays on 'Social Reconstruction after the War' by Various Writers*

(London, 1917)
'The conception of empire', in C. Bailey (ed.), *The Legacy of Rome* (Oxford, 1923)
'Politics and political philosophy', in O.H. Ball (ed.), *Sidney Ball: Memories and Impressions of 'An Ideal Don'* (Oxford, 1923)
'Greek political thought and theory in the fourth century', *Cambridge Ancient History*, vol. VI (Cambridge, 1923)
'Précis of evidence submitted', The Church Assembly, *Church and State: Report of the Archbishops' Commission on the Relations between Church and State*, 2 vols., vol. I (London, 1935)
'Christianity and economics', in M.S. Leigh (ed.), *Christianity in the Modern State* (London, 1936)
'Rival faiths?', in H. Wilson Harris (ed.), *Christianity and Communism* (Oxford, 1937)
'The Home Civil Service: The Administrative Class', in W. Robson (ed.), *The British Civil Servant* (London, 1937)
'The History Tripos', in P. Hartog *et al.*, *The Purposes of Examinations: A Symposium* (London, 1938)
'Gandhi, as bridge and reconciler', in S. Radhakrishnan (ed.), *Mahatma Gandhi: Essays and Reflections on his Life and Work* (London, 1939)
'The problem of an order in Europe', S.E. Hooper (ed.), *The Deeper Causes of the War and its Issues* (London, 1940)
'The debt of Europe to Czechoslovakia and to Comenius', in J. Needham (ed.), *The Teacher of Nations: Addresses and Essays in Commemoration of the Visit to England of the Great Czech Educationalist Jan Amos Komenský Comenius, 1641, 1941* (Cambridge, 1942)
Contribution to R. Muir, *An Autobiography and Some Essays*, ed. by S. Hodgson (London, 1943)
'For adults: The idea of People's Colleges', in R.A. Scott-James (ed.), *Education in Britain: Yesterday, To-day, To-morrow* (London, 1944)
'British and Czech democracy', in J. Opočenský (ed.), *Edward Beneš: Essays and Reflections on the Occasion of his Sixtieth Birthday* (London, 1945)
'The nature and origins of the Western political tradition', Lord Layton (intro.), *The Western Tradition* (London, 1951)
'National Council of Social Service', in E. Elath, N. Bentwich, and D. May (eds.), *Memories of Sir Wyndham Deedes* (London, 1958)

JOURNAL ARTICLES

'The rights and duties of trade unions', *Economic Review*, 21 (April 1911), 127–52
'The Roman heritage in the Middle Ages', *History* (old series), 3, 2 (1914), 85–95
'The rule of law', *Political Quarterly* (old series), 1 (May 1914), 117–40
'The discredited state: thoughts on politics before the war', *Political Quarterly* (old series), 2 (February 1915), 101–21
'The constitution of the League of Nations', *The New Europe*, 10, 6 March 1919, 180–4, 196–203, 220–6

'Nationality', *History* (new series), 4 (October 1919), 135–45
'Lord Bryce', *English Historical Review*, 37 (April, 1922), 219–24
'History and religion', *Theology*, 5 (1922), 17–24
'The aims and achievements of public elementary education', *The Modern Churchman*, 13 (1923), 402–8
'Leonard Trelawny Hobhouse, 1864–1929', *Proceedings of the British Academy*, 15 (1930), 536–54
'Authorship of the *Vindiciae Contra Tyrannos*', *Cambridge Historical Journal*, 3, 2 (1930), 164–81
'The contact of colours and civilisations', *The Contemporary Review* (November 1930), 578–87
'The life of Aristotle and the composition and structure of the *Politics*', *The Classical Review*, 45 (1931), 162–72
'New housing estates: the problem', *The Social Service Review*, 12 (1931), 47–50
'The Reformation and nationality', *The Modern Churchman*, 22 (1932), 329–43
'Democracy since the War and its prospects for the future', *International Affairs*, 13, 6 (1934), 751–71
'Group idols and their loyalties', *The Listener*, 18 July 1934, 98.
'The movement of national life, 1910–1935', *The Fortnightly Review* (May 1935), 513–26
'The romantic factor in modern politics', *Philosophy*, 11 (1936), 387–402
'Why I am a Liberal', *The Liberal Magazine* (April 1936), 94–5
'The social background of recent political changes', *The Sociological Review*, 28 (1936), 117–32
'The new reign', *The Fortnightly Review* (March 1936), 257–66
'Changing Oxford', *The Fortnightly Review* (February 1937), 175–83
'Maitland as a sociologist', *The Sociological Review*, 29, no. 2 (1937), 121–35
'Address', *Evangelical Christendom* (July/August 1938), 123–6
'Élie Halévy', *English Historical Review*, 53 (January 1938), 79–87
'The contact of cultures in India', *The Sociological Review*, 30, 2 (1938), 105–19
'Community centres and circles', *The Fortnightly Review* (March 1939), 257–66
'The rise of democracy in England', *Deutsche-Englesche Hefte*, 3 (June 1939), 76–81
'The civil service and civil liberties', *Public Administration*, 19, 3 (1941), 175–80
'John Hampden', *The Spectator*, 25 June 1943, 587–8
'Books for the Allies', *The Spectator*, 29 September 1944, 284
'Community centres and educational authorities', *The Fortnightly Review* (April 1945), 244–50
'Should we read Plato?', *John O'London's Weekly*, 45, 1283, 19 April 1946, 1
'The power of law', *The Listener*, 20 March 1947, 420–1
'From the rule of law to democracy', *The Listener*, 5 June 1948, 900
'Mr. Gladstone', *The British Weekly*, 20 May 1948, 7, 10
'The English character and attitude towards life', *England* (September 1950), 6–9
'The ideals of the Commonwealth', *Parliamentary Affairs*, 4, 1 (1950), 12–18

'The significance of the crusades', *Far and Wide* (Winter 1950–1), 33–6
'The inspiration of Emily Brontë', *Publications of the Brontë Society*, 61 (1951), 2–9
'Reflections on the party system', *Parliamentary Affairs*, 5, 1 (1951), 195–204
'Reflections on English political theory', *Political Studies*, 1 (1953), 6–12

PREFACES

C.R. Beazley, *Russia from the Varangians to the Bolsheviks* (Oxford, 1918)
J.E.W. Wallis, *The Sword of Justice: Or the Christian Philosophy of War completed in the Idea of a League of Nations* (Oxford, 1920)
C. Beard, *The Reformation of the Sixteenth Century in its Relation to Modern Thought and Knowledge* (London, 1883; new edn, 1927)
R.J.S. McDowall (ed.), *The Mind* (London, 1927)
St Augustine, *The City of God*, transl. J. Healey (London, 1931)
A Nazi School of History Textbook, 1914–1933, Friends of Europe Publications, no. 11 (London, 1934)
B. Jarrett, *The Emperor Charles IV* (London, 1935)
Institute of Sociology, *The Social Sciences: Their Relations in Theory and in Teaching*, 3 vols. (London, 1936–7)
L. Strauss, *The Political Philosophy of Hobbes: Its Basis and Genesis* (Oxford, 1936)
James Mill, *An Essay on Government* (1820; London, 1937)
M. Oakeshott, *The Social and Political Doctrines of Contemporary Europe* (Cambridge, 1939)
E. Bradby (ed.), *The University outside Europe: Essays on the Development of University Institutions in Fourteen Countries* (London, 1939)
J. Maynard, *The Russian Peasant: And Other Studies* (London, 1942)
H.E. Poole, *Perspectives for Country Men* (London, 1942)
Viscount Hinchingbrooke, *Full Speed Ahead: Essays in Tory Reform* (London, 1944)
Some Comparisons Between Universities: Proceedings of the Second Education Conference (Oxford, 1944)
E. Táborsky, *Czechoslovak Democracy at Work* (London, 1945)
J. Maynard, *Russia in Flux*, edited and abridged by S.H. Guest (New York, 1948)
A. Zóltowski, *Border of Europe: A Study of the Polish Eastern Provinces* (London, 1950)
C.M. Bowra (ed.), *Golden Ages of the Great Cities* (London, 1952)
W.R. Matthews and W.M. Atkins, *A History of St. Pauls Cathedral and the Men Associated with it* (London, 1957)
B.J. Gould, *The Jewel in the Lotus: Recollections of an Indian Political* (London, 1957)
H.V. Somerset (ed.), *A Notebook of Edmund Burke* (Cambridge, 1957)

BOOK REVIEWS

J. MacCunn, *Six Radical Thinkers* (London, 1907), *International Journal of Ethics*, 20, 2 (1910), 220–3

L. Curtis, *The Problem of the Commonwealth*, *Times Literary Supplement*, 749, 26 May 1916, 241–2

V. Brandford, *A New Chapter in the Science of Government* (London, 1919), *The Sociological Review*, 12, 2 (Autumn 1920), 137–40

The Calcutta University Commission, *Edinburgh Review*, 231, 471 (January 1920), 97–114

James Bryce, *Modern Democracies* (London, 1921), *The Observer*, 24 April 1921

A.F. Pollard, *The Evolution of Parliament* (London, 1921); and H. Belloc, *The House of Commons and Monarchy* (London, 1920), *Edinburgh Review*, 234 (July 1921), 58–73

A. Mansbridge, *The Older Universities of England* (London, 1923); *Report of the Royal Commission on the Universities of Oxford and Cambridge* (London, 1919–22); and G.E. Maclean, *Studies in Higher Education in England and Scotland* (Washington, 1917), *Edinburgh Review*, 238 (1923), 254–69

P. Vinogradoff, *Outlines of Historical Jurisprudence*, vol. II (Oxford, 1922), *English Historical Review*, 39 (1924), 424–5

A.D. Lindsay, *The Essentials of Democracy* (London, 1929); J.A. Hobson, *Wealth and Life: A Study of Values* (London, 1929); N. Rosselli, *Mazzini e Bakounine* (Turin, 1927), *Contemporary Review* (March 1930), 300–3

S.E. Finer, *The Theory and Practice of Modern Governments*, 2 vols. (London, 1932); *Contemporary Review*, 807 (March 1933), 289–97

B. Croce, *History of Europe in the Nineteenth Century*, translated by H. Furst (London, 1934) and B. Russell, *Freedom and Organisation, 1814–1914* (London, 1934), *The Sunday Times*, 28 October 1934

M. Ashley, *Oliver Cromwell: The Conservative Dictator* (London, 1937). *The Observer*, 17 October 1937

A.S.P. Wodehouse (ed.), *Puritanism and Liberty* (London, 1938), *University of Toronto Quarterly*, 8, 2 (1939), 238–41

A. Hitler, *Mein Kampf*, translated by J. Murphy (London, 1939), *The Observer*, 26 March 1939, 4

H. Rauschning, *Germany's Revolution of Destruction*, translated by A.W. Dickes (London, 1939), *The Observer*, 2 July 1939, 4

L.P. Jacks, *The Last Legend of Smokeover* (London, 1939), *Hibbert Journal*, 38, 2 (January 1940), 280–3

B. Croce, *History as the Story of Liberty*, transl. by Sylvia Sprigge (London, 1941), *The Observer*, 23 March 1941

L. Curtis, *Decision* (Oxford, 1941); Lord Lothian, *Pacifism is not Enough (Nor Patriotism Either)* (Oxford, 1941), *The Observer*, 3 August 1941, 3

D.A. Binchy, *Church and State in Fascist Italy* (London, 1941), *Manchester Guardian*, 21 October 1941

C. Dawson, *The Judgement of the Nations* (London, 1943), *The Spectator*, 12 February 1943

D.W. Brogan, *The English People: Impressions and Observations* (London, 1943), *Britain Today* (July 1943), 15–19

R.G. Collingwood, *The New Leviathan* (Oxford, 1942), *The Oxford Magazine*, 4 Feburary 1943, 162–3

A.D. Lindsay, *The Modern Democratic State*, vol. I (Oxford, 1943), *The Spectator*, 170, 26 February 1943, 200

E.H. Carr, *Nationalism and After* (London, 1945), *Britain Today* (August 1945), 41–2

K. Popper, *The Open Society and its Enemies*, 2 vols. (London, 1945), *The Sunday Times*, 18 November 1945

L.S. Amery, *Thoughts on the Constitution* (London, 1947), *Fortnightly Review* (July 1947), 177–83

A.J. Toynbee, *Civilisation on Trial* (New York, 1948), *The Spectator*, 17 December 1948, 810

OTHER PRIMARY WORKS

This section does not include all of the reviews of Barker's work mentioned in the text.

Acton, Lord. 'Nationality', *The History of Freedom and Other Essays*, ed. by J.N. Figgis (London, 1907)

Arnold, M. *Culture and Anarchy: An Essay in Political and Social Criticism* (London, 1869)

Baernreither, J.M. *English Associations of Working Men*, translated by Alice Taylor (London, 1889)

Baldwin, S. *On England* (London, 1926)

Our Inheritance (London, 1928)

Beveridge, W. 'The social sciences as a means of general education', *The Oxford Magazine*, 2 February 1933, 362–3

Bluntschli, J.K. *The Theory of the Modern State*, transl. by D.G. Ritchie, P.E. Matheson, and R. Lodge (Oxford, 1885)

Board of Education, *The Education of the Adolescent: Report of the Consultative Committee* (London, 1927)

Bosanquet, B. *The Civilisation of Christendom and Other Studies* (London, 1893)

The Philosophical Theory of the State (London, 1899)

'The English people: notes on national characteristics', *International Monthly*, 3 (1901) 71–116

'Patriotism in the perfect state', in E.M. Sidgwick (ed.), *The International Crisis in its Ethical and Psychological Dimensions* (London, 1915)

Social and International Ideals: Being Studies in Patriotism (London, 1917)

Boutmy, E. *The English People: A Study of Their Political Psychology*, transl. by E. English (London, 1904)

Bradley, F.H. *Ethical Studies* (London, 1876)

Bryant, A. *The National Character* (London, 1934)

Bryce, J. 'The law of nature', in *Studies in History and Jurisprudence*, vol. II (Oxford, 1901)

Studies in Contemporary Biography (London, 1903)
Modern Democracies, 2 vols. (London, 1921)
Caird, E. *Lay Sermons and Addresses Delivered in the Hall of Balliol College, Oxford* (Glasgow, 1907)
Cammaerts, E. *Discoveries in England* (London, 1930)
Campbell, L. *On the Nationalization of the Old Universities* (London, 1901)
Cohen-Portheim, P. *England: The Unknown Isle*, transl. A. Harris (London, 1930)
Collingwood, R.G. 'Political action', *Proceedings of the Aristotelian Society*, 29 (1928), 155–76
An Autobiography (Oxford, 1939)
The New Leviathan: Or Man, Society, Civilization, and Barbarism (Oxford, 1942)
Dibelius, W. *England*, transl. M.A. Hamilton, introduced by A.D. Lindsay (1923; London, 1930)
Dicey, A.V. *Introduction to the Study of the Law of the Constitution* (London, 1885)
Lectures on the Relation between Law and Public Opinion in England during the Nineteenth Century (London, 1905)
Figgis, J.N. *Churches in the Modern State* (London, 1913)
Fisher, H.A.L. *F.W. Maitland: A Biography* (Cambridge, 1910)
'The political writings of Rousseau', *Edinburgh Review*, 224 (1916), 43–54
'The Whig historians', Raleigh lecture on history, *Proceedings of the British Academy* (1928), 297–339
An Unfinished Autobiography (London, 1940)
Green, T.H. 'Four lectures on the English Revolution' (1867), *The Works of Thomas Hill Green*, vol. III, ed. R.L. Nettleship (London, 1889)
Liberal Legislation and Freedom of Contract (Oxford, 1881)
Prolegomena to Ethics, ed. A.C. Bradley (Oxford, 1883)
Lectures on the Principles of Political Obligation, ed. Bernard Bosanquet (London, 1895)
Haldane, R.B. *The Conduct of Life and Other Addresses* (London, 1914)
Hobhouse, L.T. *The Elements of Social Justice* (London, 1922)
Huizinga, J. *Homo Ludens: A Study of the Play Element in Culture* (1938; London, 1949)
Confessions of a European in England (London, 1958)
Keun, O. *I Discover the English* (London, 1934)
Laski, H.J. *The Danger of Being a Gentleman: And Other Essays* (London, 1939)
Lindsay, A.D. 'Political theory', in F.S. Marvin (ed.), *Developments in European Thought* (London, 1920)
'Bosanquet's theory of the General Will', *Proceedings of the Aristotelian Society* (1928), supp. vol. VIII, 31–44
The Essentials of Democracy (London, 1929)
Introduction to T.H. Green, *Lectures on the Principles of Political Obligation* (London, 1941)
The Modern Democratic State, vol. I (London, 1943)
Religion, Science, and Society in the Modern World (Oxford, 1943)

MacCunn, J. *Six Radical Thinkers* (London, 1910)
MacDougall, W. *An Introduction to Social Psychology* (London, 1908)
MacIver, R.M. 'Society and the state', *Philosophical Review*, 20 (1911), 30–45
Politics and Society, ed. D. Spitz (New York, 1969)
Mackenzie, J.S. *Arrows of Desire* (London, 1920)
Mackenzie, W.J.M. *Explorations in Government: Collected Papers, 1951–1968* (London, 1975)
Madariaga, S. de. *Englishmen, Frenchmen, Spaniards: An Essay in Comparative Psychology* (London, 1928)
Maine, H. *Ancient Law: Its Connection with the Early History of Society* (London, 1861)
Maitland, F.W. Translation of Otto Gierke's *Political Theories of the Middle Age* (Cambridge, 1900)
The Collected Papers of Frederic William Maitland, 3 vols., ed. H.A.L. Fisher (Cambridge, 1911)
Marshall, T.H. 'A British sociological career', *International Social Science Journal*, 25 (1973) 88–99
Marvin, F.S. (ed.). *The Unity of Western Civilization* (Oxford, 1915)
Maurois, A. *Three Letters on the English* (London, 1938)
Muirhead, J.H. 'Recent criticism of the Idealist theory of the General Will', *Mind*, 33 (1924), 166–75, 233–41, 361–8
Oakeshott, M. 'The theory of society', *The Cambridge Review*, 56, 12 October 1934, 11
Hobbes on Civil Association (Oxford, 1946)
Rationalism in Politics: And Other Essays (London, 1962)
On Human Conduct (Oxford, 1975)
The Voice of Liberal Learning: Michael Oakeshott on Education, ed. T. Fuller (Yale, 1989)
Oman, C. *Memories of Victorian Oxford and of Some Earlier Years* (London, 1941)
Ortega y Gassett, J. *The Revolt of the Masses* (1930; Eng. transl., London, 1932)
Orwell, G. 'The lion and the unicorn: socialism and the English genius' (1941), in *The Collected Essays, Journals, and Letters of George Orwell*, 2 vols., vol. II (London, 1968), 56–109
Oxford and Working-Class Education: Being the Report of a Joint Committee of University and Working-Class Representatives on the Relationship of the University to the Higher Education of Working People (Oxford, 1908)
Pearson, C.H. *National Life and Character: A Forecast* (London, 1893)
Pollock, F. *An Introduction to the History of the Science of Politics* (London, 1890)
Oxford Lectures and Other Discourses (London, 1890)
Jurisprudence and Legal Essays, ed. by A.L. Goodhart (London, 1961)
Pollock, F. and F.W. Maitland. *The History of English Law Before the Time of Edward I* (Cambridge, 1895)
Renier, F. *The English: Are they Human?* (London, 1931)
Ritchie, D.G. *The Principles of State Interference: Four Essays on the Political Philosophy of Mr. Herbert Spencer, J.S. Mill, and T.H. Green* (London, 1891)

'Political science at Oxford', *Annals of the American Academy of Political Science*, 2 (1891), 85–95
Darwin and Hegel, with Other Philosophical Studies (London, 1893)
Natural Rights: A Criticism of Some Political and Ethical Conceptions (London, 1894)
Studies in Political and Social Ethics (London, 1902)
Robson, W.A. *The University Teaching of the Social Sciences* (Paris, 1954)
Rowse, A.L. *The English Spirit: Essays in History and Literature* (London, 1945)
Santayana, G. *Soliloquies in England: And Later Soliloquies* (London, 1922)
Seton-Watson, R.W., E. Percy, J. Dover Wilson, Alfred E. Zimmern, and Arthur Greenwood. *The War and Democracy* (London, 1914)
Unwin, G. *Industrial Organisation in the Sixteenth and Seventeenth Centuries* (Oxford, 1904)
The Gilds and Companies of London (London, 1908)
Studies in Economic History: The Collected Papers of George Unwin, ed. by R.H. Tawney (London, 1927)
Vaughan, C.E. *The Political Writings of Jean Jacques Rousseau* (Cambridge, 1915)
Studies in the History of Political Philosophy Before and After Rousseau, 2 vols. (Manchester, 1925)
Vinogradoff, P. *The Collected Papers of Paul Vinogradoff*, 2 vols., ed. H.A.L. Fisher (Oxford, 1928)
Wallas, G. *Human Nature in Politics* (London, 1908)
The Great Society: A Psychological Analysis (London, 1914)
'Oxford and political thought', *The Nation*, 17, 15 May 1915, 227–8
Men and Ideas: Essays by Graham Wallas, ed. by M. Wallas (London, 1940)
Young, F. Brett. *The Island* (London, 1944)
Zimmern, A. *The Greek Commonwealth: Politics and Economics in Fifth-Century Athens* (Oxford, 1911)
Nationality and Government: And Other War-Time Essays (London, 1917)

SECONDARY WORKS

Abrams, P. *The Origins of British Sociology, 1834–1914* (Chicago, 1968)
Austin, G. *The Indian Constitution: Cornerstone of a Nation* (Oxford, 1966)
Barker, R. *Political Ideas in Modern Britain* (London, 1978)
Bellamy, R. (ed.) *Victorian Liberalism: Nineteenth-Century Political Thought and Practice* (London, 1990)
Black, A. *Guilds and Civil Society in European Political Thought from the Twelfth Century to the Present* (Cambridge, 1984)
Blaas, P.B.M. *Continuity and Anachronism: Parliamentary and Constitutional Development in Whig Historiography and in the Anti-Whig Reaction between 1890 and 1930* (The Hague, 1978)
Blythe, R. *The Age of Illusion: Glimpses of Britain between the Wars, 1919–1940* (Oxford, 1983)
Brasnett, M. *Voluntary Social Action: A History of the National Council of Social*

Service, 1919–1969 (London, 1969)
Boucher, D. *The Social and Political Thought of R.G. Collingwood* (Cambridge, 1989)
Bulmer, M. 'Sociology and political science at Cambridge in the 1920s: an opportunity missed and an opportunity taken', *The Cambridge Review*, 27 April 1981, 156–9
Essays on the History of British Sociology (Cambridge, 1985)
Burrow, J.W. 'The village community and the uses of history', in N. McKendrick (ed.), *Historical Perspectives: Studies in English Thought and Society in Honour of J.H. Plumb* (London, 1974)
A Liberal Descent: Victorian Historians and the English Past (Cambridge, 1981)
Whigs and Liberals: Continuity and Change in English Political Thought (Oxford, 1988)
'Victorian historians and the Royal Historical Society', *Transactions of the Royal Historical Society*, 5th series, 39 (1989), 125–40
Cannadine, D. *G.M. Trevelyan: A Life in History* (London, 1992)
Carey, J. *The Intellectuals and the Masses: Pride and Prejudice among the Literary Intelligence, 1880–1939* (London, 1992)
Catlin, G.E.G. 'Sir Ernest Barker, 1874–1960', *Proceedings of the British Academy*, 46 (1960), 341–51
Chapman, R.A. *Ethics in the British Civil Service* (London, 1988)
Chase, M. *Elie Halévy: An Intellectual Biography* (New York, 1980)
Chester, N. *Economics, Politics, and Social Studies in Oxford, 1900–85* (London, 1986)
Clogg, R. 'Politics and the academy: Arnold Toynbee and the Koraes Chair', *Middle Eastern Studies*, 21, 4, special issue (October 1985)
Cocks, R.J. *Foundations of the Modern Bar* (London, 1983)
Sir Henry Maine: A Study in Victorian Jurisprudence (Cambridge, 1988)
Collini, S. 'Sociology and Idealism in Britain, 1880–1920', *Archives Européennes de Sociologie*, 19 (1978), 3–50
Liberalism and Sociology: L.T. Hobhouse and Political Argument in England, 1880–1914 (Cambridge, 1979)
Public Moralists: Political Thought and Intellectual Life in Britain, 1850–1930 (Oxford, 1991)
'Intellectuals in Britain and France in the twentieth century: confusions, contrasts – and convergence?', in J. Jennings (ed.), *Intellectuals in Twentieth-Century France: Mandarins and Samurais* (Oxford, 1993)
Collini, S., D. Winch, and J. Burrow. *That Noble Science of Politics: A Study in Nineteenth-Century Intellectual History* (Cambridge, 1983)
Colls, R. and P. Dodd (eds.) *Englishness: Politics and Culture, 1880–1920* (London, 1986)
Cosgrove, P. *The Rule of Law: Albert Venn Dicey, Victorian Jurist* (London, 1980)
Dangerfield, G. *The Strange Death of Liberal England* (London, 1935)
Daniels, G. *George Unwin: A Memorial Lecture* (Manchester, 1926)
Deane, H.A. *The Political Ideas of Harold Laski* (New Haven, 1955)
Doyle, B. *English and Englishness* (London, 1989)

Dyson, K. *The State Tradition in Western Europe: A Study of an Idea and Institution* (Oxford, 1980)
Engel, A.J. *From Clergyman to Don: The Rise of the Academic Profession in Nineteenth-Century Oxford* (Oxford, 1983)
Eyck, F. *G.P. Gooch: A Study in History and Politics* (London, 1982)
Fisher, D. 'Philanthropy and the social sciences in Britain, 1919–1939: the reproduction of a conservative ideology', *The Sociological Review*, 28, 2 (1980), 277–315
Franco, P. *The Political Philosophy of Michael Oakeshott* (New Haven, 1990)
Furbank, P.N. 'Posers for posterity: self-protection and self-projection in the great Victorian authors', review of M. Millgate, *Testamentary Acts: Browning, Tennyson, James, Hardy* (Oxford, 1992), *Times Literary Supplement*, 17 July 1992, 3–4
Freeden, M. *Liberalism Divided: A Study in British Political Thought, 1914–1939* (Oxford, 1986)
Gay, P. *The Bourgeois Experience: Victoria to Freud*, vol. I: *Education of the Senses* (New York, 1984)
Gibbins, J.R. 'Liberalism, Nationalism and the English Idealists', *History of European Ideas*, 15 (1992), 491–7
Gordon, P. and J. White. *Philosophers as Educational Reformers: The Influence of Idealism on British Educational Thought and Practice* (London, 1979)
Grainger, J.H. *Patriotisms: Britain, 1900–1939* (London, 1986)
Grant, R. *Oakeshott* (London, 1990)
Gray, J. *Liberalisms: Essays in Political Philosophy* (London, 1989)
Greenleaf, W.H. *The British Political Tradition*, 4 vols. (London, 1983–8)
Halévy, E. *The Era of Tyrannies: Essays on Socialism and War* (1938; London, 1967)
Halsey, A.H. *Decline of Donnish Dominion: The British Academic Professions in the Twentieth Century* (Oxford, 1992)
Hanak, H. *Great Britain and Austria–Hungary During the First World War: A Study in the Formation of Public Opinion* (London, 1962)
Harris, J. *William Beveridge: A Biography* (London, 1977)
'Society and the state in twentieth-century Britain', in F.M.L. Thompson (ed.), *The Cambridge Social History of Britain, 1750–1950*, 3 vols., vol. III, *Social Agencies and Institutions* (Cambridge, 1990)
'Political thought and the welfare state 1870–1940: an intellectual framework for British social policy', *Past and Present*, 135 (1992), 116–41
Harvie, C. *The Lights of Liberalism: University Liberals and the Challenge of Democracy, 1860–1886* (London, 1976)
Havel, V. *Summer Meditations on Politics, Morality, and Civility in a Time of Transition* (London, 1992)
Hernon, J.M., Jr. 'The last Whig historian and consensus history: George Macaulay Trevelyan, 1876–1962', *American Historical Review*, 81 (1976), 66–97
Heyck, T.W. *The Transformation of Intellectual Life in Victorian England*

(London, 1982)
Himmelfarb, G. *Poverty and Compassion: The Moral Imagination of the Late Victorians* (New York, 1991)
Hirst, P.Q. *The Pluralist Theory of the State: Selected Writings of G.D.H. Cole, J.N. Figgis, and H.J. Laski* (London, 1989)
Holden, B. *The Nature of Democracy* (London, 1970)
Holloway, H.A. 'A.D. Lindsay and the problems of mass democracy', *Western Political Quarterly*, 16, 4 (1963), 798–813
Homberger, E. 'Intellectuals, Englishness, and the "myths" of Dunkirk', *Revue Française de Civilisation Britannique*, 4 (1986), 82–100
Hynes, S. *A War Imagined: The First World War and English Culture* (New York, 1991)
Inge, W.R. *England* (London, 1926)
Inglis, F. *Radical Earnestness: English Social Theory, 1880–1980* (Oxford, 1982)
Jann, R. *The Art and Science of Victorian History* (Columbus, Ohio, 1985)
Kymlicka, W. *Liberalism, Community, and Culture* (Oxford, 1989)
Jurausch, K.H. *The Transformation of Higher Learning, 1860–1930* (Chicago, 1983)
Jones, G. *Social Darwinism and English Thought: The Interaction between Biological and Social Theory* (Brighton, 1980)
Kelley, D.R. *The Human Measure: Social Thought in the Western Legal Tradition* (Cambridge, Mass., 1990)
Kenyon, J.P. *The History Men: The Historical Profession in England since the Renaissance* (London, 1983)
Keynes, J.M. 'Economic possibilities for our grandchildren' (1930), *The Collected Writings of John Maynard Keynes*, vol. IX: *Essays in Persuasion* (London, 1972)
Langan, M. and B. Schwarz (eds.) *Crises in the British State, 1880–1930* (London, 1985)
LeMahieu, D.L. *A Culture for Democracy: Mass Communication and the Cultivated Mind in Britain Between the Wars* (Oxford, 1988)
Light, A. *Forever England: Femininity, Literature and Conservatism between the Wars* (London, 1991)
Macedo, S. *Liberal Virtues: Citizenship, Virtue, and Community in Liberal Constitutionalism* (Oxford, 1990)
Maddox, G. 'The christian democracy of A.D. Lindsay', *Political Studies*, 34, 3 (1986), 441–55.
Meadowcroft, J. 'Conceptions of the state in British political thought, 1880–1914', unpublished D.Phil. thesis, University of Oxford, 1990
McNeill, W.H. *Arnold Toynbee: A Life* (Oxford, 1989)
Millgate, M. *Testamentary Acts: Browning, Tennyson, James, Hardy* (Oxford, 1992)
Milne, A.J.M. 'The common good and rights in T.H. Green's ethical and political theory', in A. Vincent (ed.), *The Philosophy of T.H. Green* (Aldershot, 1986)

Mogi, S. *Otto Von Gierke: His Political Teaching and Jurisprudence* (London, 1932)
Moorman, M. *George Macaulay Trevelyan: A Memoir* (London, 1980)
Morriss, P. 'Professor Greenleaf's collectivism', in *Politics*, 12, 1 (1992), 34–7
Morrow, J. 'British Idealism, "German philosophy" and thc First World War', *The Australian Journal of Politics and History*, 28 (1982), 380–90
Nicholls, D. *The Pluralist State* (London, 1975)
Nicholson, P.P. *The Political Philosophy of the British Idealists: Selected Studies* (Cambridge, 1990)
Oakeshott, M. *The Social and Political Doctrines of Contemporary Europe* (Cambridge, 1939)
Ogg, D. *Herbert Fisher, 1865–1940: A Short Biography* (London, 1947)
Parekh, B. 'The cultural particularity of liberal democracy', *Political Studies*, 40 (1992), special issue on 'Prospects for democracy', 160–75
Parker, C. 'Bernard Bosanquet, historical knowledge, and the history of ideas', *Philosophy of the Social Services*, 18 (1988), 213–30
The English Historical Tradition since 1850 (Edinburgh, 1990)
Perkin, H. *The Rise of Professional Society: England since 1880* (London, 1989)
Pocock, J.G.A. 'Deconstructing Europe', *London Review of Books*, 19 December 1991, 6–10
Qualter, T. *Graham Wallas and the Great Society* (London, 1980)
Rich, P. 'T.H. Green, Lord Scarman, and the issue of ethnic minority rights in English liberal thought', *Ethnic and Racial Studies*, 10 (1987), 149–68
'Imperial decline and the resurgence of English national identity, 1918–1979', in T. Kushner and K. Lunn, *Traditions of Intolerance: Historical Perspectives on Fascism and Race Discourse in Britain* (Manchester, 1989)
Richter, M. *The Politics of Conscience: T.H. Green and his Age* (London, 1964)
Ridley, F.F. (ed.) *Studies in Politics: Essays to Mark the 25th Anniversary of the Political Studies Association* (Oxford, 1975)
Robbins, P. *The British Hegelians, 1875–1925* (New York, 1982)
Roper, M. and J. Tosh (eds.) *Manful Assertions: Masculinities in Britain since 1800* (London, 1991)
Rothblatt, S. *Tradition and Change in English Liberal Education: An Essay in History and Culture* (London, 1976)
Samuel, R. (ed.) *Patriotism: The Making and Unmaking of English National Identity*, 3 vols. (London, 1989)
Schwarz, B. 'Conservatism, nationalism, and imperialism', in J. Donald and S. Hall (eds.). *Politics and Ideology* (Milton Keynes, 1986)
Scott, D. *A.D. Lindsay: A Biography* (Oxford, 1971)
Scruton, R. 'Gierke and the corporate person', *The Philosopher on Dover Beach* (Manchester, 1990)
Sennett, R. *The Fall of Public Man* (Cambridge, 1974)
Seton-Watson, H. and C. *The Making of a New Europe: R.W. Seton-Watson and the Last Years of Austria–Hungary* (London, 1981)
Shaw, C. and M. Chase (eds.) *The Imagined Past: History and Nostalgia* (Manchester, 1989)

Simhony, A. 'Idealist organicism: beyond holism and individualism', *History of Political Thought*, 12, 3 (1991), 515–35

Slee, P. *Learning and a Liberal Education: The Study of Modern History in the Universities of Oxford, Cambridge, and Manchester, 1800–1914* (Manchester, 1986)

Smith, A.D. *The Ethnic Origins of Nations* (London, 1986)

Stapleton, J. 'Academic political thought and the development of political studies in Britain, 1900–1950', unpublished D.Phil. thesis, University of Sussex, 1986

'The national character of Ernest Barker's Political Science', *Political Studies*, 37 (1989), 171–87

'Pluralism as English cultural definition: the social and political thought of George Unwin', *Journal of the History of Ideas*, 52 (1991), 665–84

'Localism versus centralism in the Webbs' political thought', *History of Political Thought*, 12 (Spring, 1991), 147–65

Stone, L. and J.C. Fawtier Stone. *An Open Elite? England, 1540–1880* (London, 1984)

Symonds, R. *Oxford and Empire: The Last Lost Cause* (London, 1986).

Taylor, M.W. *Men Versus the State: Herbert Spencer and Late Victorian Individualism* (Oxford, 1992)

Thompson, D.F. *The Democratic Citizen* (Cambridge, 1970)

Thornton, A.P. *The Imperial Idea and Its Enemies*, 2nd edn (London, 1985)

Tivey, L. and A. Wright (eds.) *Political Thought since 1945: Philosophy, Science, Ideology* (Aldershot, 1992)

Turner, F.M. *The Greek Heritage in Victorian Britain* (New Haven, 1981)

Vincent, A. *Theories of the State* (Oxford, 1987)

'Classical liberalism and its crisis of identity', *History of Political Thought*, 11 (1990), 143–61

Vincent, A. and R. Plant. *Politics, Philosophy, & Citizenship: The Life and Thought of the British Idealists* (Oxford, 1984)

Wallace, S. *War and the Image of Germany: British Academics, 1914–1918* (Edinburgh, 1988)

West, F. *Gilbert Murray: A Life* (New York, 1984)

Wiener, M.J. *Between Two Worlds: The Political Thought of Graham Wallas* (Oxford, 1971)

English Culture and the Decline of the Industrial Spirit, 1850–1980 (Cambridge, 1981)

Williamson, P. 'The doctrinal politics of Stanley Baldwin', in M. Bentley (ed.), *Public and Private Doctrine* (Cambridge, 1993)

Wilson, F.M. *Strange Island: Britain through Foreign Eyes, 1935–1940* (London, 1950)

Winter, J.M. *Socialism and the Challenge of War: Ideas and Politics in Britain, 1912–1918* (London, 1974)

Wright, A.W. *G.D.H. Cole and Socialist Democracy* (Oxford, 1979)

Wright, D.G. 'The Great War, government propaganda and English "men of letters", 1914–18', *Literature and History*, 7 (1978), 70–100

Wright, P. *On Living in an Old Country: The National Past in Contemporary Britain* (London, 1985)

Zylstra, B. *From Pluralism to Collectivism: The Development of Harold Laski's Political Thought* (Assen, 1968)

Index

The entry under Ernest Barker's name has been confined to references to his personal life, career, and writings. References to his political and social thought and other interests will be found under the relevant headings. Throughout the index his name has been abbreviated to EB.

Ideas in Context

Edited by Quentin Skinner (general editor), Lorraine Daston, Wolf Lepenies, Richard Rorty and J.B. Schneewind

1. RICHARD RORTY, J.B. SCHNEEWIND and QUENTIN SKINNER (eds.)
Philosophy in History
*Essays in the historiography of philosophy**

2. J.G.A. POCOCK
Virtue, Commerce and History
*Essays on Political thought and history, chiefly in the eighteenth century**

3. M.M. GOLDSMITH
Private Vices, Public Benefits
Bernard Mandeville's social and political thought

4. ANTHONY PAGDEN (ed.)
The Languages of Political Theory in Early Modern Europe*

5. DAVID SUMMERS
The Judgment of Sense
*Renaissance nationalism and the rise of aesthetics**

6. LAURENCE DICKEY
Hegel: Religion, Economics and the Politics of Spirit, 1770–1807*

7. MARGO TODD
Christian Humanism and the Puritan Social Order

8. LYNN SUMIDA JOY
Gassendi the Atomist
Advocate of history in an age of science

9. EDMUND LEITES (ed.)
Conscience and Casuistry in Early Modern Europe

10. WOLF LEPENIES
Between Literature and Science: The Rise of Sociology*

11. TERENCE BALL, JAMES FARR and RUSSELL L. HANSON (eds.)
Political Innovation and Conceptual Change*

12. GERD GIGERENZER *et al.*
The Empire of Chance
*How probability changed science and everyday life**

13. PETER NOVICK
That Noble Dream
*The 'objectivity question' and the American historical profession**

14. DAVID LIEBERMAN
The Province of Legislation Determined
Legal theory in eighteenth-century Britain

15. DANIEL PICK
Faces of Degeneration
A European disorder, c.1848–c.1918

16. KEITH BAKER
Approaching the French Revolution
*Essays on French political culture in the eighteenth century**

17. IAN HACKING
The Taming of Chance*

18. GISELA BOCK, QUENTIN SKINNER and MAURIZIO VIROLI (eds.)
Machiavelli and Republicanism*

19. DOROTHY ROSS
The Origins of American Social Science*

20. KLAUS CHRISTIAN KOHNKE
The Rise of Neo-Kantianism
German Academic Philosophy between Idealism and Positivism

21. IAN MACLEAN
Interpreting and Meaning in the Renaissance
The Case of Law

22. MAURIZIO VIROLI
From Politics to Reason of State
The Acquisition and Transformation of the Language of Politics 1250–1600

23. MARTIN VAN GELDEREN
The Political Thought of the Dutch Revolt 1555–1590

24. NICHOLAS PHILLIPSON and QUENTIN SKINNER (eds.)
Political Discourse in Early Modern Britain

25. JAMES TULLY
An Approach to Political Philosophy: Locke in Contexts*

26. RICHARD TUCK
Philosophy and Government 1572–1651*

27. RICHARD R. YEO
Defining Science
William Whewell, Natural Knowledge and Public Debate in Early Victorian Britain

28. MARTIN WARNKE
The Court Artist
The Ancestry of the Modern Artist

29. PETER. MILLER
Defining the Common Good
Empire, Religion and Philosophy in Eighteenth-Century Britain

30. CHRISTOPHER J. BERRY
The Idea of Luxury
*A Conceptual and Historical Investigation**

31. E.J. HUNDERT
The Enlightenment's 'Fable'
Bernard Mandeville and the Discovery of Society

32. JULIA STAPLETON
Englishness and the Study of Politics
The Social and Political Thought of Ernest Barker

Titles marked with an asterisk are also available in paperback